T0311088

The Dynamics of Governance and Sustainable Development Goals in the Global South

Edited by Hong Liu, Celia Lee, Chris Alden

WILEY

for

University of Durham and John Wiley & Sons, Ltd

This edition first published 2024

Registered Office
John Wiley & Sons Ltd, The Atrium, Southern Gate, Chichester, West Sussex, PO19 8SQ, UK

Editorial Offices
350 Main Street, Malden, MA 02148-5020, USA
9600 Garsington Road, Oxford, OX4 2DQ, UK
The Atrium, Southern Gate, Chichester, West Sussex, PO19 8SQ, UK

For details of our global editorial offices, for customer services, and for information about how to apply for permission to reuse the copyright material in this book please see our website at www.wiley.com.

Library of Congress Cataloging-in-Publication Data
Library of Congress Cataloging-in-Publication data is available for this book.
ISBN 9781394271276

A catalogue record for this book is available from the British Library.

Cover photo credit: Guillaume Meurice for Pexels

Set in 10/11pt and Helvetica LT Std by Straive

Printed and bound in Singapore
by Markono Print Media Pte Ltd

1   2024

Contents

The articles in this book were first published in 2022 in the journal Global Policy, Volume 13 Issue S1, available on Wiley Online Library.

Special Issue Articles

Research Articles

Policy Insights Article

Book Review

Partners

Global Policy's interdisciplinary and joined-up academic approach builds on links with a number of leading global universities and institutions. These networks create opportunities for key forms of collaboration and exchange, and help ensure that the Journal is truly global in its editorial approach and strategy.

NTU Singapore

A research-intensive public university, Nanyang Technological University, Singapore (NTU Singapore) has 33,000 undergraduate and postgraduate students in the Engineering, Business, Science, Humanities, Arts, & Social Sciences, and Graduate colleges. It also has a medical school, the Lee Kong Chian School of Medicine, set up jointly with Imperial College London.

Ranked amongst the world's top universities by QS, NTU has been placed the world's top young university for the past seven years. The University's main campus is frequently listed among the Top 15 most beautiful university campuses in the world and it has 57 Green Mark-certified (equivalent to LEED-certified) building projects, of which 95% are certified Green Mark Platinum.

Under the NTU Smart Campus vision, the University harnesses the power of digital technology and tech-enabled solutions to support better learning and living experiences, the discovery of new knowledge, and the sustainability of resources.

Nanyang Centre for Public Administration

Nanyang Centre for Public Administration (NCPA) at NTU is a leading institution in Asia that provides quality education and research as well as to promote good governance in the region and beyond. Among its 20,000 alumni, many are holding decision-making positions at all levels of government in their countries, including ministerial-level leaders, mayors and heads of organisations. Our students hail from many nations, including China, Vietnam, Myanmar, Cambodia, the Philippines, Laos, Malaysia, Thailand, India and Ukraine.

Received: 17 January 2022 | Accepted: 21 January 2022

DOI: 10.1111/1758-5899.13075

The Dynamics of Governance and Sustainable Development Goals in the Global South

Hong Liu[1] ⓘ | Celia Lee[1] ⓘ | Chris Alden[2]

[1]Nanyang Centre for Public Administration, Nanyang Technological University, Singapore, Singapore

[2]London School of Economics and Political Science—IDEAS, London, UK

Correspondence
Celia Lee, Nanyang Centre for Public Administration, Nanyang Technical University, 50 Nanyang Avenue Block S3.2-B4 Singapore 639798, Singapore.
Email: kplee@ntu.edu.sg

Abstract

This special issue on 'The Dynamics of Governance and Sustainable Development Goals in the Global South', with a focus on the 'Asian Models of Governance', aims to fill the gap by contributing to expanding and advancing the transnational knowledge transfer literature by bringing new cases from the Global South. It also hopes to further advance the discussions translating some aspects of Asian experiences of governance in developing an outcome-driven knowledge and policy transfer model for SDGs. The articles in this issue of *Global Policy* were selected from papers first presented at the London School of Economics – IDEAS and Nanyang Technological University – Nanyang Centre for Public Administration (LSE-IDEAS and NTU-NCPA) Joint Workshop on the Dynamics of Knowledge Transfer and Governance in the Global South, held at the London School of Economics in November 2019.

1 | INTRODUCTION

The Sustainable Development Goals (SDGs), also known as the Global Goals, consists of 17 goals which build on the successes of the Millennium Development Goals (MDGs) and aim to end poverty, protect the planet and ensure peace and prosperity. The 17 goals are interconnected and the success of one will involve tackling issues associated with another.

With its 17 SDGs and 169 targets, the 2030 Agenda for Sustainable Development[1.] demonstrates the international commitment to achieving worldwide sustainable development in its social, economic and environmental dimension (United Nations, 2015). What makes the SDGs special is the broad acceptance and commitment of the international community, the comprehensive definition of sustainable development in its different dimensions made measurable through 232 indicators, and the understanding that these sustainability goals are universal, integrated and indivisible. The emergence of the goals can be understood in the context of and as a response to global problems emerging in the wake of globalization processes and increasing global interconnectedness.

Governance constitutes a crucial part of the SDGs, while baseline public administration serves as a standalone development end in the 16th SDG, governance is an essential enabler of all other SDGs (SDGs, 2018). Governance refers to structures, processes and systems that define decision-making and interactions among various stakeholders. It is also broadly referred to as the exercise of functions and power through a country's economic, social, and political institutions.

Governance models have been predominantly based upon Western experiences and knowledge systems, especially influenced by the Anglo-American liberal-democracy system (Cheung, 2013; Kim, 2017; Wang & Liu, 2020). This is partly due to transnational knowledge transfer which is generally regarded as a one-way, 'from north to south' knowledge flow, under the assumption that Western countries (that is, the core region of the Organisation for Economic Co-operation and Development, or OECD) know best and so a transfer of knowledge, technology and expertise needs to take place from 'developed' to 'developing' countries (Lewis, 2017; Stone et al., 2020; UNDP, 2018).

Transnational knowledge diffusion, therefore, accelerates policy transfer, and it has developed into an important pillar of development cooperation (UNDP, 2016). Such transfer consists mostly of already-established best practices, and the actors of knowledge transfer are often international organizations (IOs) such as the International Monetary Fund (IMF), the World Bank (WB), or the European Union (EU) as well as national donor agencies in development aid. Partly as a result of direct or indirect coercive policy transfer (Dolowitz & Marsh, 1996), the policy advice is then fed into the developing countries' national policy advisory systems in order to obtain financial aids from these international organizations (Halligan, 1995; Hustedt, 2019).

However, in the past few decades, successful lessons from developing countries are often more relevant for other developing countries, reflecting the similarity of their opportunities and challenges. As a result, South–South cooperation has increasingly become an important source of knowledge and skills development, highly relevant to sustainable economic development (Gray, 2009; Lin & Wang, 2016; Oqubay & Ohno, 2019). For many decades, South–South cooperation featured at the periphery of developmental debates, remaining mostly an aspirational endeavour among the non-aligned countries. South–South cooperation was derived from the adoption of the Buenos Aires Plan of Action for Promoting and Implementing Technical Cooperation among Developing Countries (BAPA), which was formally recognized by United Nations in 1978 and outlined definitions. The intensification of cooperation flows between developing countries over the past decade, mostly pushed by emerging powers in the Global South such as China, Brazil, India, Turkey, Vietnam and Saudi Arabia has, however, significantly changed this picture. As a result, the Global South has gained a greater say in shaping global development debates and ensuing policies and practice in recent years.

As the largest provider of development assistance outside OECD-DAC community, China plays a key role in this endeavour (Amann & Barrientos, 2014; IDS, 2014; Scoones et al., 2016; Zhang & Smith, 2017). China's rapid economic growth in the past 30 years has stood out as an eye-catching alternative to the general pattern of modernization in the West and provided an example for some developing countries to follow suit. Following the 2008–09 financial crisis, China outperformed other major economies – from the second quarter of 2007 to the second quarter of 2014, China's economy grew by 78 per cent (Ross et. al., 2016). As a consequence, more and more developing countries in Asia, Africa and Latin America show their interest in the 'China Model' or the so-called 'Beijing Consensus', with leaders of some developing countries eager to emulating it (Oqubay & Lin, 2019; Ross et al., 2016; Wang

& Liu, 2020; Zhao, 2010). The appeal of China as an alternative model of economic growth is just one of the examples of the 'Asian Aspiration' (Mills et al., 2020; see also Oqubay & Ohno, 2019) which has been exemplified by not only China, but also Japan, South Korea and Singapore, among others. Singapore has become one of the most sought after developmental models for the nations in Southeast Asia and beyond (Lee, 2021; Saner & You, 2014; Yeo et al., 2019).

Despite the emergence of Asian models of governance and growing phenomenon of knowledge transfers spreading among developing countries (Cheung, 2013; Drechsler, 2013; Lai, 2016; Liu & Wang, 2018, 2021; Ross et al., 2016; Tugendhat & Alemu, 2016), mainstream studies on transnational knowledge has a strong bias toward (often conditionality-based) advice originating in the core western world and focuses nearly exclusively on the link from a source to a target of knowledge transfer (Heinrich, 2021; Stone et al., 2020). To be sure, the Chinese model of economic development and political governance grows out from its specific institutional realities and politico-economic structure (e.g., Bell, 2015; Chen & Naughton, 2017), and there are certain overlapping areas between the 'Washington Consensus' and the 'Beijing Consensus' in terms of state-market relations and variegated ways of institutional building (Asongu & Acha-Anyi, 2020; De Graaff et al., 2020). China's economic success has conducive lessons for the developing world, it is necessary to conceptualize and problematize how knowledge diffusion fuels policy transfer and translate into governance models in the context of international cooperation and relevance to the SDGs.

The necessity of re-examining the Chinese model of development, as a case of the Asian Aspiration, has been further propelled by the Belt and Road Initiative (BRI) launched in 2013.

Under the BRI and in line with China's 'Going Global' blueprint to expand its domestic economy and access untapped markets, Chinese firms were competitively handpicked by the Chinese Ministry of Commerce (MOFCOM) to venture into and further develop these special economic zones (SEZs) (Giannecchini & Taylor, 2018; Rohne, 2013). While it has been argued that the Chinese government actively endorses such sharing of 'wisdom' with other developing countries (Jiang, 2019) and that the BRI has potential synergies with the 2030 Sustainable Development Agenda, along with its Sustainable Development Goals (Lewis, et al., 2021), Fukuyama (2016) contends that for the first time, China is seeking to export its development model to other countries. He further claims that 'China's model will blossom outside of China, raising incomes and thus demand for Chinese products to replace stagnating markets in other parts of the world'.

The on-going contestations about the impacts of the BRI on global geopolitics, national political economy, and the environment as well as recipient nations' capacities to repaying the massive loans (c.f., Liow et al., 2021) have highlighted the importance of examining the rise of China in the context of transnational knowledge transfer in the Global South. It is against such as backdrop that this special issue explores, among others, the questions of to what extent China offers a distinctive model of economic and sustainable development and if so has the transfer of knowledge has been effective in other developing countries' contexts.

This special issue on 'The Dynamics of Governance and Sustainable Development Goals in the Global South', with a focus on the 'Asian Models of Governance', aims to fill the gap by contributing to expanding and advancing the transnational knowledge transfer literature by bringing new cases from the Global South. It also hopes to further advance the discussions translating some aspects of Asian experiences of governance in developing an outcome-driven knowledge and policy transfer model for SDGs.

The articles in this issue of Global Policy were selected from papers first presented at the London School of Economics – IDEAS and Nanyang Technological University – Nanyang Centre for Public Administration (LSE-IDEAS and NTU-NCPA) Joint Workshop on the Dynamics of Knowledge Transfer and Governance in the Global South, held at the London School of Economics in November 2019. The aim of the workshop was to zoom into key Asian nodes of knowledge transfer in the context of the Global South. In doing so, we hope the discussion will shed light on the dynamics and impacts of increasing exchanges between countries in the South and the ensuing departure from one-way flow of knowledge transfer (from North to South) that has dominated development cooperation discourse since post-Second World War. The workshop was also devoted to exploring how policy diffusion and transfer are entangled in processes and institutions of development cooperation and international aid through various forms such as special economic zones, foreign direct investments and training programmes.

We believe that there is potential for fresh insights about key issues in policy diffusion and transfer if we interlink the dynamics and discourse of governance for sustainable development in the Global South. The remainder of this introduction will introduce the essays in this special issue which consists of six research articles, one policy insight and one book review. They are segmented into three sections: *Transnational Knowledge Transfer and Dynamics of Governance in the Global South for Sustainable Development*: *Conceptual Explorations of the 'China Model' as an alternative path*; *Effectiveness and Outcomes of Transfer from Chinese Enterprises to Local Economy*: *Empirical Evidence from Africa and Asia*; *and Assessing the Asian Models of Governance in Determining SDG*

Outcomes. Finally, we conclude with discussions of the implications of the Chinese experiences of economic growth for other South countries through a developmental lens.

2 | STRUCTURE OF THE SPECIAL ISSUE

The Special Issue consists of research articles, a policy insight and a book commentary. In the research articles section, Hong Liu opens the research articles section by tracing the genesis of transnational knowledge transfer in the Global South to the Bandung Conference in 1955 and examining China's shifting strategies toward the Global South. Underlining China's growing engagement has been its belief in the shared experiences and aspirations of developing countries, as well as the enduring value of Bandung and of the Chinese model as an alternative path to economic growth, poverty alleviation, and governance reforms. He purports that China's model of economic development has constituted a main arena of knowledge transfer, which has gradually assumed a governance dimension. The model has been perceived as helping address global development problems and deepening South–South cooperation. He argues that the outcome of China's engagement with the Global South is contingent upon national and international political economy and calls for incorporating domestics interests of the Global South to ensure the smooth operation and sustainable development of relevant policy, thus bringing long-term benefits to all stakeholders.

Peng Wang and colleagues draw attention to sustainability management and the wide prevalence of the SDGs in the discourse of business and society by way of understanding the impact of culture on sustainable development and on the globalization of emerging economies. They examine the role played by sensemaking and present how Chinese culture influenced by Taoist philosophy impacts upon sustainable development in China's globalization endeavours, including Chinese overseas acquisitions and globalization of traditional Chinese medicine. They conclude that a nuanced understanding of the role played by culture such as Taoist philosophy is important to advance research on sustainability management from a microfoundational perspective.

In many developing countries, the garment sector is seen as a 'stepping stone' towards industrialization. They rely on foreign investment to enter the sector by engaging in simple assembly production and aim to gradually upgrade along the global value chain by building networks and capabilities. Neil Balchin and Linda Calabrese review and compare the developments of the garment sector in Bangladesh, Cambodia, Lesotho and Madagascar and highlight that foreign investors contribute differently to upgrading and creating linkages. They focus on the role of inward investment in the garment sector and on the approaches taken in specific countries to develop integrated value chains, facilitate backward linkages and support the upgrading of domestic firms. Due to the unequal foreign investment by European, Chinese, and other Asian enterprises, there emerge different models of production, ranging from cut-make-trim to original brand manufacturing, and divergent patterns of embeddedness in the host countries, which in turn determine the process and outcomes of knowledge spillovers.

Ana Cristina Dias Alves and Celia Lee present two cases of Chinese-led SEZs in Ethiopia and Cambodia, with a view to investigate the dynamics of knowledge transfer in South–South exchanges and assess the extent to which it diverges from more traditional patterns of exchange in their interactions and outcomes and stand up to the mutual-benefit and horizontality rhetoric. SEZs can be a useful tool for developing countries unable to upgrade infrastructure, human capital and institutional frameworks across the entire economy on their own and that are constrained by economic bottlenecks and conflicting priorities. In line with the SDGs, Alves and Lee suggest that capacity building should empower vulnerable groups by providing them with relevant knowledge, skills and information to better access wider benefits from infrastructure, such as access to markets, jobs and services. Motivated by the broader aim of contributing to the understanding of knowledge transfer (KT) flows within the global south, this paper sheds light on the modalities of KT in these zones to assess the effectiveness and outcomes of the transfer in the light of the prominence of SEZs in the planning of the economic corridors along the Belt and Road Initiative. The biggest impact of these zones is felt in FDI influx, job creation and improvement of overall investment environment. However, the potential for a more transformative impact is modest owing to evidence that in both zones the emphasis largely falls on explicit knowledge transfer (basic hard and soft skills to floor plant workers, or middle managers).

Using 2019 Chinese Overseas Enterprises and Employees Survey (OCEES), Jianxun Kong and Yidi Zhou explore the convergence of Chinese enterprise and employee (E&E) evaluation in Southeast Asia. It aims to understand how the variables of union participation, types of industries and length of work experience mediated the degree of matching between organizational and individual corporate social responsibility (CSR) performance. Their findings reveal that the firms with labour union report more CSR performance than others whilst employees in construction sector report their firms' CSR performance is higher and those from manufacture and service sectors. They conclude that good CSR performance would improve the company's impression among the host country citizens, in addition

to creating convenience for them to live in different countries and cultures. Chinese companies in countries like Vietnam, Cambodia and Malaysia accomplished CSR with both sides (enterprise and employee) satisfied to a substantive degree, whereas those in other Southeast Asian countries display a large disparity between firm and employee levels.

The SDG-related implications of polycentric urban development are multifaceted and complex, but many scholars view polycentric urban development in generally positive terms. In the third section, Eric Heikkila and Ying Xu argue that urbanization policies are a critical factor in determining SDG outcomes, explicitly SDG 11 on sustainable cities and communities. China's model of urbanization has played a crucial role in sustainable development of cities. Polycentric urban forms have the potential to reduce average commuting times, thereby impacting greenhouse gas emissions. According to them, this model focuses specifically on governmental policies to promote polycentricity, with multiple urban centres of a similar scale within metropolitan areas, rather than a traditional single, dominant central business district. Polycentricity may also enhance access to employment and other opportunities for marginalized households. Using Changsha as a case study, this essay uncovers two key findings. First, the fundamental economic drivers of urbanization are the similar in China as anywhere else. Second, China's unique governance system does provide significant capacity for staunching this economic rent dissipation. They conclude that potential benefits from polycentric urban development (such as reduced travel times, improved access to essential services, and lower CO_2 emissions) depend largely on effective local governance.

In his policy insight, Andrew Massey places the SDGs in the context of good governance. He contends that none of the other fifteen SDGs can be achieved without the coordination and delivery of SDGs 16 and 17, which are at the core of public administration and the delivery of good governance. He emphasizes that governance should include multiple stakeholders from the civil society such as economic, professional and social interest groups, into a reflection of what it means to govern and to make and implement public policy. Using examples of the United Nation's annual public service innovation awards, he points to the importance of contextually specific 'best practice' that the configuration of a state's public administration reflects the political and social values of a country. Hence the implementation of the 2030 agenda and the SDGs will only be similarly successful if there is a comparable recognition of local context.

This special issue ends with a review by Michael Charney of *Food security in Small Island States*. He contends that the volume's key contribution is the collective assessments of responses in different Small Island States (SIDS) to the food security challenges they all face. The various case studies reveal a diverse panoply of options where SIDS have attempted to transform small island food systems to make them more resilient and sustainable. He concludes that the present volume successfully lays out the scope of the issue of food insecurity and policy responses to food vulnerability. However, the larger existential challenge SIDS face depend for their resolution on how far more powerful states with larger industrial and commercial bases can continue to cooperate on reducing carbon emissions. Without concerted global solutions, whether local innovations and adaptation are effective in responding to the challenges of food insecurity locally remains to be an open question.

3 | CONCLUDING REMARKS

This special issue, we hope, extends and deepens the policy transfer literature by comparatively examining the practices of the China model of governance through the lens of South–South cooperation and SDGs. China's model has its unique 'Chinese characteristics' in its combination of economic dynamism with the state's political control of the society. While other economies cannot mechanically copy China's successful experiences, they can draw useful lessons, including through the SEZs and training programmes. Host governments need to take greater ownership of the knowledge transfer process rather than relying on automatic spill-overs arising from foreign direct investments. When governments learn from other countries, it must be in the public interest as a new or adjusted policy can affect the fabric of the society. Finally, as various articles in this special issue have highlighted, South countries should also recognize the contextual differences between China and other developing countries in terms of size, political regime, cultural and socio-economic factors which in turn shape the process and outcomes of transnational knowledge transfer.

ACKNOWLEDGEMENTS
We are grateful for all the conference speakers and participants for their invaluable contributions, especially to Dr Akebe Oqubay, Senior Minister of the Ethiopian Government, and Professor Fu Xiaolan of Oxford University for their inspiring keynote speeches. We thank the capable assistance rendered by Dr Eva Maria-Nag and her colleagues at *Global Policy* in the reviewing, editing and publishing process of this special issue. Funding support from LSE-IDEAS and the Nanyang Centre for Public Administration of Nanyang Technological University is gratefully acknowledged. The reviews and interpretations are solely those of the individual authors' and they do not necessarily represent the positions of the special issue editors and their institutions.

ORCID
Hong Liu https://orcid.org/0000-0003-3328-8429
Celia Lee https://orcid.org/0000-0002-0807-4018

ENDNOTE
1. The 2030 Agenda for Sustainable Development is a plan of action for people, planet and prosperity. It also seeks to strengthen universal peace in larger freedom. It was adopted at the United Nations Sustainable Development Summit on 25 September 2015.

REFERENCES
Amann, E. & Barrientos, A. (2014) *Is there a new Brazilian model of development? Main findings from the IRIBA research programme.* IRIBA working paper 13. University of Manchester.
Asongu, S.A. & Acha-Anyi, P.N. (2020) A survey on the Washington consensus and the Beijing Model: reconciling development perspectives. *International Review of Economics*, 67(2), 111–129.
Bell, D.A. (2015) *The China model.* Princeton, NJ: Princeton University Press.
Chen, L. & Naughton, B. (2017) A dynamic China model: the co-evolution of economics and politics in China. *Journal of Contemporary China*, 26(103), 18–34.
Cheung, A.B.L. (2013) Can there be an Asian model of governance? *Public Administration and Development*, 33(4), 249–261.
Dolowitz, D. & Marsh, D. (1996) Who learns what from whom: a review of the policy transfer literature. *Political Studies*, 44(2), 343–357.
Drechsler, W. (2013) Three paradigms of governance and administration: Chinese, Western and Islamic. *Society and Economy*, 35(3), 319–342.
Fukuyama, F. (2016) Exporting the Chinese model, Available from: https://www.project-syndicate.org/commentary/china-one-belt-one-road-strategy-by-francis-fukuyama-2016-01 [Accessed 18th December 2021].
Giannecchini, P. & Taylor, I. (2018) The eastern industrial zone in Ethiopia: catalyst for development? *Geoforum*, 88, 28–35.
De Graaff, N., ten Brink, T. & Parmar, I. (2020) China's rise in a liberal world order in transition – introduction to the forum. *Review of International Political Economy*, 27(2), 191–207.
Gray, T. (2009) An emerging south-south coalition strategy: China, Africa and Latin America. *Peace and Conflict Studies*, 16(2), 82–100.
Halligan, J. (1995) Policy advice and the public sector. In: Peters, B.G. & Savoie, D.T. (Eds.) *Governance in a changing environment.* Montreal, QC: McGill-Queen's University Press, pp. 138–172.
Heinrich, A. (2021) The advice they give: knowledge transfer of international organisations in countries of the former Soviet Union. *Global Social Policy*, 21(1), 9–33.
Hustedt, T. (2019) Studying policy advisory systems: beyond the Westminster-bias? *Policy Studies*, 40(3–4), 260–269.
Institute of Development Studies. (2014) China and international development: challenges and opportunities. In: Gu, J., Zhang, X., Li, X. & Bloom, G. (Eds.) *IDS bulletin.* Brighton: Institute of Development Studies.
Jiang, Y. (2019) Chinese wisdom: new norms for development and global governance. In: Brown, K. (Ed.) *China's 19th party congress: start of a New Era.* London: World Scientific Publishing Europe, pp. 177–203.
Kim, P.S. (2017) The development of modern public administration in East Asia. *International Review of Administrative Sciences*, 83(2), 225–240.
Lai, H. (2016) *China's governance model: flexibility and durability of pragmatic authoritarianism.* London: Routledge.

Lee, C. (2021) *Talent strategies and leadership development of the public sector: insights from Southeast Asia.* London: Routledge.

Lewis, D. (2017) Should we pay more attention to South-North learning? Human service organizations: management. *Leadership & Governance*, 31(4), 327–331.

Lewis, D.J., Yang, X., Moise, D. & Roddy, S. (2021) Dynamic synergies between China's belt and road initiative and the UN's sustainable development goals. *Journal of International Business Policy*, 4(1), 58–79.

Lin, Y. & Wang, Y. (2016) *Going beyond aid: new ideas of development cooperation in a multipolar world.* Beijing: Peking University. (In Chinese).

Liow, J., Liu, H. & Gong, X. (Eds) (2021) *Research Handbook on the Belt and Road Initiative.* Cheltenham: Edward Elgar Publishing.

Liu, H. & Wang, T. (2018) China and the Singapore model: perspectives from the mid-level cadres and implications for transnational knowledge transfer. *The China Quarterly*, 236(December), 988–1011.

Liu, H. & Wang, T. (2021) The institutionalization and effectiveness of transnational policy transfer: the China-Singapore Suzhou industrial park as a case study. *Public Administration and Development*, 41(3), 103–114. https://doi.org/10.1002/pad.1956

Mills, G., Obasanjo, O., Desalegn, H. & van der Merwe, E. (2020) *The Asian aspiration: why and how Africa should Emulate Asia.* London: Hurst & Company.

Oqubay, A. & Lin, Y. (Eds) (2019) *China-Africa and an economic transformation.* Oxford: Oxford University Press.

Oqubay, A. & Ohno, K. (Eds) (2019) *How nations learn: technological learning, industrial policy, and catch-up.* Oxford: Oxford University Press.

Rohne, E. (2013) *Chinese-initiated special economic zones in Africa: a case study of Ethiopia's Eastern Industrial Zone.* Master Thesis. School of Economics and Management, Lund University.

Ross, J., Zheng, J.H. & Prime, K.S. (2016) What can be learned from China's success? *Journal of Chinese Economic and Business Studies*, 14(1), 51–68.

Saner, R. & Yiu, L. (2014) Learning to grow: A human capital-focused development strategy, with lessons from Singapore. *International Development Policy*, 5(3), 1–15.

Scoones, I., Amanor, K., Favareto, A. & Qi, G. (2016) A new politics of development cooperation? Chinese and Brazilian engagements in African agriculture. *World Development*, 81, 1–12.

Stone, D., Porto de Oliveira, O. & Pal, L.A. (2020) Transnational policy transfer: the circulation of ideas, power and development models. *Policy and Society*, 39(1), 1–18.

Sustainable Development Goals. (2018) Global Hub on the Governance for the SDGs, Available from: https://sustainabledevelopment.un.org/partnership/?p=34170 [Accessed 18th December 2021].

Tugendhat, H. & Alemu, D. (2016) Chinese agricultural training courses for African officials: between power and partnerships. *World Development*, 81, 71–81.

United Nations. (2015) *The 17 sustainable development goals.* Available from: https://sdgs.un.org/goals [Accessed 18th December 2021].

United Nations Development Programme (UNDP). (2016) Scaling-up South-South cooperation for sustainable development. Bureau for Policy and Programme Support, December 2016. New York.

United Nations Development Programme (UNDP). (2018) The speed of urbanization around the world. Department of Economic and Social Affairs Population Division, December 2018. New York.

Wang, T.Y. & Liu, H. (Eds) (2020) *An emerging Asian model of governance and transnational knowledge transfer.* London: Routledge.

Yeo, G., Tan, K.Y. & Tan, G.K. (2019) Learning and catch-up in Singapore: lessons for developing countries. In: Oqubay, A. & Ohno, K. (Eds.) *How nations learn: technological learning, industrial policy, and catch-up.* Oxford: Oxford University Press, pp. 173–206.

Zhang, D. & Smith, G. (2017) China's foreign aid system: structure, agencies, and identities. *Third World Quarterly*, 38(10), 2330–2346.

Zhao, S.S. (2010) The China Model: can it replace the Western model of modernization? *Journal of Contemporary China*, 19(65), 419–436.

AUTHOR BIOGRAPHIES

Hong Liu is the Tan Lark Sye Chair Professor of Public Policy and Global Affairs at the School of Social Sciences, Nanyang Technological University in Singapore, where he also serves as Director of the Nanyang Centre for Public Administration. His recent publications include *The political economy of transnational governance*: *China and Southeast Asia in the 21st century* (Routledge, 2022).

Celia Lee is Research Fellow at the Nanyang Centre for Public Administration. Her recent publications include *Talent strategies and leadership development in the public sector* and *Insights from the Southeast Asia and catalysing innovation and digital transformation in combating the Covid-19 pandemic: whole-of government collaborations in ICT, R&D, and business digitization in Singapore.*

Chris Alden is Professor in International Relations at the London School of Economics and Political Science (LSE) and Director of LSE IDEAS. His research focus is on Foreign Policy Analysis and Asia-Africa relations. He is Senior Research Associate at the South African Institute of International Affairs and the University of Pretoria.

How to cite this article: Liu, H., Lee, C. & Alden, C. (2022) The dynamics of governance and sustainable development goals in the global south. *Global Policy*, 13(Suppl. 1), 5–10. Available from: https://doi.org/10.1111/1758-5899.13075

Received: 8 August 2021 | Revised: 15 September 2021 | Accepted: 21 September 2021

DOI: 10.1111/1758-5899.13034

RESEARCH ARTICLE

China engages the Global South: From Bandung to the Belt and Road Initiative

Hong Liu ⓘ

School of Social Sciences, Nanyang Technological University, Singapore, Singapore

Correspondence
Hong Liu, School of Social Sciences, Nanyang Technological University, 50 Nanyang Ave., Singapore 639798, Singapore.
Email: liuhong@ntu.edu.sg

Funding information
Nanyang Technological University, Grant/Award Number: 04INS000136C430

Abstract

This article addresses China's engagement with the Global South regarding the transnational transfer of knowledge and policy. It argues that China's active participation in the Bandung Conference constituted historical capital in legitimating its (leadership) role in the Global South and as an alternative modernity. The past decade has witnessed the growing importance of the Global South for China. Apart from a geopolitical motive, China's expanding economic ties with the developing world serve as an overarching framework facilitating transnational knowledge transfer, with the centrality of development reinforced by an institutionalization drive. The essay concludes that China's engagement with the Global South in the context of the Belt and Road Initiative has been shaped by the complex logics of domestic political economy and changing global geopolitics, not all of which are within China's control. A stakeholder-centric approach, therefore, will be beneficial to all countries concerned.

1 | INTRODUCTION

Defined as 'a process in which knowledge about policies, administrative arrangements, institutions etc. in one time and/or place is used in the development of policies, administrative arrangements and institutions in another time and/or place' (Dolowitz & Marsh, 1996, p. 344), knowledge transfer is a way of learning from nations that have already gone through given developmental trajectories. In tandem with the accelerated movements of capital, goods, and people, the gradual shift of the economic center of gravity from the Industrial North to the Global South has facilitated transnational flows of ideas and practices, including different development models in the developing world. This represents a major departure from the old pattern of North-South transfer. As Pollitt (2015, p. 4) argues, the age of 'Anglosphere' dominance in public administration on the global stage is ending, partly because

'other regions of the world are becoming economically and politically more influential and self-confident, and [...] have long administrative traditions of their own'.

The genesis of knowledge transfer in the Global South can be traced back to the Bandung Conference of 1955 in Indonesia. Attended by leaders from 29 Asian and African countries, mostly newly independent, the Bandung Conference signaled a momentous shift in global politics and prompted the emergence of the Global South, which has become increasingly important in the international arena, especially since the growth in influence of non-Western countries such as China (Dirlik, 2007; Gray & Gills, 2016). How does China approach the Global South? What have been the evolving patterns, characteristics, and policy implications of China's engagement with the Global South? How have they been shaped by the ideals of Bandung and, more recently, by the Belt and Road Initiative (BRI)? This essay will attempt to answer these questions.

Based upon data in English, Chinese and Bahasa and the author's fieldwork in two dozen BRI-related countries, this essay makes three arguments. First, it is essential to historicize China's engagement with the Global South. Bandung remains a fundamental reference point for Chinese knowledge transfer and for legitimating China's role in the Global South as an alternative modernity. Second, unlike China's rendezvous with the Global South during the Cold War, driven by ideology and revolution, China's growing economic ties with the developing world in the form of investment, trade, and overseas industrial parks have helped increase the Global South's importance and serve as an overarching framework facilitating knowledge transfer. The centrality of development as a discourse and practice has been enhanced by the establishment and reinforcing of well-endowed institutions that have gained in stability and value in terms of dealing with the Global South. Third, China's efforts to transfer knowledge in the context of the BRI have been significantly shaped by the domestic political economy of the South as well as by changing global geopolitics, especially the US–China rivalries characterized by American President Joe Biden as 'a struggle between different political systems'. To avoid returning to Cold War-style ideological confrontations, major powers need to take cognizance of the needs and interests of recipient countries in the Global South. This in turn will help institutionalize mutually beneficial knowledge transfer both within the Global South and between North and South.

After its emergence in the 1970s and especially since the 1990s, the Global South has figured increasingly in scholarly and policy circles. In China, comparable concepts are 'developing nations', 'the Third World', and, increasingly, 'South-South Cooperation' (SSC). First coined in the 1950s, SSC is defined as 'a key organizing concept and a set of practices in pursuit of these historical changes [human betterment, etc.] through a vision of mutual benefit and solidarity among the disadvantaged of the world system. It conveys the hope that development may be achieved by the poor themselves through their mutual assistance to one another, and the whole world order transformed to reflect their mutual interests vis-à-vis the dominant global North' (Gray & Gills, 2016, p. 557).

2 | BANDUNG'S LEGACIES

2.1 | Bandung as transnational knowledge transfer

From the perspective of international relations theory building, Acharya (2016. p. 342) highlights the importance of the Bandung Conference 'not only for any serious investigation into the evolution of the post-war international order, but also for the development of

Policy Implications

- The Global South should formulate and effectively implement development-oriented public policies to support economic growth in association with China's growing presence.
- Capacity building in human capital be institutionally embedded into China's engagement with the Global South.
- China and the Global South should forge better mutual understanding through closer collaboration in education, knowledge exchange, and technological innovation.
- To avoid returning to Cold War-style ideological confrontations, major powers should take a stakeholder-centered perspective regarding the needs and interests of recipient countries.

Global [international relations] (IR) as a truly universal discipline: a global international relation". Philips (2016) considers Bandung in a broader historical and global context and the four 'faces' (order-challenging, order-affirming, order-building and order-transforming) that have shaped political and academic debates. Viewed from the perspective of knowledge exchange, Bandung represents an effort by newly independent nations to seek new visions of modernity different from those of their former metropolitan masters. Bandung humanism denotes a systemic process through which non-Western nations identify commonalities and seek mutual inspiration (Liu & Zhou, 2019).

The case of post-Independence Indonesia illuminates China's first major engagement with the Global South. It demonstrates several characteristics that still shape China's relationship with the developing world, including the role of historical capital, the embeddedness of knowledge transfer in the engagement strategies, the projection of China's soft power, and the significance of national and international political economy in determining the outcomes of the engagement.

Two factors shaped pre-Bandung Sino-Indonesian interactions (unless otherwise indicated, the data for following praraphies are derived from Liu, 2011). The first was Indonesia's convoluted search for paths of development that would fit its circumstances. As Prime Minister Mohammad Natsir declared in his 1951 Independence Day speech: 'Everywhere there prevails a feeling of dissatisfaction, a feeling of frustration, a feeling of hopelessness". A few days before the Bandung Conference, Education Minister Prijono spoke of the need to seek inspiration from the East instead of continuing to look to the West. This helped bring China's development model into Indonesian focus. In the early 1950s, policy makers believed so strongly in the reproducibility of China's experiences that some were convinced that 'China's today is Southeast Asia's tomorrow'. This belief derived partially from perceived commonalties among Asian-African countries, as highlighted by Premier Zhou Enlai in a February 1955 letter to his Indonesian counterpart:

> The Afro-Asian Conference is the first conference of its kind in history held to further cordial relations and cooperation between Afro-Asian countries. This conference is also convoked to further explore and promote [Afro-Asian countries'] mutual interest, friendly relations and neighborly relations. The convocation of this conference reflects momentous changes in this region of the world, it also reflects the wishes of Afro-Asian countries to control their own fate, cooperate with other countries in the world on equal standing, and grow daily in resolution (Zhou, 1955).

China scored highly in Bandung on the diplomatic front, convincing participants to incorporate its Five Principles of Peaceful Coexistence into the Ten Principles of Bandung. The five principles (mutual respect for sovereignty and territorial integrity, mutual non-aggression, non-interference in each other's internal affairs, equality and mutual benefit, and peaceful coexistence) remain essential to China's foreign policy and have been reconstructed as a foundation for the ideals of 'the community of common destiny' foregrounding the BRI.

The efforts to project positive images about China's developments were reinforced by institutionalized mechanisms such as diplomatic missions, organized tourism, and the export of publications to Indonesia. (Bahasa publications, most of them about China's 'remarkable' socio-economic development, were second in number only to those in English.) China was perceived as a model of social engineering, economic growth, and cultural revitalization. Indonesia adopted some aspects of Chinese practice, ranging from 'Guided Democracy', intellectuals' role in society, and civilian–military relations.

In a plural society such as post-colonial Indonesia, however, China became increasingly internalized and politicized, the contestations about whether or not some aspects of the China model could be adapted were invariably intertwined with competing segments of a politically divided nation embroiled in the Cold War. The polarization of power and ideology – represented partially by China and America on the opposite spectrums and their respective Indonesian allies – was one factor leading to the downfall of Sukarno in 1965, marking the end of China's revolutionary engagement.

China's efforts in the Global South shifted to Africa, in pursuit of a more pragmatic policy, and achieved a huge political victory in 1971 when China was admitted to the United Nations and replaced Taiwan on the UN Security Council, with African support (Shinn, 2019; Zhang, 2014).

In short, Bandung represented the Global South's search for new development models among its peers. It was in this context of seeking an Asian-African formula for development, that Indonesia and other countries appropriated aspects of the Chinese model (cf. Lovell, 2019).

2.2 | China as an alternative modernity?

Bandung has not lost its historical appeal and contemporary relevance, although the context has changed. The closing decades of the 20th century witnessed the resurgence of the Global South as an entity with shared aspirations, symbolized by the setting-up of an SSC framework in 1978 at the UN Conference on Technical Cooperation among Developing Countries. The UNDP project of 2003, 'Forging a Global South', is described as a 'new paradigm of development' that will allow the South to command its own future (Dirlik, 2007).

Elements of Indonesia's earlier perception of China as a developmental state revived. An editorial in *Kompas* in 2001 expressed wonderment at China's 'spectacular and fascinating' progress and advocated 'learning from China's example in development'. Dahlan Iskan, CEO of the *Jawa Pos* Group, urged the Indonesians to learn from China's model of development. In Vietnam, younger policy makers adopted what they called a 'Chinese model' of slowly opening the economy while retaining control of the political system, while Laotians considered 'China kind of symbolizes modernity' (Kurlantzick, 2007, p. 119). Public opinion surveys in the early 2010s showed that Vietnam, Thailand, and Indonesia identified most strongly in Southeast Asia with the Chinese model of development (Welsh & Chang, 2015). However, there has been a decline of trust among Southeast Asian elites. While 76.3 per cent considered China as the most influential power economically and 49.1 per cent strategically and politically, the China trust deficit grew from 60.4 per cent in 2020 to 63 per cent in 2021, much higher than Japan and the EU (Seah et al., 2021). The lack of trust is undermining China's appeal as a feasible model of development. In Latin America, Ratigan (2021) has shown that although Peruvians generally trust the Chinese government, only a small proportion prefers China as a model for Peru, while those who strongly value democracy are less likely to prefer China as a model.

In Africa, however, China continued to rank second in 18 countries behind the United States (23 per cent vs. 32 per cent), and outranked Africa's former colonial powers (11 per cent) (Sanny & Selormey, 2020). Based upon opinion surveys from 2005 to 2018, Xie and Jin (2021) find that public attitudes toward China in developing or less-developed countries are economy-oriented, with China's involvement in the local economy leading to a more positive attitude, in stark contrast to the developed countries' ideologically driven and negative perceptions of China. Similarly, Friedrichs (2019, p. 1648) contends that China enjoys 'considerable popularity in the Middle East and Africa, not only among elites but also at street level' and that 'China has a strong record of economic growth that provides a welcome alternative to the so-called Washington consensus''.

The notion of China as an alternative modernity redefines an important dimension of the ontological relationship between the South and the North. As Eisenstadt (2000, pp. 2–3) points out, 'Modernity and Westernization are not identical; Western patterns of modernity are not the only "authentic" modernities, though they enjoy historical precedence and continue to be a basic reference point for others'.

An officially approved history of Chinese diplomacy has argued that the Bandung Conference was 'truly a milestone in the 20th century.... It promoted independence movements across Asia and Africa and prompted the emergence of developing nations as a major power in global politics' (Zhang, 2014, pp. 60–64). The term 'Silk Road' first gained currency after the Bandung Conference 'as part of the lexicon of anticolonial solidarity'', which prompted new interest in 'the linguistic dimension of connected history' (Chin, 2021, p. 17). It was no coincidence that Chinese President Xi Jinping announced the '21st Century Maritime Silk Road Initiative' in his speech to the Indonesian Parliament in October 2013, in which Bandung featured prominently: 'With the principles of peaceful co-existence and seeking common ground while shelving differences at its core, the Bandung spirit remains an important norm governing state-to-state relations, and has made indelible contribution to the building of new international relations' (Wu, 2013).

Chinese–Indonesian relations demonstrate that the transnational exchange of knowledge and policy regarding models of development has been an integral component of SSC. From a practitioners' perspective, 'the exchange of resources, technology, and knowledge between developing countries' constitutes SSC's core activities (UNICEF China, 2019; emphasis in the original). The feasibility of such exchanges is based upon (real or perceived) commonalities, shared goals, mutual benefits, and respect for sovereignty among non-Western nations as well as the aspirations of each for economic development and nation-building. Friedrichs (2019) argues that shared frameworks of meaning and culture form the core of social constructivism and help explain China's popularity in Africa and the Middle East. Qian Qichen, Foreign Minister

(1988–1998), wrote: 'Being fellow developing countries with a shared history of oppression by imperialism and colonialism, China and African nations have a mutual understanding of each other's pursuit of independence and freedom, and there is a natural sense of affinity' (Qian, 2003, pp. 254–255). Confident of the applicability of China's economic model, Justin Lin Yifu, former senior vice president of the World Bank, declared that '[a]s China's economic clout grows, so will its influence in global governance' (Lin, 2017).

3 | THE GLOBAL SOUTH AND THE BRI

3.1 | China's growing economic linkages with the Global South

According to the IMF, China's share of global GDP adjusted for purchasing-power parity (PPP) increased from 13.71 per cent in 2010 to 18.78 per cent in 2020 and is projected to increase to 20.37 per cent in 2026. China's growing economic influence in and multi-layered connections with the developing world have shaped its engagement with the Global South. China attaches greater significance to the developing world in terms of strategy, knowledge transfer, resources allocation, and institutionalization.

Intra-Asian trade, of which China is a key motor, now accounts for 60 per cent of the region's total trade, a substantial increase on the late 1970s, when only 20 per cent of total exports were intra-Asian. Intra-regional flows form 59 per cent of foreign direct investment, 74 per cent of Asian air travelers, and 71 per cent of Asian investment in start-ups. Chinese trade with ASEAN (the Association of Southeast Asian Nations) increased by more than 30 per cent annually in the early 21st century. In 2011, ASEAN was China's third-largest trading partner, and it overtook the USA in 2019. Since early 2020, ASEAN has replaced the EU as China's largest trading partner. The formation of the China–ASEAN Free Trade Area in 2010 created an economic entity with a combined GDP of $6.6 trillion, 1.9 billion people and a total trade of $4.3 trillion. Chinese FDI to ASEAN countries doubled between 2013 and 2018, to $14 billion (Liu, 2022b).

China's economic ties with Africa also increased. In 2009 China emerged as Africa's leading trading partner and surpassed the World Bank as Africa's top lender. Trade between Africa and China grew from $1 billion in 2000 to $182.5 billion in 2018. China and India have become Africa's top two trading partners. Their combined share of Africa's exports grew to 23.3 per cent in 2018, up from 3.5 per cent in 1998. This shows that the growing economic linkage between China and Southeast Asia/Africa is part of the rise of the Global South, regarded as the most important characteristic feature and driver of tectonic shifts in the global economy over the last four to five decades. The South in 2019 accounted for over 57 per cent of global trade (Akyeampong & Fofack, 2019; see also Oqubay & Lin, 2019). Equally important is the growing intra-Global South trade. Developing economies' exports to other developing economies surpassed their exports to developed economies. South-South trade represented an estimated $4.28 trillion or 52 per cent of total developing economies' exports in 2018 (WTO, 2019). In 2017, at Davos, Xi Jinping underscored that emerging and developing economies contribute 80 per cent of global economic growth (Fuchs & Rudyak, 2019). China's growing investment in BRI countries has led to rapid flows of population. The number of Chinese migrants in BRI regions in 2015 increased substantially over the early 1990s. The largest percentage increase is in Western Asia (524 per cent), Eastern Africa (297 per cent) and Southern Africa (126 per cent) (Muttarak, 2017).

China has forged extensive state-to-state linkages with the Global South. A survey by the Lowry Institute shows that average annual visits to China and the US by world leaders changed dramatically in China's favor. During the Bush presidency (1989–1993), the average annual visit by world leaders to the US was 65.8, in contrast to five to China. In 2018, the number to China was 127 compared with only 22 to the US. Far more leaders of the South visited China than the US between 2010 and 2019: African leaders visited China 172 times (83 to the US), Asian leaders visited China 287 times (compared with 90 times to the US), and South American leaders visited China 30 times (compared with 25 times to the US). This, concluded the Lowry report, 'is both a symptom of [China's] growing power and one of its causes' (Thomas, 2021).

In short, as the largest country in the Global South, over the past two decades China has substantially expanded its economic imprint not only in the world but also with other developing countries, a major driving force behind China's multi-layered engagement since the BRI's launch in 2013.

3.2 | The Chinese state and the Global South since 2013

In 2013, Xi Jinping announced the BRI, which has since become China's foremost diplomatic and economic strategy in engaging with the world, especially developing nations. According to the Refinitiv BRI Database, 2631 projects had a combined value of $3.7 trillion in 2019, and nearly 2600 enterprises participated in the signature project. Of these, more than 55 per cent are non-Chinese. Although it was reported in June 2020 that some 20 per cent of BRI projects had been 'seriously affected' or 'somewhat affected' by COVID-19,

around 40 per cent had suffered little adverse impact. The BRI remains China's most important foreign policy initiative (Liu, 2022b). It is also key platform in China's engagement with the Global South. Despite numerous studies on the BRI (e.g. Blanchard, 2021; Liow et al., 2021; Schneider, 2021), few approach it from a Global South perspective. While there is a mixture of motives behind China's latest engagement with the developing world, including political (such as promoting the One-China policy), diplomatic and commercial (Fuchs & Rudyak, 2019), this essay argues that the BRI makes the Global South ever more important in China's international strategy.

China's post-2013 engagement with the Global South has embraced both continuity and change. In addition to the cherished Bandung legacy, it continues the transition started in the 1980s, namely, from ideology to economy. Three characteristics define China's new approach: development as a bridge between the BRI and the Global South; the institutionalization of multilateral and bilateral mechanisms to bolster South-South cooperation and China's leadership role; and the augmentation and deepening of knowledge transfer with the Global South, with the 'China Solution' as an alternative model of development to that of the Global North.

Speaking at the Asian-African Summit in Jakarta in 2015, Xi Jinping cited Deng Xiaoping's comment that 'South-South cooperation was such a well-put term that we must give whoever invented it a big medal'. He reiterated that 'developing countries ought to look to one another for comfort and come to each other's aid in times of difficulty … [and] to realize their respective development blueprints'. Their cooperation should include 'dialogue and exchange on governance, communication and coordination on major international and regional issues, and enhancement of forces making for world peace and common development' (Xi, 2015a). The White Paper 'China's International Development Cooperation in the New Era' underscores the BRI as 'significant public goods China offers to the whole world and a major platform for international development cooperation' (State Council Information Office, 2021).

Institutionalization is a key characteristic of China's recent engagement with the Global South. The effectiveness of transnational policy transfer is contingent on institutionalization – defined by Samuel Huntington as 'the process by which organizations and procedures acquire value and stability' (cited in Liu & Wang, 2021) at both ends of the exchange. Since 2000, China has either set up or actively participated in multilateral mechanisms and fora specifically related to the Global South. Xi (2015a) calls for 'more effective institutions and mechanisms' and the adaption of existing mechanisms to 'encourage dialogue and exchanges among regional organizations of developing countries and explore new frameworks for South-South cooperation'.

TABLE 1 Chinese publications on the Global South, 1980–2020

Keyword	Total numbers, 1980–2012 (annual average)	Total numbers, 2013–2020 (annual average)	Change of annual average (per cent)
South-South cooperation (*Nannan Hezuo*)	538 (17)	648 (81)	+376
Developing countries (*Fazhanzhong Guojia*)	4024 (125)	1498 (187)	+50
Third world (*Disan Shijie*)	1900 (59)	322 (40)	−32
Three keywords combined	6462 (201)	2468 (308)	+53

Source: Collated on 19 July 2021 from the CNKI (only Chinese-language publications are included for the statistical analysis).

Such new mechanisms include the Asian Infrastructure Investment Bank (AIIB) and the New Development Bank of BRICS.

Both as a blueprint for and a vehicle of China's efforts to promote connectivity, the South has become an expansive notion that merges with the discourse of global connectivity (Kohlenberg & Godehardt, 2021). Chinese-led regional multilateralism in Central and Eastern Europe, Africa and Latin America is thought to be based on Chinese-backed norms of non-binding agreements, voluntarism and consensus, which is in turn derived from the tradition of South–South cooperation. This process of institutionalization has been shaped by developing nation member states' own social and political interests, which lead to an adjustment of China's behavior (Alden & Alves, 2017; Jakóbowski, 2018).

The state has provided substantial financial support to beef up institutionalization. Between 2013 and 2018, China allocated RMB270.2 billion (approximately US$41.83 billion) to foreign assistance in the form of grants (47.3 per cent), interest-free loans (4.18 per cent), and concessional loans (48.52 per cent), with Africa being the largest recipient (44.65 per cent) and Asia the second largest (36.82 per cent). In 2015, Xi Jinping announced the creation of the South–South Cooperation Assistance Fund (SSCAF) with an initial contribution of $2 billion, to help developing countries carry out the UN 2030 Agenda for Sustainable Development. Two years later, an additional contribution of US$1 billion to the SSCAF was announced at the First Belt and Road Forum for International Cooperation in Beijing (State Council Information Office, 2021). Martin Khor, Executive Director of the UN-affiliated South Centre, hailed the funding as 'a big boost to South-South Cooperation' and a 'game changer' in international relations (Khor, 2015). It has been pointed that China's economic strength has provided leverage to it international cooperation regime and that the Chinese approach is regarded as a more attractive option for the Global South (Vadell et al., 2020).

Apart from the regional and multilateral platforms, China has set up new domestic mechanisms to serve its engagement with the Global South. The China International Development Cooperation Agency (CIDCA), a deputy-ministerial level organization, was established in 2018 under the State Council. Hailed by Beijing as 'a significant move to safeguard world peace and promote common development' as well as 'a milestone in China's foreign aid journey', the CIDCA 'aims to formulate strategic guidelines, plans and policies for foreign aid, coordinate and offer advice on major foreign aid issues, advance the country's reforms in matters involving foreign aid, and identify major programs and supervise and evaluate their implementation'. It has been argued that Chinese model of development aid demonstrates differences from the Western model, with the former deriving from China's distinctive historical experience of engagement with its peripheries, China's own experiences of colonialism and socialist development, values of self-reliance, mutual benefit (win-win) and non-interference and a concept of common values (Dunford, 2020).

The third characteristic of China's engagement is the strengthening of knowledge exchange. China's participation in the SSC movements, institutionally and financially, increases China's voice in terms of the development model and new global governance. According to Xi Jinping, 'the Bandung Spirit is not only relevant to Asian–African cooperation and South–South cooperation, it also provides important inspiration and useful reference for greater North-South cooperation''. Announcing that China would offer 100,000 training opportunities for candidates from developing countries in Asia and Africa, he urged developing countries to 'promote the reform of global economic governance' and to 'improve the global development framework' (Xi, 2015a, 2015b). The Institute of South–South Cooperation and Development was subsequently established at Peking University. With Justin Lin Yifu as the founding Dean, the Institute aims 'to share the experience of state management, to deal with polities, to help other developing countries cultivate high-end government management personnel and to jointly discuss a development road of multi-elements' (Ministry of Commerce, 2016).

China's transnational knowledge transfer includes technical assistance, knowledge sharing, and the training of technical personnel. China's reform and opening-up in 1978 led to a strategic shift of focus from 'war and revolution' to 'peace and development', including economic aid and other forms of mutually beneficial cooperation (Alden, 2005; Li, 2016). This transition has been enhanced under the BRI by schemes to train public officials and technical staff and large numbers of scholarships for students. From 2013 to 2018, China staged more than 7000 training sessions and seminars for foreign officials and technical personnel and in-service education programs involving some 200,000 people. Such projects cover more than 100 subjects, including politics and diplomacy, public administration, national development, poverty reduction, health care, education and scientific research, culture and sports, and transport (State Council Information Office, 2021). China-led special economic zones and overseas industrial parks familiarize Southern countries with Chinese economic practices, thus entailing a policy mobility dimension (Liang et al., 2021).

3.3 | Changing discourses

Alongside the Chinese state's new approach to the Global South come changes in academic and public discourses. The term 'Global South' has not entered the mainstream academic and public lexicon, perhaps because there are comparable concepts with which Chinese readers are more familiar, including the Third World, developing countries, and SSC. A keyword search conducted in July 2021 on *Quanqiu Nanfang* (Global South) in the China National Knowledge Infrastructure (CNKI), the most comprehensive database of journal articles, theses, newspaper essays, and yearbooks published in China since 1915, yielded just eight entries throughout the years. However, as Table 1 shows, the number of references to the Global South-related keywords has increased dramatically, except for the term Third World, reflecting recent global trends (Dirlik, 2007). Apart from confirming the greater prominence of South–South cooperation in Chinese policy narratives (Kohlenberg & Godehardt, 2021), a survey of relevant publications underscores three recurring themes in discourses about the Global South.

The first theme is the enduring importance of the Bandung legacy for China's present policy toward the Global South. According to Ruan (2015), Executive Vice President of the China Institute of International Studies under the Ministry of Foreign Affairs, 'as a participant of the Bandung Conference, an advocate of the Bandung Spirit, and a practitioner of the Bandung Road', China continues to treasure its relationships with developing countries, which serve as a foundation of its foreign policy. The establishment of the China-led BRI, AIIB and Silk Road Fund reflects such a development.

The second theme is the logic of connecting the BRI with the Global South. The launch of the BRI and associated mechanisms has provided a platform for expanding China's ties with developing countries. According to Zha (2018, pp. 206–207) of Peking University, South-South cooperation is no longer 'revolution and mutual repulsion', and the exploration of development paths is not limited to one-way guidance from the West. Instead, China's SSC experience provides 'a mirror and point of reference for the BRI', especially in promoting policy coordination and people-to-people connections, two of the BRI's five pillars.

The third theme is the Chinese governance model's applicability. China's model of economic development has been a main topic of knowledge transfer, and this discourse is now assuming a governance dimension. According to Luo (2019, pp. 7-8), Director of Institute of Chinese Diplomacy at the CCP Central Party School, China's governance experience connotes with self-reliance, developmentalism, effective government and plural consensus. This experience has become an important focus and growing point for the in-depth development of South-South Cooperation. It has helped solve global development problems and deepen South-South knowledge exchange. As such, Chinese governance 'has a positive impact on the development and perfection of the world order'.

In sum, the past decade has witnessed China's growing engagement with the Global South in terms of trade, investment, aids, and the flow of people and ideas. This engagement has been driven by the state with well-endowed institutionalization. It has also been bolstered by policy narratives and academic discourses, as evidenced by the increasing number of publications on it. The launch in January 2021 of *China and the Global South*, a Chinese-English electronic journal, by the Intellisia Institute (a Guangzhou-based independent think-tank), represents a further step to deepening knowledge about the Global South. China's expanding engagement with the Global South is therefore a symbol of and a driving force behind the rise of China on the global stage.

4 | CONTESTING THE GLOBAL SOUTH

4.1 | China as a revisionist power?

China's approach to the Global South has received mixed receptions. Skeptics are concerned by what they see as China's strategy to export its model of economic development and political governance to other countries. Fukuyama (2016) characterizes the BRI as a competition between 'Chinese and Western strategies to promote economic growth' and says that 'the outcome of this struggle will determine the fate of much of Eurasia in the decades to come''.

However, many Southern countries, especially in Africa, seem to be more receptive to the Chinese experience of development. Jorge Chediek, Director of the UN Office for South–South Cooperation, remarked that 'China is a model for developing countries, and the BRI provides the rest of the world with the opportunity to share in China's great experiences' (cited in Xu, 2019). Oqubay and Lin (2019, pp. ix–x) emphasize that 'the lessons from China—policy ownership and strategic planning—increasingly inform national development strategies in many African countries'. China is able to share its development experiences to promote industrialization and technological innovation through concrete project building and knowledge-sharing platforms (Cheong et al., 2016; Han & Webber, 2020; Li, 2016). A recent study by senior African politicians and academics cites a 2019 survey in which 67 per cent of respondents agreed that Asia, especially China, is the world region that Africa has most to learn from and concludes: 'Many Africans aspire to "be like China"' (Mills et al., 2020, pp. 9–10). Rather than a case of debt-trap diplomacy, as some commentators label the BRI, Brautigam (2020, p. 12) argues that 'the story of Chinese lending is far more complicated, interesting and potentially developmental than it is currently portrayed'. China's economic rise, far from happening at the expense of Southeast Asia, has (according to the SOAS economist Anne Booth) benefited the economies of both Southeast Asia and China (cited in Liu, 2022b).

Furthermore, other studies suggest that China does not want, and lacks the capacity, to overhaul the postwar world order. China still embraces 'the Westphalian principles of state sovereignty […], while adapting to the liberal norms of globalization', and is 'dissatisfied not with the fundamental rules of the order but its status in the hierarchy of the order' (Zhao, 2018, p. 643; see also Lukin & Fan, 2019; Hooijmaaijers, 2021). Investigations of China's international development finance show that China's attitude to global economic governance is one of 'Business as Usual' and that 'the China model is not so revolutionary as many analysts suppose', and that the World Bank has emulated the Chinese approach (Babones et al., 2020; Zeitz, 2021). Similarly, Justin Lin Yifu's 'China Model' is regarded as part of mainstream economic theorizing and 'complementary to the global capitalist system' (Åberg & Becker, 2020).

My own studies (Lim & Liu, 2021; Liu, 2022b; Liu & Lim, 2019) also show that recipient countries' political economy plays a significant role in deciding the extent to which the Chinese model of development is adopted. For example, the eventual outcome of Sino-Malaysian interaction depends on three conditions: fulfillment of Malaysia's longstanding pro-Malay policy, a mutual vision between the state and federal authorities, and advancement of both nations' geopolitical interests. While Malaysia has attracted Chinese investment, it rejects the political and ideological influences that might come with the economic linkages or conflict with Malaysian political and cultural values. As Prime Minister Mahathir put it in 2019, 'I believe that China will have a great influence over the whole world in the future, but for the moment, it is not for us to promote Chinese ideas and ideologies' (Liu, 2022a, p. 168).

4.2 | The logics of political economy and global geopolitics

Although China has increasingly engaged with the Global South, the outcome of knowledge/policy transfer is contingent upon factors many of which are beyond China's control. These include recipient nations' domestic political economy and global geopolitics, especially escalating US-China rivalries. In the case of Sukarno's Indonesia, domestic political consideration played a major part in determining whether and what knowledge from China was adopted. Alden (2005, p. 153) underscores that Africa's interests in China 'complement much of the agenda being promoted by Beijing. Governing and business elites within Africa see new opportunities in China: trade and investment opportunities, ways to bolster regime stability, and strategically significant partnerships'. Arkebe Oqubay, senior minister in the Ethiopian government, and Justin Yifu Lin have demonstrated that China's rise in Africa began at a time 'when Africans themselves were engaged in a major soul-searching exercise to find out why the continent's development path had gone wrong' after more than fifty years and continuous ties with the Global North since the end of colonial rule. 'The growing fatigue with neoliberal policy experiments that is driving a search for an alternative development model has led many African leaders to take a closer look at China's recent development experience in the hope of drawing important lessons from it' (Oqubay & Lin, 2019; see also Mills et al., 2020). Hodzi (2020, p. 902) argues that Africans have selected elements of the China model that serve their interests while deriving maximum benefits from China and that Beijing 'is being forced to reconsider and be pragmatic in the norms it advances to African countries—something akin to the proverbial "across the river by feeling the stones"'.

Other studies highlight the need to conceptualize the interlinked nature of domestic state-society models and the global political economy in an attempt to understand China's rising influence (de Graaff et al., 2020). A major recent development in this regard is the renewed partnership between the US and its Western allies, symbolized by the G7 Summit in June 2021 (Carbis Bay, 2021). Though physically absent, China featured prominently in the Summit, which stressed 'our commitment to international cooperation, multilateralism and an open, resilient, rules-based world order'. More significantly, the USA and its allies launched a new initiative, Build

Back Better World (B3W), aimed at creating an orchestrated and direct alternative to China's BRI. Lauded as 'a values-driven, high-standard, and transparent infrastructure partnership led by major democracies to help narrow the $40+ trillion infrastructure need in the developing world,' the B3W has four areas of focus—climate, health and health security, digital technology, and gender equity and equality—with catalytic investments from our respective development finance institutions. While questions pertaining to the new plan's finance, coordination, and operations loom large, such a coordinated effort is likely to pose major challenges to the BRI and further strengthen China's engagement with the Global South in years to come.

The US and its allies have characterized China as a 'systemic challenge'. According to the Economist (2021), by framing the relationship as 'a zero-sum contest', Biden has effectively ruled out co-existence and 'is overestimating America's influence and underestimating how much potential allies have to lose by turning their back on China'. Commentators have identified the fallacies of the 'misplaced ideological hostility' and the danger of 'ideological competition' (Pepinsky & Weiss, 2021; Zhao, 2021). In addition to understanding the domestic logics of the recipient Southern nations, it is wise to take heed of these views as well as aforementioned studies regarding the limits of the China model in the developing world.

As major donors to the developing world and the largest economies, both China and the US have their own national interests to promote. Nevertheless, it is imperative to take a stakeholder-centered approach by placing the recipient nations' interests at the center of engagements. This requires a sensible assessment of the delicate political economy and developing robust mechanisms to sustain the projects. Studies have shown the effectiveness of a multiple stakeholder perspective in elaborating 'a path dependent way but subject to the spatial embeddedness of specific projects' (Han & Webber, 2020). Working closely with Africa's existing regional programs and the ASEAN Economic Community will help promote mutual benefits (e.g. Lisinge, 2020; Liu, 2022b; Oqubay & Lin, 2019).

Both the US and China wish to cooperate on global climate change. Together with recipient nations and international organizations, the two countries may come up with effective solutions to such global challenges, for both the BRI and the B3W. Finally, it is essential to go beyond the zero-sum mindset and to allow the Global South, China included, into the emerging global governance structure set up after the Second World War, when the Global South was an infant player in the international political economy. In this regard, Bandung heralded a new era for the South, which continues to require transnational knowledge exchanges across all countries, both North and South.

5 | CONCLUSION

The genesis of China's systemic engagement with the Global South can be traced back to the Bandung Conference, which continues to underpin China's attitude to the developing world. Underlining this engagement has been China's belief in the shared experiences and aspirations of developing countries, as well as the enduring value of Bandung and of the Chinese model as a path to economic growth, poverty alleviation, and global governance reforms.

China's increasing economic linkages with the developing world and the potential geopolitical benefits have helped further the role played by the Global South in China's international strategies. It is evidenced not only by the growing discourses in policy and academic arenas, but also by the strengthening (both structurally and financially) of bilateral and multilateral institutions for engaging with the developing world. The BRI has served as a platform for facilitating and expanding this institutionalization. It is further bolstered by the establishment of the China International Development Cooperation Agency as a domestic organization strategizing and coordinating activities related to the Global South.

The outcome of China's engagement with the Global South, including transnational knowledge transfer, depends not just on China's will and efforts but, more importantly, on how countries in the South appropriate it to serve their domestic needs. Forging a sensible understanding of these interests will ensure the smooth operation and sustainable development of relevant knowledge and policy, thus bringing long-term benefits to China and other countries.

Finally, one must avoid reducing the complex and multi-faceted relationship between China and the West to a mere ideological struggle. China has no intention of overhauling the global order, or even the capacity to do so; rather, it aims to provide a feasible alternative path of development. Its engagement with the Global South is subject to structural and narrative constraints that are beyond its control. Dragging the developing world into the so-called 'rivalry of the century' and forcing it to take sides will harm the future development not only of the Global South but global powers including the US and China.

ACKNOWLEDGMENTS
The author is grateful to Akebe Oqubay and Chris Alden for enhancing his understanding about Sino-African interactions and to Gregor Benton for his constructive comments. Funding for this research is provided by a grant from Nanyang Technological University (04INS000136C430). The author is solely responsible for the views and any remaining errors in this essay.

ORCID
Hong Liu https://orcid.org/0000-0003-3328-8429

REFERENCES

Åberg, J.H. & Becker, D. (2020) China as exemplar: Justin Lin, new structural economics, and the unorthodox orthodoxy of the China model. *Politics & Policy*, 48(5), 815–835. Available from: https://doi.org/10.1111/polp.12376

Acharya, A. (2016) Studying the Bandung conference from a Global IR perspective. *Australian Journal of International Affairs*, 70(4), 342–357. Available from: https://doi.org/10.1080/10357718.2016.1168359

Akyeampong, E. & Fofack, H. (2019) Special issue on 'Africa and China: emerging patterns of engagement'. *Economic History of Developing Regions*, 34(3), 251–258. Available from: https://doi.org/10.1080/20780389.2019.1684691

Alden, C. (2005) China in Africa. *Survival*, 47(3), 147–164. Available from: https://doi.org/10.1080/00396330500248086

Alden, C. & Alves, A. (2017) China's regional forum diplomacy in the developing world: socialisation and the 'Sinosphere'. *Journal of Contemporary China*, 26(103), 151–165. Available from: https://doi.org/10.1080/10670564.2016.1206276

Babones, S., Åberg, J.H. & Hodzi, O. (2020) China's role in global development finance: China challenge or business as usual? *Global Policy*, 11(3), 326–335. Available from: https://doi.org/10.1111/1758-5899.12802

Blanchard, J.M. (2021) Belt and Road Initiative (BRI) Blues: powering BRI research back on track to avoid choppy seas. *Journal of Chinese Political Science*, 26, 235–255. Available from: https://doi.org/10.1007/s11366-020-09717-0

Brautigam, D. (2020) A critical look at Chinese "debt-trap diplomacy": the rise of a meme. *Area Development and Policy*, 5(1), 1–14. Available from: https://doi.org/10.1080/23792949.2019.1689828

Carbis Bay (2021) G7 Summit Communiqué, 13 June 13 2021. Available at: https://www.g7uk.org/wp-content/uploads/2021/06/Carbis-Bay-G7-Summit-Communique-PDF-430KB-25-pages-3.pdf [Accessed 15 June 2021].

Cheong, K.C., Wong, C.Y. & Goh, K.L. (2016) Technology catch-up with Chinese characteristics: What can southeast Asia learn from China? *The Round Table*, 105(6), 667–681. Available from: https://doi.org/10.1080/00358533.2016.1246853

Chin, T. (2021) The Afro-Asian Silk Road: Chinese experiments in postcolonial premodernity. *PMLA/Publications of the Modern Language Association of America*, 136(1), 17–38. Available from: https://doi.org/10.1080/00358533.2016.1246853

De Graaff, N., ten Brink, T. & Parmar, I. (2020) China's rise in a liberal world order in transition – introduction to the FORUM. *Review of International Political Economy*, 27(2), 191–207. Available from: https://doi.org/10.1080/09692290.2019.1709880

Dirlik, A. (2007) Global South: predicament and promise. *The Global South*, 1(1), 12–23.

Dolowitz, D. & Marsh, D. (1996) Who learns what from whom: a review of the policy transfer literature. *Political Studies*, 44(2), 343–357. Available from: https://doi.org/10.1111/j.1467-9248.1996.tb00334.x

Dunford, M. (2020) Chinese and Development Assistance Committee (DAC) development cooperation and development finance: implications for the BRI and international governance. *Eurasian Geography and Economics*, 61(2), 125–136. Available from: https://doi.org/10.1080/15387216.2020.1716821

Economist. (2021) Biden's New China Doctrine, *Economist*, 440 (9254), 17 July, p. 11.

Eisenstadt, S.N. (2000) Multiple modernities. *Daedalus*, 129, 1–29.

Friedrichs, J. (2019) Explaining China's popularity in the Middle East and Africa. *Third World Quarterly*, 40(9), 1634–1654. Available from: https://doi.org/10.1080/01436597.2019.1592670

Fuchs, A. & Rudyak, M. (2019) The motives of China's foreign aid. In: Zeng, K.A. (Ed.) *Handbook on the international political economy of China*. Edward Elgar Publishing, pp. 392–410.

Fukuyama, F. (2016) *Exporting the Chinese model*, Project Syndicate, 12 January. Available at: https://www.project-syndicate.org/onpoint/china-one-belt-one-road-strategy-by-francis-fukuyama-2016-01 [Accessed 2 March 2021].

Gray, K. & Gills, B. (2016) South–South cooperation and the rise of the Global South. *Third World Quarterly*, 37(4), 557–574. Available from: https://doi.org/10.1080/01436597.2015.1128817

Han, X. & Webber, M. (2020) From Chinese dam building in Africa to the Belt and Road Initiative: Assembling infrastructure projects and their linkages. *Political Geography*, 77, 102102. Available from: https://doi.org/10.1016/j.polgeo.2019.102102

Hodzi, O. (2020) African political elites and the making(s) of the China model in Africa. *Politics & Policy*, 48(5), 887–907. Available from: https://doi.org/10.1111/polp.12380

Hooijmaaijers, B. (2021) China, the BRICS, and the limitations of reshaping global economic governance. *The Pacific Review*, 34(1), 29–55. Available from: https://doi.org/10.1080/09512748.2019.1649298

Jakóbowski, J. (2018) Chinese-led regional multilateralism in Central and Eastern Europe, Africa and Latin America: 16 + 1, FOCAC, and CCF. *Journal of Contemporary China*, 27(113), 659–673. Available from: https://doi.org/10.1080/10670564.2018.1458055

Khor, M. (2015) *China's boost to South-South cooperation*. Available at: https://www.southcentre.int/question/chinas-boost-to-south-south-cooperation/ [Accessed 20 July 2021].

Kohlenberg, P. & Godehardt, N. (2021) Locating the "South" in China's connectivity politics. *Third World Quarterly*, 42(9), 1963–1981. Available from: https://doi.org/10.1080/01436597.2020.1780909

Kurlantzick, J. (2007) *Charm offensive: How China's soft power is transforming the world*. Yale University Press.

Li, A. (2016) Technology transfer in China-Africa relation: myth or reality. *Transnational Corporations Review*, 8(3), 183–195. Available from: https://doi.org/10.1080/19186444.2016.1233718

Liang, Y., Zeng, J., Kuik, C.-C., Zhou, Z. & Zhou, K. (2021) Policy transfer and scale reconstruction of China's overseas industrial parks: A case study of the Malaysia-China Kuantan Industrial Park. *Journal of Geographical Sciences*, 31, 733–746. Available from: https://doi.org/10.1007/s11442-021-1868-2

Lim, G. & Liu, H. (2021) Soaring Garuda meets rising dragon: the political economy of the Belt and Road Initiative in Indonesia. In: Liow. J., Liu, H. & Xue, G. (Eds.) *Research handbook on the Belt and Road Initiative*. Edward Elgar Publishing, pp. 123–136.

Lin, J.Y. (2017) What China can teach developing nations about building power, New York Times, 5 December. Available from: https://www.nytimes.com/2017/12/05/opinion/xi-jinping-china-rises.html [Accessed June 20, 2021]

Liow, J., Liu, H. & Xue, G. (Eds.) (2021) *Research handbook on the Belt and Road Initiative*. Edward Elgar Publishing. Available from: https://www.e-elgar.com/shop/gbp/research-handbook-on-the-belt-and-road-initiative-9781789908701.html [Accessed 23 November 2021].

Lisinge, R. (2020) The Belt and Road Initiative and Africa's regional infrastructure development: implications and lessons. *Transnational Corporations Review*, 12(4), 425–438. Available from: https://doi.org/10.1080/19186444.2020.1795527

Liu, H. (2011) *China and the shaping of Indonesia, 1949–1965*. National University of Singapore Press and Kyoto University Press. Available from: https://nuspress.nus.edu.sg/products/china-and-the-shaping-of-indonesia [Accessed 23 November 2021].

Liu, H. (2022a) Beyond strategic hedging: Mahathir's China policy and the changing political economy in Malaysia, 2018–2020. In: Heiduk, F. (Ed.) *Asian geopolitics and the US-China rivalry*. Routledge, pp. 159–176. Available from: https://doi.org/10.4324/9781003106814-10

Liu, H. (2022b) *The political economy of transnational governance: China and Southeast Asia in the 21st century*. Routledge.

Available from: https://www.routledge.com/The-Political-Econo my-of-Transnational-Governance-in-Asia-China-and-South east/Liu/p/book/9780367608804 [Accessed 23 November 2021].

Liu, H. & Lim, G. (2019) The political economy of a rising China in Southeast Asia: Malaysia's responses to the Belt and Road Initiative. *Journal of Contemporary China*, 28(116), 216–231. Available from: https://doi.org/10.1080/10670564.2018.1511393

Liu, H. & Wang, T. (2021) The institutionalization and effective-ness of transnational policy transfer: The China-Singapore Suzhou Industrial Park as a case study. *Public Administration and Development*, 41(3), 103–114. Available from: https://doi. org/10.1002/pad.1956

Liu, H. & Zhou, T. (2019) Bandung humanism and a new understand-ing of the Global South: An introduction. *Critical Asian Studies*, 51(2), 141–143. Available from: https://doi.org/10.1080/14672 715.2018.1564625

Lovell, J. (2019) *Maoism: A global history*. Random House. Available from: https://www.penguinrandomhouse.com/books/602335/ maoism-by-julia-lovell/ [Accessed 23 November 2021].

Lukin, A. & Fan, X. (2019) What is BRICS for China? *Strategic Analysis*, 43(6), 620–631. Available from: https://doi.org/10. 1080/09700161.2019.1669896

Luo, J. (2019) Zhongguo yu Fazhanzhong Guojia de Zhiguo Lizheng Jinyan Jiaoliu: Lishi, Lilun yu Shijie Yiyi [Exchanges of gover-nance experiences between China and developing countries: history, theory and world significance]. *Xiya Feizhou [West Asia and Africa]*, 2, 3–23.

Mills, G., Obasanjo, O., Desalegn, H. & van der Merwe, E. (2020) *The Asian aspiration: Why and how Africa should emulate Asia*. Hurst & Company.

Ministry of Commerce (2016) *Institute of South-South Cooperation and Development (ISSCAD) established in Peking University*. Available at: http://english.mofcom.gov.cn/article/newsreleas e/significantnews/201605/20160501314609.shtml [Accessed 30 July 2021].

Muttarak, R. (2017) Moving along the Belt and Road: Implications of China's "one belt, one road" strategies on Chinese migration. *Translocal Chinese: East Asian Perspectives*, 11(2), 312–332. Available from: https://doi.org/10.1163/24522015-01102007

Oqubay, A. & Lin, J.Y. (2019). Introduction. In Oqcubay, A. & Lin, J.Y. (Eds.) *China–Africa and an economic transformation*. Oxford University Press, pp. 1–18. Available from: https://oxford.unive rsitypressscholarship.com/view/10.1093/oso/9780198830 504.001.0001/oso-9780198830504-chapter-1 [Accessed 23 November 2021].

Pepinsky, T. & Weiss, J.C. (2021) The clash of systems? Washington should avoid ideological competition with Beijing, Foreign Affairs. Available at: https://www.foreignaffairs.com/articles/ united-states/2021-06-11/clash-systems [Accessed 31 July 2021].

Phillips, A. (2016) Beyond Bandung: The 1955 Asian-African confer-ence and its legacies for international order. *Australian Journal of International Affairs*, 70(4), 329–341. Available from: https:// doi.org/10.1080/10357718.2016.1153600

Pollitt, C. (2015) Towards a new world: Some inconvenient truths for Anglosphere public administration. *International Review of Administrative Sciences*, 81(1), 3–17. Available from: https:// doi.org/10.1177/0020852314544069

Qian, Q. (2003) *Waijiao Shiji [Ten Stories of A Diplomat]*. Shijie Zhishi Chubanshe.

Ratigan, K. (2021) Are Peruvians enticed by the "China Model"? Chinese investment and public opinion in Peru. *Studies in Comparative International Development*, 56(1), 87–111. Available from: https://doi.org/10.1007/s12116-021-09321-0

Ruan, Z. (2015) Fuyu Wanglong Jingshen Xinneihan, Goujian Xingxin Guoji Guangxi [Enriching the Bandung spirit with new substances, constructing a new model of international relation-ship]. *Qiushi*, 13, 58–60.

Sanny, J. & Selormey, E. (2020) Africans regard China's influence as significant and positive, but slipping, Afro Barometer, dispatch no. 407, 17 November. Available from: https://afrobarometer. org/publications/ad407-africans-regard-chinas-influence-signi ficant-and-positive-slipping [Accessed 23 November 2021].

Schneider, F. (Ed.) (2021) *Global perspectives on China's Belt and Road Initiative: Asserting agency through regional connectivity*. Amsterdam University Press. Available from: https://www.aup. nl/en/book/9789048553952/global-perspectives-on-china-s-belt-and-road-initiative [Accessed 23 November 2021].

Seah, S., Ha, H.T., Martinus, M. & Thao, P.T. (2021) *The state of Southeast Asia: 2021*. ISEAS-Yusof Ishak Institute. Available from: https://www.iseas.edu.sg/wp-content/uploads/2021/01/ The-State-of-SEA-2021-v2.pdf [Accessed 23 November 2021].

Shinn, D.H. (2019). China–Africa ties in historical context. In: Oqubay, A. & Lin, J.Y. (Eds.) *China-Africa and an economic transfor-mation*. Oxford University Press, pp. 61–83. Available from: https://oxford.universitypressscholarship.com/view/10.1093/ oso/9780198830504.001.0001/oso-9780198830504-chapter-4 [Accessed 23 November 2021].

State Council Information Office of the People's Republic of China (2021) *China's international development coopera-tion in the new era*. Available at: http://en.cidca.gov.cn/2021-- 01/10/c_581228.htm [Accessed 23 July 2021].

Thomas, N. (2021, July 28). *Far more world leaders visit China than America*. Available at: https://www.lowyinstitute.org/the-inter preter/far-more-world-leaders-visit-china-america [Accessed 2 August 2021].

UNICEF China. (2019) *South-South cooperation explained*. Available at: https://www.unicef.cn/en/south-south-cooperation-explained [Accessed 21 March 2021].

Vadell, J., Brutto, G.L. & Leite, A.C.C. (2020) The Chinese South-South development cooperation: An assessment of its structural transformation. *Revista Brasileira de Política Internacional*, 63(2), 1–22. Available from: https://doi.org/10.1590/0034-73292 02000201

Welsh, B. & Chang, A. (2015) Choosing China: Public percep-tions of 'China as a model'. *Journal of Contemporary China*, 24(93), 442–456. Available from: https://doi.org/10.1080/10670 564.2014.953847

World Trade Organization. (2019) *World trade statistical review 2019*. Available at: https://www.wto.org/english/res_e/statis_e/ wts2019_e/wts2019_e.pdf [Accessed 18 June 2021].

Wu, J. (2013) President Xi gives speech to Indonesia's parliament, China Daily, 2 October. Available at: https://www.chinadaily. com.cn/china/2013xiapec/2013-10/02/content_17007915_2. htm [Accessed 20 June 2021].

Xi, J. (2015a) *Carry forward the Bandung spirit for win-win cooper-ation*, speech at the Asian-African Summit in Jakarta. Available at: https://www.fmprc.gov.cn/mfa_eng/topics_665678/xjpdb jstjxgsfwbfydnxycxyfldrhyhwlhy60znjnhd/t1259844.shtml [Accessed 20 July 2021].

Xi, J. (2015b) *Speech at "high-level roundtable on South-South co-operation"*, UN Headquarters. Available at: https://www.fmprc. gov.cn/mfa_eng/topics_665678/xjpdmgjxgsfwbcxlhgcl70znx lfh/t1302399.shtml [Accessed 20 July 2021].

Xie, Y.U. & Jin, Y. (2021) Global attitudes toward China: trends and correlates. *Journal of Contemporary China*. Available from: https://doi.org/10.1080/10670564.2021.1926088

Xu, L. (2019) *China takes extraordinary initiatives in South-South cooperation*. Available at: https://www.fmprc.gov.cn/mfa_eng/ topics_665678/xjpdmgjxgsfwbcxlhgcl70znxlfh/t1302399.shtml [Accessed 21 March 2021].

Zeitz, A.O. (2021) Emulate or differentiate? Chinese development finance, competition, and World Bank infrastructure funding.

The Review of International Organizations, 16(2), 265–292. Available from: https://doi.org/10.1007/s11558-020-09377-y

Zha, D. (2018) Nannan Hezuo Yindong Lichen: Dui Yidaiyilu de Qishi [History of South-South cooperation: lessons for the Belt and Road Initiative], *Zhongguo Guoji Zhanlue Pinglun. China International Strategy Review*, 1, 196–207.

Zhang, L. (2014) *Dangdai Zhongguo Waijiao Jianshi [A short history of contemporary Chinese diplomacy]*. Shanghai Renmin Chubanshe.

Zhao, S. (2018) A revisionist stakeholder: China and the post-world war II world order. *Journal of Contemporary China*, 27(113), 643–658. Available from: https://doi.org/10.1080/10670564.2018.1458029

Zhao, S. (2021) The US–China rivalry in the emerging bipolar world: Hostility, alignment, and power balance. *Journal of Contemporary China*, 1–17. Available from: https://doi.org/10.1080/10670564.2021.1945733

Zhou, E. (1955) *Letter from Zhou Enlai to Ali Sastroamidjojo*, 10 February, History and Public Policy Program Digital Archive, PRC FMA 207-00003-01, 16-17. Available at: https://digitalarchive.wilsoncenter.org/document/114659 [Accessed 9 May 2020].

AUTHOR BIOGRAPHY

Hong Liu is the Tan Lark Sye Chair Professor of Public Policy and Global Affairs at the School of Social Sciences, Nanyang Technological University in Singapore, where he also serves as Director of the Nanyang Centre for Public Administration. His recent publications include *The political economy of transnational governance: China and Southeast Asia in the 21st century* (Routledge, 2022).

How to cite this article: Liu, H. (2022) China engages the Global South: From Bandung to the Belt and Road Initiative. *Global Policy*, 13(Suppl. 1), 11–22. Available from: https://doi.org/10.1111/1758-5899.13034

Received: 12 August 2021 | Revised: 3 January 2022 | Accepted: 4 January 2022

DOI: 10.1111/1758-5899.13055

Sensemaking and Sustainable Development: Chinese Overseas Acquisitions and the Globalisation of Traditional Chinese Medicine

Peng Wang[1] | Eugenia Yijun Xing[2] | Xiaotao Zhang[3] | Yipeng Liu[4]

[1]Beijing Hospital of Traditional Chinese Medicine, Capital Medical University, Beijing, China

[2]Brunel University London, Uxbridge, UK

[3]Central University of Finance and Economics, Beijing, China

[4]University of Reading, Reading, UK

Correspondence
Yipeng Liu, University of Reading, Reading, UK.
Email: yipeng.liu@henley.ac.uk

Eugenia Yijun Xing, Brunel University London, Uxbridge, UK.
Email: eugenia.xing@brunel.ac.uk

Funding information
Beijing Moral Cultivation Research Society, Grant/Award Number: jckt2017-22; Schoeller Foundation for Business and Society, Grant/Award Number: Schoeller Fellowship

Abstract

Despite the increasing attention paid to sustainability management and the wide prevalence of the United Nation's SDGs (Sustainable Development Goals) in the discourse of business and society, there is little nuanced understanding of the impact of culture on sustainable development in international contexts, and on the globalisation of emerging economies in particular. By juxtaposing the literature streams of sensemaking, micro-foundations, and collaborative partnerships, this paper presents an investigation into how culture and sensemaking influence sustainable development. Our research context – Chinese globalisation endeavours – includes Chinese overseas acquisitions and the globalisation of traditional Chinese medicine. This paper illuminates the role played by sensemaking and Taoist philosophy with regard to sustainable development. Taking a micro-foundational perspective, we show how both cultural and institutional contexts can influence sustainable development in Chinese globalisation endeavours enacted in the form of collaborative partnerships.

1 | INTRODUCTION

Sustainability matters for the long-term survival of humankind, and its significance has been urgently highlighted in the United Nations Sustainable Development Goals (United Nations, 2015). The achievement of sustainability necessitates the collective endeavours of an innovative action by individuals, organisations, and society from multiple levels and involving diverse stakeholders (Starik & Kanashiro, 2020; Starik & Marcus, 2000). Specifically, given their economic size and dynamic development, emerging economies and the developing world can play an important role in contributing to the design and implementation of climate governance (Held et al. 2014).

However, the extant research seems to be elusive with regard to sustainable development. As acknowledged, sustainability and corporate social responsibility (CSR) have both commonalities and distinctive characteristics (Bansal & Song, 2017). The prevailing discrepancy calls for a nuanced and contextualised understanding of sustainability and sustainable development. We argue that the sensemaking literature (Maitlis & Christianson, 2014) may provide revealing and useful insights to understand sustainable development. For instance, the notion of ecological sensemaking suggests that both the social and ecological processes matter by encouraging a holistic and a multi-level approach (Whiteman & Cooper, 2011).

Global contexts can inform and impact global policy (Bakonyi et al. 2021). The increasing globalising endeavours enacted by Chinese organisations tend to favour collaborative partnerships, such as overseas mergers and acquisitions (Xing et al. 2017) and partnerships between healthcare providers (Xing et al. 2020a). However, global collaborative partnerships are complex global affairs that entail additional challenges that the involved stakeholders need to interpret and respond to in order to construct sustainable development practices. In particular, institutional differences can have a strong bearing on the dynamics of sustainable development. Thus, sensemaking with institutions (Weber & Glynn, 2006) can influence sustainable development in important ways in the context of global collaborative partnerships.

Furthermore, there is little nuanced understanding of the impact of culture on sustainable development in international contexts, and on the globalisation of emerging economies in particular. Building upon micro-foundational insights into collaborative partnerships (Liu et al. 2017) and sustainability management (Cooper et al. 2017), we argue that cultural and philosophical underpinnings can shed revealing light on sustainable development. For instance, Taoist leadership can inspire and cultivate employee green behaviours (Xing & Starik, 2017). The cultural proximity between Chinese traditional culture and African Ubuntu can facilitate mutual understanding and the enactment of hybrid Human Resource Management (HRM) practices in collaborative partnerships (Xing et al. 2016). Therefore, this paper aims to present an exploration of how culture and sensemaking influence sustainable development in Chinese globalisation endeavours. The research context includes Chinese overseas acquisitions and the globalisation of traditional Chinese medicine in the form of collaborative partnerships.

Our study makes three theoretical contributions to sensemaking and sustainable development in global contexts. First, it contributes to a nuanced and contextualised understanding of sensemaking by exploring the complex interactions that take place between sensemaking and institutions in the context of Chinese globalisation endeavours. Second, it contributes to demonstrating, from a micro-foundational perspective, the role played by culture and philosophy in advancing sustainability and sustainable development research. Third, our findings highlight the joint influence of culture and sensemaking in shaping the dynamics of global collaborative partnerships. This paper is organised as follows. We first review the theoretical underpinnings of sensemaking, collaborative partnerships, and micro-foundational theoretical perspectives. We then present the research context of Chinese globalisation endeavours. We conclude by discussing the theoretical, managerial, and policy implications.

2 | THEORETICAL BACKGROUND

2.1 | Sensemaking and meanings of sustainability

Sensemaking theory has a long history in management and organisation studies (Maitlis & Christianson, 2014). The signature of sensemaking theory is the question: 'How can I know what I think when I see what I say?' (Weick, 1995). As a complex process, sensemaking centres on two key components: (1) events as triggers for sensemaking, which leads to the creation of intersubjective meaning; and (2) the role played by action in sensemaking. Proactive enactment and reactive retrospect are two essential perspectives simultaneously involved in sensemaking. Events are not identified, scanned, and analysed, but enacted through their salience (Weick & Sutcliffe, 2006). When people engage in sensemaking, they invoke ever increasing abstraction, which means that they may move away from their initial impressions while demonstrating a certain degree of agency by engaging in action. For instance, during strategic change in academia sensemaking, process intertwines with identity construction and issue interpretation (Gioia & Thomas, 1996). Sensemaking can affect the willingness of people to disengage from their initial story and adopt a new one that is more sensitive to the particulars of the present context. Thus, context and the broader environment can have a bigger say in influencing the sensemaking process and the individual and organisational actors involved.

Although one persistent criticism levelled at Karl Weick's original sensemaking theory is its neglect of the role of larger social and historical contexts (Weber & Glynn, 2006), recent research began to highlight the importance of institutional contexts and global challenges and issues. Of particular importance is the notion of ecological sensemaking, which reveals how both the social and ecological processes matter while encouraging a holistic view and a multi-level perspective (Whiteman & Cooper, 2011). Along this line of reasoning, it is worth mentioning the commonalities and distinctive characteristics found in sustainability and corporate social responsibility (CSR) (Bansal & Song, 2017). The salience of this discrepancy calls for a nuanced and contextualised understanding of sustainability. Simply put, sustainability matters for the long-term survival of humankind, and its significance has been urgently highlighted in the United Nations Sustainable Development Goals (United Nations, 2015).

Arguably, sensemaking theory and recent empirical evidence may offer some revealing insights in regard to advancing the meanings of sustainability. Departing from the content-based models of CSR, a process model based on sensemaking theory helps to explain how managers think and act holistically with respect to their key stakeholders and the world in regard to CSR-related activities (Basu & Palazzo, 2008). Differing from moral reasoning, which is rooted in 'rationalist approaches', the sensemaking perspective offers an alternative approach to understanding how individuals respond to ethical issues at work (Sonenshein, 2007). A study conducted on Fairtrade minimum prices has suggested sensemaking to explain how actors can collectively agree on what is ethical in complex situations and how they cope with the challenges arising from the stark inequalities found in extreme contexts (Reinecke & Ansari, 2015). To summarise, sensemaking offers a useful theoretical perspective for individuals to seek and find meaningfulness through work while highlighting the multi- and cross-level interactions that occur among individual, organisational, and institutional factors in the sensemaking process (Aguinis & Glavas, 2019). In a similar vein, the achievement of sustainability necessitates multi-level collective endeavours of and innovative action by individuals, organisations, and society involving diverse stakeholders (Starik & Kanashiro, 2020; Starik & Marcus, 2000).

2.2 | Collaborative partnerships and the micro-foundational perspective

Collaborative partnerships constitute an important organisational form in organisations and management studies. Research conducted on this organisational form has yielded a rich body of knowledge, shedding light on several complex organisational phenomena. Collaborative partnerships include various organisational forms – such as mergers and acquisitions (M&As) (Liu & Meyer, 2020), university-industry partnerships (Liu & Huang, 2018), joint ventures (Collinson & Liu, 2019), public-private partnerships (Liu et al. 2020; Xing et al. 2020a), and entrepreneurial partnerships (Liu & Almor, 2016; Xing et al. 2018) – the key characteristics of which are centred on the social interactions of individuals and organisational actors across traditional organisational boundaries.

The micro-foundations movement that has emerged in strategy and management research (Felin et al. 2015) provides a perspective that is useful to understand the underlying mechanisms and organisational tensions found in the context of collaborative partnerships. Micro-foundations can be derived theoretically from multiple disciplines, including psychology, behavioural sciences, sociology, anthropology, and philosophy, among others. Investigating human factors as the micro-foundations of collaborative partnerships can advance our collective understanding of the phenomena in important ways (Liu et al. 2017). Furthermore, micro-foundational approaches can advance international management, global business, and innovation research (Liu et al. 2021). For instance, genetic distance can positively influence the performance of the cross-border Research and Development (R&D) activities of emerging markets multinational enterprises (EMNEs) (Xu et al. 2021). In essence, a better understanding of micro-level behavioural antecedents and social interaction provides an opportunity to advance our understanding of the macro-level processes and outcomes of management practices (Barney & Felin, 2013).

In the international entrepreneurship research stream, resilience may serve as a micro-foundation of effectuation strategy that entrepreneurs can leverage to cope with risk and stressful situation (Liu, 2020a). Furthermore, university capability, as a micro-foundation of the triple helix model, helps disentangle the intertwined interactions among university, industry, and government (Liu & Huang, 2018). In designing and launching global business incubation platforms, international migrant entrepreneurs can orchestrate resources with multiple stakeholders through entrepreneurial partnerships (Liu, 2020b). In leadership research, a leader's identity work can help explain the dynamics of sociocultural integration in Chinese M&As (Xing & Liu, 2016). As for international M&A research, from a micro-foundational perspective, boundary spanners can significantly influence the reverse knowledge transfer from target to acquirer in the context of Chinese cross-border acquisitions (Liu & Meyer, 2020).

2.3 | The micro-foundations of sustainability and their philosophical underpinnings

Building upon the micro-foundational perspective, some pioneering research has shed insightful light on why and how behavioural micro-foundations may advance our understanding of sustainability and behavioural changes (Cooper et al. 2017). For instance, the adoption of a unique micro-foundational approach to grammatical gender marking to measure women-oriented cultural effects has shown how the percentage of women sitting on an organisation's board of directors has a direct effect on such organisation's attitude towards environmental sustainability (Shoham et al. 2017). From a social identity perspective, an organisational ethic of care can drive employees to become involved in sustainability-related behaviours at work (Carmeli et al. 2017). Furthermore, context can shape the manifestations of sustainability dynamic capabilities by linking different individual-level characteristics and organisational practices and processes (Strauss et al. 2017). A recent study has demonstrated how the regional economic development context can influence the attitudes of individual owner-managers towards sustainability (tangible vs. intangible) underpinned by moral identity as one micro-foundation in German small-to-medium-sized firms (Kraus et al. 2020).

Despite the micro-foundation movement in sustainability studies, scant research has paid attention to philosophical and cultural resources as micro-foundational underpinnings. One rare study has revealed how Taoist leadership can influence employee green behaviours (Xing & Starik, 2017). Along this line of philosophical inquiry, Taoism can explain leaders' behaviours in regard to the three different forms of reflexivity found in the way they believe in Wu Wei, namely: flow, self-protection and an excuse for failing (Xing & Sims, 2012). Furthermore, Taoist leadership can be observed in the 'Haier is a Sea' letter written by Zhang Ruimin, Haier's chief executive officer (CEO) (Xing, 2016), which exemplifies Lao Zi's view that 'the highest virtue is like that of water. Water benefits everything in the world without contending'. Apart from Taoism, other philosophical underpinnings also have important bearings on contemporary management practices. For instance, Confucianism and Legalism can jointly affect the behaviours of individuals in the management of their relationships with their supervisors (Xing et al. 2020b). In the context of Chinese globalisation endeavours, the notion of Mid-View thinking, from a cultural and philosophical perspective, can serve as a micro-foundation of the unique 'light-touch' integration approach taken by the Chinese in their dual pursuit of the exploration and exploitation of knowledge in cross-border M&As (Zhang et al. 2020).

3 | CONTEXTS OF CHINESE GLOBALISATION ENDEAVOURS

For our study, we selected two contexts of Chinese globalisation endeavours – namely, Chinese overseas M&As and the globalisation of traditional Chinese medicine (TCM) – to illustrate our argument and understanding. Three reasons justify our choice. First, from the organisational perspective, these globalisation endeavours fall into the organisational form of global collaborative partnerships. Second, from the micro-foundational perspective, culture plays an important role in affecting the processes and outcomes of these globalisation endeavours. Third, from the institutional perspective, Chinese globalisation endeavours encounter various institutional contexts that differ from their home country one. From a comparative perspective, the host institutional contexts can be advanced or developing countries. Thus, our choice of contexts provides a background against which to examine the influence wielded by institutional and cultural contexts from a micro-foundational perspective.

3.1 | The case of Chinese overseas M&As

Chinese overseas M&As have received significant attention from both academics and practitioners. The focus of our study was Chinese M&As conducted in Germany, which has become the top destination for Chinese investment in Europe amid the recent developmental trends characterised by a sharp increase of Chinese cross-border M&As. In 2017, Chinese companies engaged in 247 acquisitions throughout Europe for a total amount of US$57.6 billion. Fifty-four of these transactions were conducted in Germany, putting the country at the top of the ranking, followed by 44 conducted in the UK (EY, 2018). The choices of Chinese overseas investment locations are a function of both the countries' and the industries' characteristics (Estrin et al. 2018; Holtbruegge & Kreppel, 2012). Chinese M&As in Germany mainly focus on manufacturing sector (Liu & Meyer, 2020).

3.2 | The case of the globalisation of traditional Chinese medicine

Traditional Chinese medicine is mainly recognised as alternative medicine in the West, although it has had a long history in practice in Western countries, such as in herbal and acupuncture shops (Bivins, 2010). Despite the differences that exist between TCM and Western medicine, benefits can be found in exploring their synergetic potential in providing novel health solutions for patients throughout the world (Zhou & Nunes, 2015). An exemplary illustration is Ms. Tu Youyou, an 85-year-old Chinese pharmacologist who, in 2015, became China's first medicine Nobel laureate. Ms. Tu acknowledged the influence of Western medicine methodology, which had assisted her discoveries in regard to a novel therapy against Malaria, although she had relied heavily on TCM.

As alternative medicine, TCM directly addresses the United Nation's Sustainable Development Goal 3 (to ensure healthy lives and promote well-being for all ages) by providing alternative approaches to dealing with healthcare issues and challenges. Therefore, the globalisation of TCM has been promoted by the Chinese government among their endeavours enacted within the broader framework of the Belt and Road Initiative (BRI) (Zhang et al. 2018). Furthermore, the recognition of TCM by international organisations is conducive to its gaining acceptance and legitimacy around the world. For example, the director-general of the World Health Organisation has emphasised the necessity to take a holistic approach to the treatment of symptoms and has highlighted the crucial role played by TCM in this regard, while recognising the contribution of TCM to sustainable development (WHO, 2016).

4 | TAOIST PHILOSOPHY, SUSTAINABLE DEVELOPMENT, AND CHINESE GLOBALISATION

Our analysis revealed one salient concept underpinned by Taoist philosophy – namely, the community of shared destiny. We will refer to Chinese globalisation endeavours to illustrate how this concept is manifested in connection with sensemaking in different contexts, and its implications on sustainable development practices.

Our focus was on the post-acquisition phase of Chinese cross-border M&As, where integration management plays out and synergy potential may be exploited. From the sensemaking perspective, it is essential to understand how events become triggers for sensemaking and how intersubjective meaning is created. M&A events trigger sensemaking for both acquirers and targets. Chinese globalising endeavours enacted through cross-border M&As in developed economies can be spurred by strong motives linked to learning and access to technology, advanced knowledge, and experience aimed at the pursuit of technological upgrading. For instance, brand acquisition is one key strategic asset-seeking endeavour that Chinese MNEs enact through M&As in order to enhance their reputation and gain legitimacy in the global market (Liu et al. 2018). Furthermore, Chinese manufacturing firms may use M&As to expand their service offerings and gain competitive advantages (Xing et al. 2017). However, as China's foreign acquisitions aimed at technological upgrading have grown over time, many Western countries have reviewed their own investment policies and have begun to push back against such acquisitions at the national level. In 2017, Germany passed its Foreign Trade and Payments Act, which stipulates that, when an investor from outside the Europe Union aims at acquiring more than 25 per cent of the voting rights of a German company, the German Ministry of Economics and Technology has the right to block the transaction if it poses a threat to German security or public policy. In one such instance, in July 2018, the German federal government intervened to stop the Chinese acquisition of Leifeld Metal Spinning, a toolmaker specialising in high-strength materials for aviation, space, and nuclear applications.

These institutional- and organisational-level challenges require Chinese companies to pay close attention to local contexts while defining the management practices to adopt in the post-acquisition phase. For example, the interplay of institutions, culture, and strategic choice affects human resource management in Chinese multinationals (Khan et al. 2019). Given the different institutional environments of China and Germany —emerging economy vs. advanced economy — institutions should have a bearing on the sensemaking processes of organisations. Hence, the Chinese globalising context offers the opportunity to understand how institutional contexts impact the sensemaking processes and the mechanisms used by micro-level actors in relation to macro-level factors.

We proposed a conceptual framework suite to understand sensemaking with regard to institutions in the context of cross-border M&As. The macro-level institutional context primes and triggers the micro-level formation of action. The difference of developing stage and the institutional environment affect the organisational actors' perceptions of the new phenomenon of Chinese cross-border M&As in advanced economies. The institutional development phase of Chinese and German firms, together with their home country economic and institutional environments, as institutional contexts, provide the backdrop for Chinese M&As in Germany. With their relatively limited experience in cross-border M&As, Chinese firms are eager to learn from their advanced economy counterparts. Institutional contexts implicitly affect the reasoning effected by individuals and organisational actors when dealing with post-acquisition integration.

At the micro-level, both acquirers and targets construct meanings during the unfolding of the sensemaking processes. For example, Chinese firms invite high-profile politicians from China and Germany to visit the targets and to promote the cross-border M&As as Sino-German landmark achievements. Such visits are intended to facilitate the establishment of friendly environments as one means of sensemaking. On the target side, German firms tend to acknowledge the advanced development state of their machinery and advanced manufacturing sectors, in comparison to that of the Chinese acquirers. Hence, at the micro-level, the sensemaking process can influence the macro-level institutional context. Similarly, organisational cultural differences, synergy potential, and autonomy granted to the acquired high-tech firms impact the M&A performance in important ways (Tarba et al. 2019). This also relates to the importance of human resource management in mergers and acquisitions in the global context (Tarba et al. 2020).

Furthermore, concerns are being increasingly raised in relation to the impact of Chinese M&As on employment and social standards. For instance, local communities have expressed concerns about job security and social interaction with Chinese employees. One important characteristic of the 'light-touch integration' management approach in Chinese M&As is caring about local communities. New job creation and job security are at the top of the agenda. Thus, it is important to enable local communities to flourish and prosper following the M&As. Furthermore, due to institutional differences, Chinese companies may not share their developed economy counterparts' social standards, including those relating to environmental protection, corporate social responsibility, and corporate governance. Mutual shows of respect and learning are conducive to the co-development of social standards that may benefit both acquirers and targets. This activity illustrates the notion of 'community of shared destiny' underpinned by Taoist philosophy.

In the context of TCM globalisation endeavours, we observe that collaborative partnerships between Chinese firms and their local counterparts are the main organisational form. The Chinese government has issued a number of policy guidelines and documents aimed at promoting the globalisation of TCM. Specifically, in February 2016, the State Council of the People's Republic of China issued the 'Outline of Chinese Medicine Development Strategy Plan 2016–2030'. This plan and other guidelines have motivated several countries along the BRI to explore opportunities aimed at setting up joint TCM hospitals with Chinese partners. The countries that have expressed an interest include Russia, Malaysia, France, and Australia. However, the pursuit of collaborative partnerships between Chinese healthcare providers and foreign partners faces multiple challenges (Xing et al. 2020a) that remain pertinent for TCM globalisation endeavours.

For instance, the Sino-Swiss centre is the first overseas TCM centre to obtain the ISO 9001-2015 certification. TCM centres have been establishedin Australia, France, Luxembourg, Germany, Russia, Czech Republic, Hungary and others. Table 1 gives further information about these collaborative partnerships aimed at globalising TCM. The essence of TCM favours collaboration and cooperation, thus manifesting the 'community of shared destiny' notion.

To articulate the cultural and philosophical micro-foundations of sustainability and further elucidate its intellectual roots from a cultural perspective, we refer to Chinese classic philosopher. Table 2 presents illustrative examples of classic quotations from Tao Te Ching.

5 | DISCUSSION AND IMPLICATION

5.1 | Theoretical contribution

Our study makes three theoretical contributions by: (1) examining the role played by sensemaking in the context of Chinese globalisation endeavours, and the complex interactions between sensemaking and institutions; (2) exploring the cultural and philosophical micro-foundations of sustainability and sustainable development; (3) suggesting the joint influence exerted by culture and sensemaking in shaping the dynamics of global collaborative partnerships. First, our research contributes to gaining a nuanced understanding of sensemaking theory. The relevance of sensemaking in predicting individual and organisational behaviour and the rather less contextualised understanding of sensemaking with institutions in the extant literature called for an investigation conducted from a comparative institutional perspective in order to capture the dynamics and nuances of sensemaking. Our findings reveal salient manifestation of sensemaking and sustainability. The tensions linked to sustainable development emphasise the situations encountered by global collaborative partnerships. In connection with the sustainability management literature, our study extends the recent discussion on sustainable development by articulating the importance of sensemaking in interpreting and constructing sustainable development practices in global collaborative partnership settings. By adopting such a nuanced approach to the appreciation of different forms of collaborative partnerships – either M&As (Liu & Meyer, 2020) or partnerships between healthcare providers (Xing, et al. 2020) – our findings offer additional insights into sensemaking. Our study contributes to the sensemaking and sustainable development literature by highlighting the importance of institutional contexts (Weber & Glynn, 2006); in so doing, it uncovers the interaction between the micro- and macro-levels to advance research on sensemaking. Importantly, we attempted to define an analytical framework theoretically rooted in collaborative partnerships to understand the multifaceted nature of sensemaking.

Second, our study contributes to the sustainability management literature from a micro-foundational perspective. Specifically, it links the recent vibrant micro-foundational movements in management studies and sustainability management research (Starik & Kanashiro, 2020); it does so particularly by investigating sustainability from a micro-foundational perspective (Cooper et al. 2017) in the context of globalising endeavours. The existing research on sustainability has largely tended to focus on the organisation- or system-levels (Bansal & Song, 2017), but has hitherto failed to uncover the interactions and dynamics underpinned by cultural and philosophical factors. Recent research has begun to highlight the important role played by cultural and philosophical factors in influencing sustainable management – for instance, the role played by Taoist leadership in employee green behaviours (Xing & Starik, 2017). Our findings reveal the important notion of the 'community of shared destiny', which underpins the dynamics and progress of sustainable development by strengthening the role played by cultural and philosophical micro-foundations. We also advance the micro-foundation literature by demonstrating that Taoist philosophy may serve as a micro-foundation suited to guide individual and organisational actors in their pursuit of globalising endeavours while drawing from cultural resources rooted in history and traditional philosophy.

Third, our findings shed revealing light on the factors that influence global collaborative partnerships.

By underscoring the relevance of Taoist philosophy and sensemaking, our findings reveal two important factors underpinning the dynamics and development of globalising endeavours. Our findings not only lend support to previous research on dynamics of collaborative partnerships (Liu et al. 2019) and highlight the important influence of micro-foundations (Liu, 2020b; Liu et al. 2017) on crafting practices in the form of international collaborative partnership, but also advance the collaborative partnership literature by demonstrating

TABLE 1 Examples of TCM overseas centres established through collaborative partnerships

TCM centres	Country	Main activities
China–Australia (Melbourne) Chinese Medicine Centre (Nanjing University of Chinese Medicine)	Australia	Expanding the cultural education of Chinese medicine from Australian universities to teaching activities in local community colleges, and creating a service-oriented model of 'integrating into life', which has opened up a new path for Chinese medicine and Chinese culture.
China–France (Paris) Traditional Chinese Medicine Centre	France	The 'Clinical Study of Huangkui Capsules for the Treatment of Proteinuria in Diabetic Nephropathy' funded by the French government, laying the foundation for the entry of Chinese medicine into the European Union.
China–Luxembourg Chinese Medicine Cooperative Research Centre (jointly established by Hunan University of Traditional Chinese Medicine and Luxembourg Institute of Health)	Luxembourg	Adopting the 'medicine integration' model to promote the international drug registration project with Chinese pharmaceutical companies, and to gradually establish a network of medical centres in neighbouring countries
China–German Chinese Medicine Centre	Germany	Carrying out Chinese medicine diagnosis and treatment services, including Chinese medicine training, Chinese and Western medicine research cooperation, Chinese medicine standardisation, and Chinese cultural communication etc.
The St. Petersburg Centre for Traditional Chinese Medicine (jointly established by Beijing University of Chinese Medicine and Pavlov First State Medical University)	Russia	The first Chinese medicine hospital licensed in Russia has made a milestone contribution by building a platform for cooperation in teaching and research between China and Russia with distinctive Chinese medicine diagnosis and treatment.
'China–Czech' Traditional Chinese Medicine Centre, (jointly established by Shuguang Hospital and University Hospital Hradec Králové)	Czech Republic	With the characteristics of acupuncture and moxibustion in the treatment of chronic pain, creating a cooperative development model of 'clinical-oriented, integrated medicine and education, and introduction of scientific research'.
China–Central and Eastern European Traditional Chinese Medicine Medical Training Centre (Heilongjiang University of Traditional Chinese Medicine)	Hungary	With advantages in education and training, focusing on training pertaining to internal medicine prescriptions, acupuncture meridians, and clinical practice
Tai Chi Health Centre (Shanghai University of Traditional Chinese Medicine)	Greece	The first overseas 'Tai Chi Health Centre' of the Shanghai University of Traditional Chinese Medicine is operated at the University of West Attica in Greece with the concept of health maintenance and exercises, diet therapy, etc. focusing on 'Tai Chi health'
China–Romanian Traditional Chinese Medicine Centre (jointly established by Zhejiang University of Traditional Chinese Medicine and Vasile Goldiş University)	Romania	Carrying out cooperation in the fields of Chinese medicine education and scientific research, Chinese medicine cultural promotion, Chinese medicine talent training between the two parties in the fields of liver disease, diabetes clinical research, Chinese medicine rehabilitation physiotherapy, and Chinese medicine cultivation
China–Poland Traditional Chinese Medicine Centre (jointly established by Shandong University of Traditional Chinese Medicine, TOMO School of Traditional Chinese Medicine in Gdańsk, and Medical University of Lublin, Poland)	Poland	integrating medical education, medical care, scientific research, cultural exchanges, trade services and other functions, taking advantage of Confucian and Mencius culture to promote Chinese medicine in Poland
China–Montenegro Centre for Traditional Chinese Medicine	Montenegro	Carrying out systematic research on the traditional medicine of Montenegro, and promoting the development and utilisation of Montenegro's medicinal plant resources

that institutional differences may serve as a trigger to enact sensemaking processes. Although TCM has been studied from other perspectives, mainly medicine, it has rarely been examined from the globalisation perspective. Our research addressed this gap from a theoretical perspective by referring to global collaborative partnerships. Including M&As (King et al. 2020) and international joint ventures (Collinson & Liu, 2019),

TABLE 2 Illustrative examples of Taoist philosophy and implications

Key concept from Taoism	Excerpts from *Tao Te Ching*	Implications on sustainable development
Community of shared destiny	Blunt the sharpness, Untangle the knot, Soften the glare, Merge with dust. Oh, hidden deep but ever present! I do not know from whence it comes. It is the forefather of the gods. (Chapter 4)	• Sensemaking with institutions • Collaborative partnership • Caring for the community
Community of shared destiny	Surrender yourself humbly; then you can be trusted to care for all things. Love the world as your own self; then you can truly care for all things. (Chapter 13)	• Collaborative partnership • Caring for the community
Community of shared destiny	Ordinary men hate solitude. But the Master makes use of it, embracing his aloneness, realising he is one with the whole universe. (Chapter 42)	• Sensemaking with institutions • Collaborative partnership

global collaborative partnerships constitute as an important organisational form to comprehend globalisation. Importantly, culture can influence the dynamics of sensemaking with institutions, particularly from a philosophical micro-foundational perspective. In connecting culture and sensemaking, our study contributes to the theoretical advancement of global collaborative partnership research. It may thus significantly expand the understanding of collaborative partnerships by highlighting the influence of Taoist philosophy – in conjunction with sensemaking – in the context of Chinese globalising endeavours enacted through global collaborative partnerships. In doing so, it contributes to gaining a nuanced understanding of the role played by Taoism by articulating the contextual characteristics of global collaborative partnerships.

5.2 | Policy and managerial implications

This study has several implications for Chinese managers working in both enterprises and healthcare organisations, and for policy makers. First, Chinese managers should pay close attention to partnership situations and to their influence on the pursuit of globalising endeavours, which involve constant risk, ambiguity, and uncertainty throughout their developmental trajectory. Partnership is an effective means to navigate through the complexity and uncertainty by leveraging local knowledge and resources. Importantly, managers need to take the time to design appropriate collaborative partnerships by reflecting upon their past experiences and current situations. Through this process of reflection, managers may draw valuable resources from cultural and institutional contexts. Specifically, the interplay between sensemaking and culture may represent a resource base for managers. Our research highlights that sensemaking may play a crucial role for

managers in dealing with partnership situations arising during the development of their globalising endeavours. Understanding the sociocultural perspective of M&A (Sarala et al. 2016) can affect managers' behaviours and responses, especially from the sensemaking and institutions perspective.

In regard to policy implications, governments around the globe tend to turn to attracting foreign investment for economic development, innovation, and growth, which is an especially salient policy option in emerging economies (Collinson & Liu, 2019). Our research on sensemaking with institutions highlights the importance of sensemaking for potentially successful global partnerships. Any focus on the promotion and development of foreign investment should not ignore the institutional differences. In the context of fighting against the global health crisis COVID-19, governments in both developed and developing economies need to implement grand, novel and proactive policies (Lee et al. 2021; Liu et al. 2020). In today's uncertain global environment, globalisation face new challenges and opportunities. Policy makers need to engage and respond to these new challenges and opportunities with creativity, solidarity, and imagination, to navigate through crisis, uncertainties, and complexities. Also, the global gravity shift from 'West-Leads-East' to 'West-Meets-East' requires various types of training and education that fall outside of the conventional offerings. We argue that governments could systematically design and implement policy initiatives aimed at cultivating skillsets and capabilities that are conducive to globalisation in the new era. Specifically, the cultivation of global talent endowed with cultural sensitivity and quality international experience will be the key to moving forward (Liu, 2019). Furthermore, power is an important aspect in sensemaking (Schildt et al. 2020). In the global policy domain, soft power (Nye, 1990) can play an even more critical role in enabling organisational actors to make sense with institutions in their globalisation endeavours.

6 | CONCLUSION

This article examined the role played by sensemaking and culture in Chinese globalisation endeavours. In particular, it referred to illustrative cases of Chinese overseas acquisitions and the globalisation of traditional Chinese medicine in the form of global collaborative partnerships. We thus identified the cultural and institutional factors that influence sustainable development practices. Our study suggests that a nuanced understanding of the role played by Taoist philosophy is important in order to advance research on sustainability management from a micro-foundational perspective. By highlighting the roles played by culture and philosophy, our exploratory study represents an attempt to illuminate the complex interplay between sensemaking and sustainable development in different institutional contexts.

ACKNOWLEDGEMENT
This research has been supported by the 'Research on promoting harmonious doctor-patient relationship based on the construction of traditional Chinese medicine hospital culture', Beijing Moral Cultivation Research Society (Project number: jckt2017-22). Prof. Yipeng Liu is appreciative of Schoeller Fellowship from the Schoeller Foundation for Business and Society.

ORCID
Yipeng Liu 🄳 https://orcid.org/0000-0002-4918-925X

REFERENCES
Aguinis, H. & Glavas, A. (2019) On corporate social responsibility, sensemaking, and the search for meaningfulness through work. *Journal of Management*, 45(3), 1057–1086.

Bakonyi, J., Kappler, S., Nag, E.M. & Opfermann, L.S. (2021) Precarity, mobility and the city: introduction to the special issue. *Global Policy*, 12(S2), 5–9.

Bansal, P. & Song, H.-C. (2017) Similar but not the same: Differentiating corporate sustainability from corporate responsibility. *Academy of Management Annals*, 11(1), 105–149.

Barney, J. & Felin, T. (2013) What are microfoundations? *The Academy of Management Perspectives*, 27(2), 138–155.

Basu, K. & Palazzo, G. (2008) Corporate social responsibility: A process model of sensemaking. *Academy of Management Review*, 33(1), 122–136.

Bivins, R. (2010) *Alternative medicine? A history*. Oxford University Press.

Carmeli, A., Brammer, S., Gomes, E. & Tarba, S.Y. (2017) An organizational ethic of care and employee involvement in sustainability-related behaviors: A social identity perspective. *Journal of Organizational Behavior*, 38(9), 1380–1395.

Collinson, S. & Liu, Y. (2019) Recombination for innovation: performance outcomes from international partnerships in China. *R&D Management*, 49(1), 46–63.

Cooper, C.L., Stokes, P., Liu, Y. & Tarba, S.Y. (2017) Sustainability and organizational behavior: A micro-foundational perspective. *Journal of Organizational Behavior*, 38(9), 1297–1301.

Estrin, S., Meyer, K.E. & Pelletier, A. (2018) Emerging Economy MNEs: How does home country munificence matter? *Journal of World Business*, 53(4), 514–528.

EY (2018) Chinese firms pay record sums for European companies, especially in Germany and the UK. Available from: https://www.ey.com/ch/en/newsroom/news-releases/news-release-ey-chinese-firms-pay-record-sums-for-european-companies [Accessed 31 March 2018].

Felin, T., Foss, N.J. & Ployhart, R.E. (2015) The microfoundations movement in strategy and organization theory. *The Academy of Management Annals*, 9(1), 575–632.

Gioia, D.A. & Thomas, J.B. (1996) Identity, image, and issue interpretation: Sensemaking during strategic change in academia. *Administrative Science Quarterly*, 41(3), 370–403.

Held, D., Roger, C. & Nag, E.-M. (2014) *Climate governance in the developing world*. John Wiley & Sons.

Holtbruegge, D. & Kreppel, H. (2012) Determinants of outward foreign direct investment from BRIC countries: an explorative study. *International Journal of Emerging Markets*, 7(1), 4–30.

Khan, Z., Wood, G., Tarba, S.Y., Rao-Nicholson, R. & He, S. (2019) Human resource management in Chinese multinationals in the United Kingdom: The interplay of institutions, culture, and strategic choice. *Human Resource Management*, 58(5), 473–487.

King, D.R., Bauer, F., Weng, Q., Schriber, S. & Tarba, S. (2020) What, when, and who: Manager involvement in predicting employee resistance to acquisition integration. *Human Resource Management*, 59(1), 63–81.

Kraus, P., Stokes, P., Cooper, S.C., Liu, Y., Moore, N., Britzelmaier, B. et al. (2020) Cultural antecedents of sustainability and regional economic development-a study of SME 'Mittelstand' firms in Baden-Württemberg (Germany). *Entrepreneurship & Regional Development*, 32(7–8), 629–653.

Lee, C., Lee, J.M. & Liu, Y. (2021) Catalysing innovation and digital transformation in combating the Covid-19 pandemic: whole-of government collaborations in ICT, R&D, and business digitization in Singapore. *Public Money & Management*, https://doi.org/10.1080/09540962.09542021.01966197

Liu, Y. (2019) *Research handbook of international talent management*. Edward Elgar.

Liu, Y. (2020a) Contextualizing risk while building resilience: Returnee vs. local entrepreneurs in China. *Applied Psychology: An International Review*, 69(2), 415–443.

Liu, Y. (2020b) The micro-foundations of global business incubation: Stakeholder engagement and strategic entrepreneurial partnerships. *Technological Forecasting and Social Change*, 161(December), 120294.

Liu, Y. & Almor, T. (2016) How culture influences the way entrepreneurs deal with uncertainty in inter-organizational relationships: The case of returnee versus local entrepreneurs in China. *International Business Review*, 25(1), 4–14.

Liu, Y., Collinson, S., Cooper, C. & Baglieri, D. (2021) International business, innovation and ambidexterity: A micro-foundational perspective. *International Business Review*, Available online 12 April 2021: 101852.

Liu, Y. & Huang, Q. (2018) University capability as a micro-foundation for the Triple Helix model: the case of China. *Technovation*, 76-77(August–September), 40–50.

Liu, Y., Lattemann, C., Xing, Y. & Dorawa, D. (2019) The emergence of collaborative partnerships between knowledge-intensive business service (KIBS) and product companies: the case of Bremen, Germany. *Regional Studies*, 53(3), 376–387.

Liu, Y., Lee, J.M. & Lee, C. (2020) The challenges and opportunities of a global health crisis: The management and business implications of COVID-19 from an Asian perspective. *Asian Business & Management*, 19(3), 277–297.

Liu, Y. & Meyer, K.E. (2020) Boundary spanners, HRM practices, and reverse knowledge transfer: The case of Chinese cross-border acquisitions. *Journal of World Business*, 55(2), 100958.

Liu, Y., Öberg, C., Tarba, S.Y. & Xing, Y. (2018) Brand management in Mergers and Acquisitions: Emerging market multinationals venturing into advanced economies. *International Marketing Review*, 35(5), 710–732.

Liu, Y., Sarala, R.M., Xing, Y. & Cooper, C.L. (2017) Human side of collaborative partnerships: A microfoundational perspective. *Group & Organization Management*, 42(2), 151–162.

Maitlis, S. & Christianson, M. (2014) Sensemaking in organizations: Taking stock and moving forward. *Academy of Management Annals*, 8(1), 57–125.

Nye, J.S. (1990) Soft power. *Foreign Policy*, 80(Autumn), 153–171.

Reinecke, J. & Ansari, S. (2015) What is a 'fair' price? Ethics as sensemaking. *Organization Science*, 26(3), 867–888.

Sarala, R.M., Junni, P., Cooper, C.L. & Tarba, S.Y. (2016) A sociocultural perspective on knowledge transfer in mergers and acquisitions. *Journal of Management*, 42(5), 1230–1249.

Schildt, H., Mantere, S. & Cornelissen, J. (2020) Power in sensemaking processes. *Organization Studies*, 41(2), 241–265.

Shoham, A., Almor, T., Lee, S.M. & Ahammad, M.F. (2017) Encouraging environmental sustainability through gender: A micro-foundational approach using linguistic gender marking. *Journal of Organizational Behavior*, 38(9), 1356–1378.

Sonenshein, S. (2007) The role of construction, intuition, and justification in responding to ethical issues at work: The sensemaking-intuition model. *Academy of Management Review*, 32(4), 1022–1040.

Starik, M. & Kanashiro, P. (2020) *Advancing a multi-level sustainability management theory*. Emerald Publishing Limited.

Starik, M. & Marcus, A.A. (2000) Introduction to the special research forum on the management of organizations in the natural environment: A field emerging from multiple paths, with many challenges ahead. *Academy of Management Journal*, 43(4), 539–547.

Strauss, K., Lepoutre, J. & Wood, G. (2017) Fifty shades of green: How microfoundations of sustainability dynamic capabilities vary across organizational contexts. *Journal of Organizational Behavior*, 38(9), 1338–1355.

Tarba, S.Y., Ahammad, M.F., Junni, P., Stokes, P. & Morag, O. (2019) The impact of organizational culture differences, synergy potential, and autonomy granted to the acquired high-tech firms on the M&A performance. *Group & Organization Management*, 44(3), 483–520.

Tarba, S.Y., Cooke, F.L., Weber, Y., Ahlstrom, D., Cooper, C.L. & Collings, D.G. (2020) Mergers and acquisitions in the global context: The role of human resource management. *Journal of World Business*, 55(2), 101048.

The State Council of the People's Republic of China, 'TCM gets healthy Silk Road boost', http://english.gov.cn/news/top_news/2017/01/19/content_281475545591726.htm.

United Nations (2015) *Sustainable development goals*. http://www.un.org/sustainabledevelopment/accessed [Accessed 22 February 2017]

Weber, K. & Glynn, M.A. (2006) Making sense with institutions: Context, thought and action in Karl Weick's theory. *Organization Studies*, 27(11), 1639–1660.

Weick, K.E. (1995) *Sensemaking in organizations*. Sage Publications.

Weick, K.E. & Sutcliffe, K.M. (2006) Mindfulness and the quality of organizational attention. *Organization Science*, 17(4), 514–524.

Whiteman, G. & Cooper, W.H. (2011) Ecological sensemaking. *Academy of Management Journal*, 54(5), 889–911.

WHO (2016) *The contribution of traditional Chinese medicine to sustainable development: keynote address at the international conference on the modernization of traditional Chinese medicine*. WHO.

Xing, Y. (2016) A Daoist reflection on sea-like leadership and enlightened thinking. *Management and Organization Review*, 12(4), 807–810.

Xing, Y. & Liu, Y. (2016) Linking leaders' identity work and human resource management involvement: the case of sociocultural integration in Chinese mergers and acquisitions. *The International Journal of Human Resource Management*, 27(20), 2550–2577.

Xing, Y., Liu, Y., Tarba, S.Y. & Cooper, C.L. (2016) Intercultural influences on managing African employees of Chinese firms in Africa: Chinese managers' HRM practices. *International Business Review*, 25(1), 28–41.

Xing, Y., Liu, Y., Tarba, S. & Cooper, C.L. (2017) Servitization in mergers and acquisitions: Manufacturing firms venturing from emerging markets into advanced economies. *International Journal of Production Economics*, 192(October), 9–18.

Xing, Y., Liu, Y. & Cooper, S.C.L. (2018) Local government as institutional entrepreneur: Public–private collaborative partnerships in fostering regional entrepreneurship. *British Journal of Management*, 29(4), 670–690.

Xing, Y., Liu, Y. & Lattemann, C. (2020a) Institutional logics and social enterprises: Entry mode choices of foreign hospitals in China. *Journal of World Business*, 55(5), 100974.

Xing, Y., Liu, Y., Tarba, S. & Wood, G. (2020b) A cultural inquiry into ambidexterity in supervisor–subordinate relationship. *The International Journal of Human Resource Management*, 31(2), 203–231.

Xing, Y. & Sims, D. (2012) Leadership, Daoist Wu Wei and reflexivity: Flow, self-protection and excuse in Chinese bank managers' leadership practice. *Management Learning*, 43(1), 97–112.

Xing, Y. & Starik, M. (2017) Taoist leadership and employee green behaviour: A cultural and philosophical microfoundation of sustainability. *Journal of Organizational Behavior*, 38(9), 1302–1319.

Xu, C., Xiong, Y., Sun, Y. & Liu, Y. (2021) Genetic distance, international experience and the performance of cross-border R&D for EMNEs. *Journal of International Management*, 27(2), 100853.

Zhang, W., Alon, I. & Lattemann, C. (2018) *China's Belt and Road Initiative: Changing the rules of globalization*. Springer.

Zhang, X., Liu, Y., Tarba, S.Y. & Del Giudice, M. (2020) The microfoundations of strategic ambidexterity: Chinese cross-border M&As, Mid-View thinking and integration management. *International Business Review*, 29(6), 101710.

Zhou, L. & Nunes, J.M.B. (2015) *Knowledge sharing in Chinese hospitals: Identifying sharing barriers in traditional chinese and western medicine collaboration*. Springer.

AUTHOR BIOGRAPHIES

Peng Wang is Associate Professor at Beijing Hospital of Traditional Chinese Medicine and Capital Medical University in Beijing, China. His research interests are traditional Chinese medicine theory and practice, hospital management and public policy, and internationalisation of traditional Chinese medicine.

Eugenia Yijun Xing is Chair Professor in Human Resource Management and Director of Healthcare Management, Culture and Leadership (College-level) at Brunel University London, UK. Her research interests include leadership, indigenous management theory, healthcare management, Chinese traditional culture, and philosophy.

Xiaotao Zhang is Professor at the Central University of Finance and Economics in Beijing, China. His research interests include international trade and policy, foreign direct investment, and multinational enterprises.

Yipeng Liu is Fellow of the Academy of Social Sciences. He has worked as Professor and Research Director with leading universities, business schools, and research institutions in the UK, Europe, and Asia. His research expertise covers entrepreneurship and innovation, global talent management, business sustainability, and emerging markets.

How to cite this article: Wang, P., Xing, E.Y., Zhang, X. & Liu, Y. (2022) Sensemaking and sustainable development: Chinese overseas acquisitions and the globalisation of traditional Chinese medicine. *Global Policy*, 13(Suppl. 1), 23–33. Available from: https://doi.org/10.1111/1758-5899.13055

Received: 21 August 2021 | Revised: 11 January 2022 | Accepted: 15 January 2022

DOI: 10.1111/1758-5899.13059

RESEARCH ARTICLE

Foreign Investment and Upgrading in the Garment Sector in Africa and Asia

Linda Calabrese[1,2] | Neil Balchin[3]

[1]Overseas Development Institute (ODI), London, UK

[2]King's College London, London, UK

[3]Commonwealth Secretariat, London, UK

Correspondence
Linda Calabrese, Overseas Development Institute, 203 Blackfriars Rd, London SE1 8NJ, UK.
Email: l.calabrese@odi.org.uk

Abstract

In many developing countries, the apparel industry is seen as a 'stepping stone' towards industrialisation. Countries rely on foreign investment to enter the garment sector by engaging in simple assembly production and aim to gradually upgrade along the value chain by building their networks and capabilities. By comparing case studies in Africa and Asia, this article shows that foreign investors contribute differently to upgrading and creating linkages. The study reviews the historical experiences of Bangladesh, Cambodia, Lesotho and Madagascar to understand the roles played by various types of foreign investors in contributing to upgrading. The model of production of these investors and their embeddedness in the host countries' markets shape their contribution towards upgrading. This has important policy implications, suggesting that government policies aiming to develop the garment sector beyond the assembly stage need to correctly identify and attract the investors that are most likely to be or become 'embedded'. The case studies also highlight the importance of creating a domestic class of entrepreneurs that can actively contribute to the development of the garment industry.

1 | INTRODUCTION

In many developing countries the garment sector is seen as a 'stepping stone' towards industrialisation. Garment manufacturing can be kickstarted with limited domestic capital and a skilled workforce. Leveraging foreign investment, developing countries can start producing garments quickly, achieving short-term benefits in terms of employment and exports, but also longer-term benefits such as skills development and creation of linkages. However, given the generally limited requirements in terms of capital intensity, investment and skills, international firms in this sector can also be footloose and volatile (Rotunno et al. 2013). Therefore,

countries that want to unlock long-lasting benefits need to make sure to leverage foreign investment to upgrade their production structure.

In the context of global value chains (GVCs), along which most of the global garment industry is organised, upgrading involves organizational learning to improve the position of firms in international trade networks. Upgrading is not a given, and it depends on a variety of factors. This article assesses the role of foreign investment in promoting upgrading along the garment value chain by looking at case studies in Africa and Asia. The research question is whether foreign firms have differentiated spillovers in the export-oriented garment manufacturing sector in host countries. We argue that this is the case, and the main factor is the 'embeddedness' of foreign firms and investors (Morris & Staritz, 2014; Morris et al. 2011; Staritz & Morris, 2013) in the domestic garment industry.

We adopt a comparative sectoral case study approach. Considering the question from a comparative angle, looking at new entrants in the garment value chain in Africa and Asia, allows us to build on the existing development and business literature and to tease out differences in the ability of various types of foreign investment to support upgrading. Bangladesh, Cambodia, Madagascar and Lesotho are selected as case studies, as they are relatively successful latecomers to global garment production in the respective regions, and they offer diverse insights into the role of inward investors. To follow the evolution of the garment sector in each country, we rely on an analysis of the literature, and in particular on historical accounts of the development of the garment sector in the selected countries. The use of secondary data and historical accounts makes sense for two reasons. First, in some of our countries, the origin of the garment sector goes far back in time, making it difficult to collect primary data. Second, our case studies cover countries where the garment industry has developed quite successfully, and as such they have been widely studied, making it redundant to collect additional data, except for some specific questions. Our chosen method has limitations – in particular, the literature on some countries does not explicitly consider the role of foreign investors. In those cases, we used insights on the prevalence of foreign investors in the industry, and the sector's performance in terms of upgrading, to draw answers to our question.

The study is structured as follows: Section 2 reviews the literature on learning and upgrading along the value chain in the garment sector and beyond. Section 3 reviews the experiences of Bangladesh, Cambodia, Lesotho and Madagascar. Section 4 summarises the findings from a comparative perspective and section 5 concludes.

2 | A REVIEW OF THE LITERATURE

2.1 | Upgrading in the garment value chain

The modern garment sees many different firms operating along the global value chain, each type performing different functions. At the lower end of the chain, firms undertake simple assembly (or cut–make–trim, CMT) subcontracting according to the specification and with the inputs provided by buyers or by other firms. Often located in developing countries, these CMT firms supply little more than the space of production and the labour, often at low wages, and thus have low value-added

---

Policy Implications

- To contribute to the upgrading of the garment sector, it is important to promote locally-embedded Foreign Direct Investment and domestic investment.
- If policy makers are interested in upgrading the domestic garment, they should not encourage all foreign investment equally, but should try to prioritise those that may be more 'embedded' in their domestic production network.
- Alongside this, policy makers should incentivise domestic businesses, and create a class of domestic entrepreneurs that has a strong stake in the sector.

---

and low margins. Firms undertaking original equipment manufacturing (OEM, also called full-package manufacturing or free-on-board, FOB) production are responsible for financing and sourcing the inputs, organising the production process, finishing and packaging the goods, and arranging for the final products to be shipped to a designated location. A step above are original design manufacturing (ODM) firms, which provide design functions; and original brand manufacturing (OBM) firms, which own the brand (Gereffi, 1999).

Upgrading refers to the capacity of a firm to increase the value-added of its products and processes (Giuliani et al. 2005; Humphrey & Schmitz, 2002). By upgrading, firms increase their technological capabilities or organizational and managerial skills (Lall, 1996). Firms achieve this via a conscious process of accumulated learning through experience which requires time and capital investment. Some of these skills are developed through 'codified knowledge' that can be written down and transmitted from firm to firm and from person to person. In other instances, they are formed through 'tacit knowledge' that is neither written down nor articulated orally and can only be learned through practice or imitation. Tacit knowledge requires frequent interaction between firms and individuals to be passed on, for example, through social networks in which firms are embedded (Whitfield et al. 2020).

In the context of the GVC literature, there exist various types of upgrading: process or product, functional or intersectoral upgrading (Giuliani et al. 2005; Humphrey & Schmitz, 2002). This article is concerned with functional upgrading, which entails 'moving up' the value chain acquiring superior functions in the chain, such as moving from CMT to OEM production, or from OEM to OBM, performing tasks that offer higher value-added. This requires deepening existing capabilities and acquiring new ones through a process requiring conscious planning and investment (Whitfield et al. 2020).

The frequently cited success cases of garment firms in East Asia moved through functional upgrading. Starting from CMT production, garment firms in Taiwan, South Korea, Hong Kong and Singapore started implementing additional tasks such as sourcing material and financing their operations, thus transitioning to OEM. These firms then became full-range package suppliers for foreign buyers, and coordinated complex production, trade and financial networks on their behalf (Gereffi, 1995). For countries that are currently involved in CMT production, the main question is how to follow the path of their East Asian predecessors, upgrading from CMT to become OEM, ODM and ultimately OBM manufacturing. In comparison, and as will be shown in the remainder of this article, many African producers remained stuck to the low steps of the production ladder.

2.2 | Foreign investment and garment sector upgrading

Many actors play a role in the learning and upgrading process of local firms. Some studies focus on the role of global buyers, highlighting that the ability of local firms operating within a GVC to upgrade is conditioned by the power asymmetry between them and their lead firms. In some cases, global buyers transfer knowledge to local firms, and in other instances they withhold it, thus hindering upgrading (Gereffi et al. 2005; Humphrey & Schmitz, 2002; Schmitz & Knorringa, 2000). Other studies assess the role of local firms themselves to upgrade, focusing on their agency to develop their own capabilities, learn and achieve technological progress (Pietrobelli & Rabellotti, 2011; Staritz & Whitfield, 2019). Local firms play an active role in absorbing knowledge and upgrading through their efforts to develop human capital, build ties with suppliers and component manufacturers, and gather market intelligence (Kadarusman & Nadvi, 2013).

This article focuses on the role of foreign investors in supporting upgrading in the garment industry. This has been long debated in the literature. Willingly or unwillingly, foreign firms can transfer knowledge to their local counterparts or competitors (Harding & Javorcik, 2012; Javorcik, 2004; Javorcik et al. 2018). Historically, many late developers, particularly those in Asia, have benefited from technology transfers generated through foreign direct investment (FDI) (e.g. Lee & Tan, 2006).

Insights on the role of FDI in upgrading come from several disciplines, including development economics, economic geography and international business studies (Buzdugan & Tüselmann, 2018). These bodies of literature identify several factors that affect upgrading through FDI. Some of these are related to the host country, such as its endowments and (static and dynamic) comparative advantages; tangible and intangible assets, including next-to-market and cost factors; and its business environment. Others focus on local firms' characteristics, such as their absorptive capacity (Cohen & Levinthal, 1990; Peng & Yu, 2021) influenced by factors such as their access to capital, or the technology gap between foreign and domestic firms (Amighini & Sanfilippo, 2014; Auffray & Fu, 2015).

Foreign investment may differ in their upgrading potential, based on the type of investment (greenfield, joint venture or acquisitions) and drivers of investment decisions (market-, resource-, efficiency- or strategic asset-seeking) (Farole & Winkler, 2014; Zhan et al. 2015). FDI objectives – including strategies towards investment, interest in subsidiary development, and links with productivity, skills and so on – also affect upgrading (Cantwell & Mudambi, 2011; Kano et al. 2020). Another factor that matters for the role of FDI in upgrading is the embeddedness of the subsidiary in the wider multinational corporation (MNC) network, as well as in the host countries, to access locational advantages and assets (Meyer et al. 2011). Others focus on the embeddedness of foreign investors in the domestic garment sector, highlighting its importance in upgrading (Morris & Staritz, 2014; Morris et al. 2011; Staritz & Morris, 2013). Social networks influence how firms interact with the local, regional, and global relationships in which they participate (Hess, 2004). For instance, diaspora investors usually have wide social networks linking to their country of origin, that help them leverage finance and knowledge (So et al. 2001). Foreign firms whose country of origin is geographically close to the host country are often more embedded in the host country and can more easily tap into both global and local resources (Morris, Plank et al. 2016).

However, foreign firms may also not be well suited to support local upgrading owing to their mobility and 'footloose' nature. Foreign investors may be attracted by government incentives, market access and attractive cost factors, but as soon as these conditions are no longer in place, 'footloose' investors will leave the country, with negative implications for upgrading. Therefore, attracting FDI does not, in itself, guarantee upgrading, and it can even relegate a country's domestic manufacturing to simple, routine and low-value-added CMT activities. In these cases, while learning may be rapid at first, over time there may be no incentive for the foreign investors to promote domestic upgrading over moving to new low-cost production sites (Gereffi, 2014). In reality, empirical evidence shows that the ability of FDI to promote upgrading varies widely. In some cases, foreign companies are found to invest little in building human capital (Nolintha & Jajri, 2016).

In summary, the existing literature points to a variety of outcomes in terms of FDI and upgrading, but it does not explain which investors are more conducive to upgrading, and which ones are likely to reinforce the position of local firms at the low-end of the value addition spectrum. Therefore, what should governments interested in upgrading their garment industries do? Should they open their doors to all foreign investors, or should they target specific firms which are more conducive to upgrading? Who are these investors, and what makes them different? What can historical experience teach us in this regard? The remainder of this study disentangles the impact of various types of FDI on upgrading and attempts to identify which kinds of foreign investment may be more conducive to upgrading, and why.

3 | COUNTRY CASE STUDIES: A HISTORICAL OVERVIEW

3.1 | Bangladesh

At the time of writing, Bangladesh is among the top ten largest textile and garment exporters in the world, mainly supplying Europe and the United States. The garment industry represents almost 10 per cent of the country's gross domestic product (GDP).

The beginning of the garment industry in Bangladesh dates back to the late 1970s. In 1977, a collaboration agreement (not a joint venture) between a Bangladeshi businessman and the South Korean conglomerate Daewoo led to the creation of Desh Garments Ltd (Rhee, 1990). This collaboration involved limited financial investment, with Daewoo instead focusing on providing guidance to Desh Garments, building capacity and transferring knowledge in the process.

The successful collaboration between Desh Garments and Daewoo was pivotal for the Bangladesh garment sector and had several effects:

- *Building capacity*. One hundred and thirty Bangladeshi workers and managers were trained in South Korea for six months. They returned to Bangladesh, to work in a factory built according to Daewoo's specifications (Yunus & Yamagata, 2012). The workers were exposed to the systems and operations of Daewoo and received comprehensive training in shop floor work; factory management; international procurement and marketing. The trainees went on to train other Desh employees to pass on the skills they acquired (Rhee, 1990).
- *Transferring skills*. Some of the 130 trainees went on to set up their own factories (Rhee, 1990), while those with little or no financial means became managers in, or traders for, newly established entrepreneurs (Mottaleb & Sonobe, 2011). This led to the rapid circulation of skills beyond those who took part in the original training.

- *Building trust as a supplier*. The role of Daewoo as an established firm was critical in transforming Bangladeshi firms into trusted suppliers. Daewoo initially mediated deals between Desh Garments and overseas buyers to establish Desh Garments's reputation as a credible producer, and gradually enabled other Bangladeshi firms to access the international market as trusted suppliers (Rhee, 1990).

The early stages of the modern garment industry in Bangladesh saw a prevalence of CMT-type firms, importing inputs from South Korea and exporting the final product to European and American markets. Though CMT remains the prevalent model for woven products, there now exist more vertically integrated operations, starting from cotton or yarn to produce the final products (mostly knitwear) (Fernandez-Stark et al. 2011). Bangladesh does not export textiles, but it imports cotton to produce textiles for the domestic industry, therefore showing some success at vertical integration and upgrading (Moazzem & Sehrin, 2016).

The Bangladeshi garment sector is dominated by domestic firms (Fernandez-Stark et al. 2011). This was made possible through former Desh Garments's employees who went on to set up their own businesses, or helped others do the same (Rhee, 1990). The extraordinary performance of the firm generated interest among domestic entrepreneurs who could provide finance and human capital but had little knowledge of the garment sector. They hired former Desh Garments's employees to manage their firms or worked with them as traders, which enabled the transfer of knowledge and skills (Mottaleb & Sonobe, 2011). Thus, the garment industry in Bangladesh grew through a 'demonstration effect' generated by the success of Desh Garments, and through 'labour circulation' of former Desh Garments's employees.

Once Bangladeshi entrepreneurs got a stake in the garment sector, they expanded their operations to capture more of the value of production and increase their gains. They started lobbying actively with their government, through their association, the powerful Bangladesh Garment Exporters and Manufacturers Association. Over time, the government introduced policies aimed at improving vertical integration, such as the establishment of export processing zone (EPZ) regulations which required backward linkages, encouraging the establishment of knitwear factories; and upgraded labour regimes which improved workers' rights (Fernandez-Stark et al. 2011; Moazzem & Sehrin, 2016).

Government policies also played a role in supporting the development and upgrading of local capacity in Bangladesh's garment sector. While the Bangladeshi government gradually lifted controls and restrictions on foreign investment from the late 1970s onwards, which enabled firms like Daewoo to enter the market, the government mostly only allowed investments in areas where domestic firms lacked capacity. This paved the way for the second generation of Bangladeshi firms to enter the garment sector after the initial wave of foreign investment, building on the knowledge gained about production processes and the networks of suppliers and customers established initially through the presence of a foreign company. Specific policies were introduced to create backward linkages, including financial incentives to encourage imports of raw materials and machinery for domestic textile production and EPZ regulations mandating backward linkages to spinning, weaving/knitting, dyeing and finishing, which encouraged the development of knitwear factories (Fernandez-Stark et al. 2011). Further government support for upgrading included a back-to-back letter of credit facility to aid imports of raw materials, a duty-free import allowance for capital machinery, raw materials and intermediate products used in export-oriented industries, a cash subsidy of 5 per cent of the value of fabrics for manufacturers of indigenous fabrics supplying fully export-oriented industries, and financial support – including subsidised credit – through an export promotion fund (Moazzem & Sehrin, 2016). Many of these policies were introduced in response to needs voiced by the private sector.

3.2 | Cambodia

Cambodia started producing and exporting garments in the 1990s and, by 2019, garment and textile products made up almost 60 per cent of Cambodia's total exports, a ratio among the highest in the world. The country exported over US$8 billion worth of garments and textiles, of which 99 per cent were garments, mainly to the US, Europe, Canada and Japan. Cambodia benefits from duty-free and quota-free market access through several Generalised System of Preference (GSP) schemes, including the EBA scheme for least developed countries.

In the mid-1990s, the country opened up to FDI. Foreign investors could easily set up shop in the country and enjoy the same benefits as domestic producers. Moreover, the 1994 law on investment granted tax concessions and incentives, including tax holidays, low corporate tax rates, tax-free reinvestment of profits and tax-free repatriation of earnings, and import duty exemptions. Furthermore, the Cambodian government made it easy to obtain work permits for foreign experts (Bargawi, 2005; Hossain, 2010). Market access was the single most important reason for foreign investors to set up shop in Cambodia, while low wages were of secondary importance (Bargawi, 2005).

The garment industry began to grow rapidly after 1997 when Cambodia was granted most-favoured nation status by the US and signed a framework cooperation agreement that allowed access to EU markets under the GSP. The US expanded quotas on

Cambodia's exports in 1999, enabling the rapid growth of the sector. In addition, in 2005, the EU and US limited quotas on exports from China, which prompted many Chinese producers to relocate part of their production to Cambodia. Though quotas on China were lifted in 2008, the increase in Chinese workers' wages allowed Cambodia to remain a competitive platform for garment production (Asuyama & Neou, 2012; Bargawi, 2005).

The combination of an initial lack of quotas, an open trade regime and an FDI-friendly investment environment, together with preferential access to the EU and other markets, made Cambodia a suitable destination for investment in garment manufacturing. These factors also shaped the salient features of the sector observed today. The first feature is the prevalence of CMT firms having very limited opportunities for domestic value addition. Around 60 per cent of producers work on a CMT basis, operating at low profit margins. Firms based in Cambodia import all materials and inputs from China, Hong Kong, Taiwan and South Korea, cut the fabrics and stitch them together, before exporting the final product (Asuyama & Neou, 2012; Natsuda et al. 2010).

The second, and related, feature of the Cambodian garment industry is its reliance on foreign capital. Around 90 per cent of the garment firms operating in Cambodia are foreign, with the majority coming from China, Taiwan, Hong Kong and South Korea (Hossain, 2010). Of the 615 member companies of the Garment Manufacturers Association in Cambodia, only 45 have Cambodian owners; 118 are Taiwanese-owned and 65 are Hong Kong-owned (Balchin & Calabrese, 2019). Foreign companies could thrive in Cambodia as they enjoyed access to capital and expertise that Cambodian companies, weakened by years of civil war and the presence of a limited financial system, did not have. Foreign companies also had access to networks of clients and sources of inputs and could rely on their expert managers and skilled labour (Asuyama & Neou, 2012).

The CMT model and the high degree of foreign ownership led to the third feature, the lack of vertical integration. The presence of a large number of foreign firms that are not vertically integrated in Cambodia stifles their need to invest in backward linkages domestically and makes value chain upgrading in Cambodia a challenging process (Natsuda et al. 2010). Similarly, the lack of a domestic textile industry in Cambodia has prevented the development of more integrated production, while the production models of the dominant foreign firms operating in the country, which rely on extensive international sourcing networks, have created few incentives to invest in backward linkages domestically or upgrade local suppliers and domestic value chains (Natsuda et al. 2010).

Thus, while the FDI-friendly environment facilitated foreign investment in Cambodia, the lack of a pro-active government policy to promote domestic investment has not encouraged production in the country to move beyond basic CMT activities. Consequently, in contrast to Bangladesh and Madagascar (discussed below), there is a clear absence of local exporting firms in Cambodia which, as we examine below, is also a feature of the sector in Lesotho.

3.3 | Lesotho

Lesotho is widely regarded as an African success story in export-oriented manufacturing. Preferential trade and access to key markets, together with FDI, played a key role in kick-starting industrialisation centred on garment manufacturing.

Lesotho welcomed different waves of foreign investment, spurred by varying motivations and characterised by contrasting business models. In the early 1980s, motivated by a desire to capitalise on Lesotho's low-cost labour and duty-free access to Europe, as well as to avoid apartheid-related sanctions (Morris & Staritz, 2017), some Taiwanese-owned firms based in South Africa relocated plants to Lesotho. This was followed by further waves of investment from Taiwanese firms looking to capitalise on Lesotho's underutilised MFA quotas and the country's eligibility for Africa Growth and Opportunity Act (AGOA) preferences (with the added benefit of the third-country fabric derogation) after 2000, as well as to take advantage of the country's various FDI incentives (Morris, Barnes et al. 2016; Morris & Staritz, 2017). South African regional investors also relocated production to Lesotho in successive waves from the late 1980s, initially in the wake of apartheid-related sanctions on South Africa. In the 1990s, a second wave of South African investors relocated to Lesotho in response to lower tariffs on imports into the South Africa market, which made supplying that market less attractive. A third wave of South African investment was motivated by the promise of lower costs (both labour and overheads), greater labour market flexibility and duty-free access to SACU (Morris & Staritz, 2017). Foreign firms were also attracted to Lesotho by the early-stage FDI incentives offered by the government (Morris & Staritz, 2017), which also established industrial zones and provided serviced factory shells with subsidised rent (Shakya, 2011). These zones were located close to links with South Africa's road network to facilitate the transport of textiles and apparel to ports in Durban and East London and onward for exporting.

The contrasting strategies, business models and ownership and governance structures of the Asian and South African foreign investors attracted to Lesotho have had differential implications for upgrading and the broader industrialisation of the country's garment sector. Investment from Asian (mostly Taiwanese) transnationals in Lesotho since 2000 has been concentrated primarily in production units focusing on CMT activities

to capitalise on AGOA trade rents and MFA quotas. In operating a disembedded, export-oriented production model based on preferential market access, these firms are generally not locally embedded in Lesotho, but instead use foreign networks for input suppliers and agents working with sourcing and buying offices (Morris, Barnes et al. 2016). While these firms brought knowledge and capabilities related to production set-up and processes through their initial investments, and helped link the sector in Lesotho to GVCs, they have not generated major process innovations or made significant investments to improve technology, capital or skills (Staritz & Morris, 2013). The focus on securing AGOA trade rents as part of an overriding strategy of global cost containment for exporting globally, rather than other strategic reasons for locating in Lesotho, stifles the need for investment in upgrading and skills development and disincentivises diversification (Edwards & Lawrence, 2010; Morris, Barnes et al. 2016; Staritz & Morris, 2013). Instead, with global production strategies focused on producing narrow ranges of basic products for export, local skills advancement through Taiwanese firms has mostly focused on basic production skills (e.g. on-the-job training for handling sewing machines). In addition, with market access the primary consideration, many Asian transnational producers left Lesotho after the phase-out of the MFA, leading to a notable decline in the country's exports (Whitfield & Staritz, 2021).

In contrast, South African firms investing in Lesotho operate a different production model. They are generally more locally embedded within a regional production network and have direct relationships with South African retailers. Motivated by a regional displacement strategy that hinges on relocating more functions to Lesotho (Morris & Staritz, 2017; Morris et al. 2011), these firms focused on establishing a regional value chain involving Lesotho to capitalise on lower labour costs and duty-free access to SACU markets (Kao, 2016). The South African-owned firms have recently been driving some upgrading to focus on producing shorter runs of more complicated products with higher fashion content to supply South African retailers. This contrasts with the long runs of basic or semi-basic items produced by Taiwanese firms for the US market in simple assembly facilities in Lesotho (Morris & Staritz, 2017).

In contrast to Bangladesh and Madagascar (discussed below), Lesotho has virtually no locally owned garment factories. Capacity and competitiveness limitations deter foreign-owned firms from sourcing locally from indigenous enterprises (Morris and Staritz, 2016). Further upstream, the domestic textile industry in Lesotho is non-existent and the country produces almost no fabric due to a lack of local fabric mills (apart from the Formosa Textile Mill, which produces denim textiles). This owes, at least in part, to the presence of the AGOA third-country fabric provision, which allowed firms based in Lesotho to import fabrics and engage only in the final stages of production for export, further reducing incentives to source locally. In line with this, the focus is on the downstream assembly of textile and garment products, using imported raw materials, with very limited integration upstream and little value addition. Production is highly routine and mostly concentrated in a narrow range of low unit value products in large volumes (Edwards & Lawrence, 2010).

3.4 | Madagascar

Since the early 2000s, Madagascar's economy has relied heavily on the export-oriented textiles and garment sector for jobs and revenue. The government's industrial policy was based on the adoption of a single factory EPZ model which allowed firms to benefit from a range of incentives, including duty exemption on capital transfers, tax holidays and concessions (Landry & Chen, 2021; Morris & Staritz, 2014). Alongside the EPZ incentives, preferential access to key markets (the EU, US and the Southern African Development Community, SADC) also served as an important motivation for locating production in Madagascar. Garment exports to the US were boosted heavily by the introduction of the AGOA, which stimulated growth in garment production from 2000 onwards (Morris & Sedowski, 2006). However, Madagascar's loss of AGOA benefits between 2010 and 2014, following a political crisis, prompted most of the Asian-owned firms focused on supplying the US market to relocate their operations away from Madagascar (Landry & Chen, 2021).

FDI from Asian, European diaspora and Mauritian regional investors has been a key driver of growth in Madagascar's highly export-oriented garment industry. However, in a similar manner to the sector's development in Lesotho, different types of inward investors have made varied contributions to upgrading, based on the differentiated nature of their GVC relationships, their level of local embeddedness and the varying end markets they have targeted (Staritz & Morris, 2013). Asian-owned firms investing in Madagascar operated a 'both-ends overseas' model mostly focused on CMT activities (Landry & Chen, 2021). These firms, many of whom were focused on supplying the US market and exited after the MFA phase-out at the end of 2004 or when Madagascar lost AGOA eligibility in 2010, tended to source fabric and other inputs from their own mills in Asia, which was made possible by the AGOA's single transformation provision. While the involvement of these firms helped link Madagascar-based production into GVCs, it resulted in limited upgrading. In contrast, the export-oriented European diaspora investors (primarily French) were, and continue to be, more locally embedded in Madagascar. On the back of their historical roots in the country, they have set up head offices and decision-making functions within Madagascar.

Their access to European networks and buyers provides powerful linkages to end markets (Morris, Plank et al. 2016). Similarly, the Mauritian firms with established regional production networks (and operating regional sourcing strategies) relocated basic production to Madagascar in the 1990s to access cheaper labour and capitalise on underutilised quotas. This enabled their production in Mauritius to shift to higher-value products and value chain segments (Morris, Plank et al. 2016). These firms have followed a process of upgrading that is regional in scope, and have demonstrated a higher propensity to upgrade in Madagascar compared to other foreign-owned firms (Morris & Staritz, 2014; Staritz & Morris, 2013).

Variation in the end markets targeted by different types of inward investors in Madagascar has also influenced upgrading. Whereas the Asian-owned firms operating in Madagascar export mainly to the US, the European and Mauritian investors, as well as some local Malagasy firms, export predominantly to the EU and, more recently, to South Africa. Buyers in the EU typically place greater emphasis on versatility and flexibility and often expect producers to make contributions to the design and product development, whereas US-based buyers usually provide strict specifications for producers to follow. The Asian-owned firms have taken on simple CMT activities in Madagascar as part of a strategy to undertake relatively basic long-run production for the US market. They emphasise efficiency in high-volume production to meet the specifications dictated by US buyers and thus prioritise improvements to processes rather than product or functional upgrading (Staritz & Morris, 2013).

Mauritian and European investors in Madagascar have played an influential role in regionalising exports towards South Africa and/or boosting production for the European market. Exports to the latter were not significantly affected by the elimination of MFA quotas at the end of 2004, meaning the growth of European diaspora, Mauritian and local firms supplying the European market helped the industry in Madagascar to rebound after the MFA phase-out. In addition, the diversification of exports has supported process and product upgrading in Madagascar. The loss of Madagascar's AGOA eligibility in 2010 forced them to shift to shorter-run, smaller-batch, higher-quality and more complex products to supply regional markets (especially the South African market) as well as Europe. This shift was possible because the Mauritian investors had a regionally embedded production network and were able to utilise management capabilities in a flexible manner (Morris & Staritz, 2014). The EU and South African markets, which demand smaller batches of differentiated products with higher unit values, are more stringent in processes and production capabilities. The shift to producing these types of products in Madagascar, in some cases through sub-contracting arrangements with local firms, has had positive impacts on upgrading, product quality and local skills (Kaplinsky & Wamae, 2010; Morris, Plank et al. 2016; Morris & Staritz, 2014).

Local firms in Madagascar benefited from proximity to regional assets operated by Mauritian-owned firms and their regional supply chain upgrading processes; and enjoyed access to an experienced pool of production managers as well as textiles and other inputs (Whitfield & Staritz, 2021). Through transnational social relations and networks, some local firms were able to leverage the presence of foreign-owned firms to learn and upgrade their capacities (Whitfield & Staritz, 2021). This was facilitated in different ways depending on the type and source of investment, varying from joint ventures with Mauritian investors, to buyouts of existing French firms and partnerships with French stakeholders or investors from Hong Kong (Whitfield & Staritz, 2021).

As a result, and in contrast to the absence of local firms in Cambodia and Lesotho, the split between local and foreign-owned firms operating in Madagascar's export-oriented apparel industry is fairly even – with 31 local versus 38 foreign-owned firms as of 2019 (Whitfield & Staritz, 2021). The local firms generally produce small volumes of niche and high-value garments for European markets (Whitfield & Staritz, 2021).

4 | THE ROLE OF FOREIGN INVESTMENT IN UPGRADING: A COMPARATIVE DISCUSSION

The four case studies reviewed here offer insights into the drivers of upgrading in the garment sector, highlighting the roles foreign investors play in contributing to upgrading. The literature shows how foreign investors can support or hinder upgrading, depending on both their own characteristics and those of the country and industry they operate in. But are 'foreign investors' a uniform category, generating uniform outcomes? Or does their impact on upgrading differ, even within the same country? While the literature seems to veer towards the latter, it does little to explain how various investors differ, and what is the contribution in terms of upgrading. By comparing four case studies, our article shows that what matters for foreign investors' contribution to upgrading is their level of 'embeddedness' (Morris & Staritz, 2014; Morris et al. 2011; Staritz & Morris, 2013).

In Bangladesh, a foreign firm kick-started the emergence of a competitive garment sector. Daewoo was instrumental in transferring knowledge and technical skills to Bangladeshi workers beyond the traditional shop floor, while also providing links to input suppliers and buyers in end markets, and this helped facilitate the emergence of domestic firms and enabled upgrading of local capacity. The Daewoo–Desh Garments partnership did have a positive impact on firms in the garment sector, which in the longer term contributed to developing supplying industries as well. This case illustrates the 'embeddedness' of local firms at play. As the Bangladeshi entrepreneurial class entered the garment sector, they had reasons to ensure that more of the value is captured domestically, rather than by foreign firms, and supported upgrading of the industry. This also solved the issue of mobility of capital, as (at least part of) domestic capital is bound to remain in Bangladesh, ensuring sustained upgrading.

In stark contrast, garment factories in Cambodia undertake CMT activities, and there is little evidence of diversification or vertical integration in the sector. The garment sector is dominated by Asian transnational investors operating disembedded production models, who use Cambodia as a base for exporting. All production and sourcing decisions remain in the headquarters of the foreign firms. Foreign investors have no interest in lobbying the government to promote domestic value addition, and therefore the Cambodian government has shown limited interest in incentivising value addition. In Cambodia we have a prevalence of disembedded foreign firms, which have limited stakes in the industry and therefore can leave the country whenever better opportunities arise. This type of foreign investment is not conducive to upgrading.

Lesotho offers a comparison between two different types of FDI. In a similar manner to the Cambodian case, investment from Asian transnationals has been defined by a global strategy targeting long-run production of a narrow range of basic products for export to capitalise on trade rents accruing through market access preferences, and thus focused only on CMT production while retaining the main sourcing and marketing decisions in their headquarters and drawing from a worldwide sourcing network. The benefits of this type of FDI in Lesotho have largely been limited to employment and exports. In contrast, by operating a regional production network, investment from South African firms in Lesotho's garment sector has been notably more locally embedded. By harnessing geographical proximity to the destination market of the garments, and catering to the relatively higher level of product sophistication required by South African brands, FDI from South Africa has helped to upgrade the capacity of producers in Lesotho.

The case of Madagascar similarly highlights the varied impacts of different types of FDI and their motivations on upgrading and capacity building in the domestic sector. Asian firms operating a 'both-ends overseas' production model and attracted to Madagascar by the market access opportunities helped link Madagascar-based production into GVCs but contributed little to upgrading in the sector. In contrast, Mauritian firms with established regional production networks and sourcing strategies, and French firms with historically embedded roots in the country and links to European networks, buyers and end markets, were considerably more embedded in local and regional markets, and demonstrated a greater propensity for upgrading, to meet the more demanding processes and production capabilities necessary to supply the European and South African markets. This has helped develop a local cadre of export-focused Malagasy garment firms producing smaller batches of differentiated products. It has also helped the sector in Madagascar to recover from external shocks, including the phase-out of the MFA and the loss of AGOA eligibility.

The four case studies demonstrate that foreign investment can be crucial for upgrading. FDI has played a central role in kickstarting the garment industry in all four countries, but moving up the value chain has not been straightforward. In most settings, the investment of Asian transnational firms with disembedded production units has been motivated primarily by a desire to benefit from preferential market access. This investment has generally brought little backward integration or upgrading. This is evident from the experiences of Cambodia and Lesotho, where the dominance of foreign investors has been a deterrent to value chain integration and stifled the development of indigenous capacity and the emergence of locally owned firms. In contrast, domestic or regional investors with regional production networks and diaspora investors have been more locally embedded, and have helped to drive upgrading. It is not the nationality of investors that matters here; rather it is the role they play in the value chain and the stakes they have in the host country's garment industry.

The case of Bangladesh highlights the importance of domestic producers, the recipients of the knowledge transfers of foreign firms. Our analysis builds on the 'agency' argument (see, for example, Kadarusman & Nadvi, 2013; Staritz & Whitfield, 2019) to emphasise that domestic firms are not only responsible for their own upgrading, but also contribute to creating an environment that encourages upgrading for other firms as well. In Bangladesh, domestic firms have been instrumental in lobbying their government to introduce incentives for upgrading, making Bangladesh the most vertically integrated among the four case studies. In that sense, domestic firms have shaped the domestic industry environment.

5 | CONCLUSIONS AND POLICY IMPLICATIONS

In the garment sector and beyond, foreign investment is deemed an important tool to bring in technology and transfer knowledge to local firms, thus facilitating the development of the sector. This article demonstrates that not all foreign investment is equal in this respect. It shows that it is not the nationality of the investors that matters, but rather their modes of production, business strategies and levels of embeddedness in the domestic sector. These factors shape and influence their incentives for investing in upgrading and developing local capabilities. This article builds on the finding of earlier case-study based literature (Morris & Staritz, 2014; Morris et al. 2011; Staritz & Morris, 2013) to identify embeddedness as the most crucial factor in determining whether foreign firms will support upgrading. Foreign firms that are more embedded in the domestic industrial environment relocate (part of) their more complex operations, including the decision-making process, in the host country. By doing so, they contribute to transferring knowledge and therefore to upgrading. On the contrary, more disembedded and 'footloose' firms do not have an interest in, and most likely will not have an effect on, upgrading.

This article contributes to the literature and builds on studies such as Morris, Plank et al. (2016) by showcasing different examples from Asia. The study also poses new practical considerations for countries looking to attract investment into the garment sector and other light manufacturing industries, including: how to encourage investors to become more embedded? How to design policies that will incentivise them to invest in the upgrading of firms in the countries where they work? How to maximise their spillovers to local economies? These questions have very practical policy implications. The findings of this article suggest that governments that aim to develop their garment industry should try to attract mostly 'embedded' type of foreign investors.

Our findings have important policy implications, suggesting that any host government aiming to develop their garment sector beyond the assembly stage needs to provide the right set of incentives for investors to upgrade. Beyond the initial stages of development in a sector, it is important to incentivise investors to contribute to upgrading and be willing to relocate some of the investment decisions in the country. This can be done through specific policies that support the development of the necessary skills and networks to upgrade the sector.

Beyond the role of foreign investors, this article recognises the importance of the agency of domestic firms, as highlighted by Whitfield et al. (2020). This is critical and needs to be considered in conjunction with foreign investment.

CONFLICT OF INTEREST
The authors declare that they have no known competing financial interests or personal relationships that could have appeared to influence the work reported in this paper.

ACKNOWLEDGEMENTS
The authors are thankful to Gatsby Africa, whose financial support funded the original research from

which this article is drawn. We also wish to thank Dr Celia Lee Khiaw Peng and an anonymous reviewer whose comments greatly helped us improve this study.

DATA AVAILABILITY STATEMENT

Data sharing is not applicable to this article as no datasets were generated or analysed during the current study.

ORCID

Linda Calabrese 🔟 https://orcid.org/0000-0001-9261-3602

REFERENCES

Amighini, A. & Sanfilippo, M. (2014) Impact of south-south FDI and trade on the export upgrading of african economies. *World Development*, 64(1), 1–17.

Asuyama, Y. & Neou, S. (2012) How has the cambodian garment industry evolved? In: Fukunishi, T. (Ed.) *Dynamics of the garment industry in low-income countries: Experience of Asia and Africa* (Interim Report). IDE-JETRO.

Auffray, C. & Fu, X. (2015) Chinese MNEs and managerial knowledge transfer in Africa: The case of the construction sector in Ghana. *Journal of Chinese Economic and Business Studies*, 13(4), 285–310.

Balchin, N. & Calabrese, L. (2019) *Comparative country study of the development of textile and garment sectors: Lessons for Tanzania*. ODI.

Bargawi, O. (2005) *Cambodia's garment industry – Origins and future prospects*. ESAU Working Paper. ODI.

Buzdugan, S.R. & Tüselmann, H. (2018) Making the most of FDI for development: 'New' industrial policy and FDI deepening for industrial upgrading. *Transnational Corporations*, 25(1), 1–21.

Cantwell, J.A. & Mudambi, R. (2011) Physical attraction and the geography of knowledge sourcing in multinational enterprises. *Global Strategy Journal*, 1(3–4), 206–232.

Cohen, W.M. & Levinthal, D.A. (1990) Absorptive capacity: A new perspective on learning and innovation. *Administrative Science Quarterly*, 35(1), 128–152.

Edwards, L. & Lawrence, R.Z. (2010) *AGOA rules: The intended and unintended consequences of special fabric provisions*. Working Paper 16623. National Bureau of Economic Research.

Farole, T. & Winkler, D. (2014) *Making foreign direct investment work for sub-saharan africa: Local spillovers and competitiveness in global value chains*. The World Bank.

Fernandez-Stark, K., Frederick, S. & Gereffi, G. (2011) The apparel global value chain: Economic upgrading and workforce development. In: Gereffi, G., Fernandez-Stark, K. & Psilos, P. (Eds.) *Skills for upgrading: Workforce development and global value chains in developing countries*. Center on Globalization, Governance & Competitiveness, Duke University, pp. 75–131.

Gereffi, G. (1995) Global production systems and third world development. In: Stallings, B. (Ed.) *Global change, regional response: The new international context of development*. Cambridge University Press, pp. 100–142.

Gereffi, G. (1999) International trade and industrial upgrading in the apparel commodity chain. *Journal of International Economics*, 48(1), 37–70.

Gereffi, G. (2014) A global value chain perspective on industrial policy and development in emerging markets. *Duke Journal of Comparative & International Law*, 24(3), 433–458.

Gereffi, G., Humphrey, J. & Sturgeon, T. (2005) The governance of global value chains. *Review of International Political Economy*, 12(1), 78–104.

Giuliani, E., Pietrobelli, C. & Rabellotti, R. (2005) Upgrading in global value chains: Lessons from latin american clusters. *World Development*, 33(4), 549–573.

Harding, T. & Javorcik, B.S. (2012) Foreign direct investment and export upgrading. *The Review of Economics and Statistics*, 94(4), 964–980.

Hess, M. (2004) 'Spatial' relationships? Towards a reconceptualization of embeddedness. *Progress in Human Geography*, 28(2), 165–186.

Hossain, Z. (2010) *Report on Cambodia textile and garment industry*. ACTIF - African Cotton & Textile Industries Federation.

Humphrey, J. & Schmitz, H. (2002) How does insertion in global value chains affect upgrading in industrial clusters? *Regional Studies*, 36(9), 1017–1027.

Javorcik, B.S. (2004) Does foreign direct investment increase the productivity of domestic firms? In search of spillovers through backward linkages. *The American Economic Review*, 94(3), 605–627.

Javorcik, B.S., Lo Turco, A. & Maggioni, D. (2018) New and improved: Does FDI boost production complexity in host countries? *The Economic Journal*, 128(614), 2507–2537.

Kadarusman, Y. & Nadvi, K. (2013) Competitiveness and technological upgrading in global value chains: Evidence from the indonesian electronics and garment sectors. *European Planning Studies*, 21(7), 1007–1028.

Kano, L., Tsang, E.W.K. & Yeung, H.W. (2020) Global value chains: A review of the multi-disciplinary literature. *Journal of International Business Studies*, 51(4), 577–622.

Kao, M. (2016) *Lesotho's participation in apparel value chains: An opportunity for sustainable development?, International Centre for Trade and Sustainable Development*. Available at: https://ictsd.iisd.org/bridges-news/bridges-africa/news/lesotho%E2%80%99s-participation-in-apparel-value-chains-an-opportunity-for [Accessed 31 December 2020]

Kaplinsky, R. & Wamae, W. (2010) *The determinants of upgrading and value added in the african clothing sector: The contrasting experiences of Kenya and Madagascar*. IKD Working Paper 59. Open University.

Lall, S. (1996) *Learning from the Asian tigers: Studies in technology and industrial policy*. Palgrave Macmillan.

Landry, D. & Chen, Y. (2021) Can Chinese investment lead to knowledge and technology transfers? The case of Madagascar. *Journal of Chinese Economic and Business Studies*, 19(4), 315–334.

Lee, H.H. & Tan, H.B. (2006) Technology transfer, FDI and economic growth in the ASEAN region. *Journal of the Asia Pacific Economy*, 11(4), 394–410.

Meyer, K.E., Mudambi, R. & Narula, R. (2011) Multinational enterprises and local contexts: the opportunities and challenges of multiple embeddedness. *Journal of Management Studies*, 48(2), 235–252.

Moazzem, K.G. & Sehrin, F. (2016) Economic upgrading in Bangladesh's apparel value chain during the post-mfa period: An exploratory analysis. *South Asia Economic Journal*, 17(1), 73–93.

Morris, M., Barnes, J. & Kao, M. (2016) *Global value chains, sustainable development, and the apparel industry in lesotho*. Country Case Study. ICTSD.

Morris, M., Plank, L. & Staritz, C. (2016) Regionalism, end markets and ownership matter: Shifting dynamics in the apparel export industry in Sub Saharan Africa. *Environment and Planning A: Economy and Space*, 48(7), 1244–1265.

Morris, M. & Sedowski, L. (2006) The competitive dynamics of the clothing industry in Madagascar in the post-MFA environment. Available at http://hdl.handle.net/11427/19848 [Accessed 28 June 2020]

Morris, M., Staritz, C. & Barnes, J. (2011) Value chain dynamics, local embeddedness, and upgrading in the clothing sectors of Lesotho and Swaziland. *International Journal of Technological Learning, Innovation and Development*, 4(1–3), 96–119.

Morris, M. & Staritz, C. (2014) Industrialization trajectories in Madagascar's export apparel industry: Ownership, embeddedness, markets, and upgrading. *World Development*, 56(4), 243–257.

Morris, M. & Staritz, C. (2017) Industrial upgrading and development in Lesotho's apparel industry: global value chains, foreign direct investment, and market diversification. *Oxford Development Studies*, 45(3), 303–320.

Mottaleb, K.A. & Sonobe, T. (2011) An inquiry into the rapid growth of the garment industry in Bangladesh. *Economic Development and Cultural Change*, 60(1), 67–89.

Natsuda, K., Goto, K. & Thoburn, J. (2010) Challenges to the Cambodian garment industry in the global garment value chain. *The European Journal of Development Research*, 22(4), 469–493.

Nolintha, V. & Jajri, I. (2016) The garment industry in Laos: Technological capabilities, global production chains and competitiveness. *Asia Pacific Business Review*, 22(1), 110–130.

Peng, H. & Yu, J. (2021) Absorptive capacity and quality upgrading effect of OFDI: Evidence from China. *Pacific Economic Review*, 26(5), 651–671.

Pietrobelli, C. & Rabellotti, R. (2011) Global value chains meet innovation systems: Are there learning opportunities for developing countries? *World Development*, 39(7), 1261–1269.

Rhee, Y.W. (1990) The catalyst model of development: Lessons from Bangladesh's success with garment exports. *World Development*, 18(2), 333–346.

Rotunno, L., Vézina, P.-L. & Wang, Z. (2013) The rise and fall of (Chinese) African apparel exports. *Journal of Development Economics*, 105, 152–163.

Schmitz, H. & Knorringa, P. (2000) Learning from global buyers. *The Journal of Development Studies*, 37(2), 177–205.

Shakya, M. (2011) Apparel exports in Lesotho: The state's role in building critical mass for competitiveness. In: Chuhan-Pole, P. & Angwafo, M. (Eds.) *Yes Africa can: Success stories from a dynamic continent*. The World Bank, pp. 219–229.

So, A.Y., Lin, N. & Poston, D. (Eds). (2001) *The Chinese triangle of mainland China, Taiwan, and Hong Kong : Comparative institutional analyses*. Greenwood Press.

Staritz, C. & Morris, M. (2013) *Local embeddedness, upgrading and skill development: Global value chains and foreign direct investment in lesotho's apparel industry*. Capturing the Gains Working Paper 20.

Staritz, C. & Whitfield, L. (2019) Local firm-level learning and capability building in global value chains. In: Ponte, S., Gereffi, G. & Raj-Reichert, G. (Eds.) *Handbook on global value chains*. Edward Elgar Publishing, pp. 385–402.

Whitfield, L., Staritz, C., Melese, A.T. & Azizi, S. (2020) Technological capabilities, upgrading, and value capture in global value chains: Local apparel and floriculture firms in Sub-Saharan Africa. *Economic Geography*, 96(3), 195–218.

Whitfield, L. & Staritz, C. (2021) Local supplier firms in Madagascar's apparel export industry: Upgrading paths, transnational social relations and regional production networks. *Environment and Planning A: Economy and Space*, 53(4), 763–784.

Yunus, M. & Yamagata, T. (2012) The garment industry in Bangladesh. In: Fukunishi, T. (Ed.) *Dynamics of the garment industry in low-income countries: Experience of Asia and Africa* (Interim Report). IDE-JETRO.

Zhan, J., Mirza, H. & Speller, W. (2015) The impact of larger scale agricultural investments on communities in South East Asia: A first assessment. *Revue internationale de politique de développement*, (6). https://doi.org/10.4000/poldev.2029

AUTHOR BIOGRAPHIES

Linda Calabrese is a Research Fellow with the International Economic Development Group, ODI and a Leverhulme Doctoral Fellow at the Lau China Institute, King's College London.

Neil Balchin holds a PhD in Economics from the University of Cape Town and is currently an Economic Adviser at the Commonwealth Secretariat, focusing on trade policy analysis. This article is based on work undertaken in his former capacity as a Research Fellow at the Overseas Development Institute (ODI).

How to cite this article: Calabrese, L. & Balchin, N. (2022) Foreign Investment and Upgrading in the Garment Sector in Africa and Asia. *Global Policy*, 13(Suppl. 1), 34–44. Available from: https://doi.org/10.1111/1758-5899.13059

Received: 31 August 2021 | Revised: 14 January 2022 | Accepted: 14 January 2022

DOI: 10.1111/1758-5899.13060

RESEARCH ARTICLE

Knowledge Transfer in the Global South: Reusing or Creating Knowledge in China's Special Economic Zones in Ethiopia and Cambodia?

Ana Cristina Alves[1] | Celia Lee[2]

[1]School of Social Sciences, Nanyang Technological University, Singapore City, Singapore

[2]Nanyang Centre for Public Administration, Nanyang Technological University, Singapore City, Singapore

Correspondence
Celia Lee, Nanyang Centre for Public Administration, Nanyang Technological University, 50 Nanyang Avenue Block S3.2-B4 50 Nanyang Avenue, Block S3.2-B4, Singapore City, Singapore.
Email: kplee@ntu.edu.sg

Abstract

Chinese special economic zones (SEZs) have played a key role in attracting massive foreign investment and in facilitating knowledge and technology transfer to local companies. This explains the mushrooming of Chinese-led SEZs and industrial parks in parts of Southeast Asia and Africa since the early 2000s, and more recently its prominence in the planning of the economic corridors along the Belt and Road Initiative. Our interest in SEZs derives from the fact that they provide novel grounds to investigate the dynamics of knowledge transfer (KT) in South–South exchanges and the extent to which it diverges from more traditional exchanges. This study undertakes a comparative analysis of KT in the Eastern Industrial Zone (EIZ) in Ethiopia, and the Sihanoukville Special Economic Zone (SSEZ) in Cambodia. The case studies suggest that, although the provision of training by Chinese investors has added value to the labour force, its transformative impact is limited owing to the concentration on explicit KT modalities at lower skills levels and the top–down approach to KT by Chinese companies. These limitations are largely a function of the wide absorptive capacity gap between China and the host countries studied and the absence of more conducive industrial policies.

1 | INTRODUCTION

For their part, Chinese companies should also make greater efforts to disseminate implicit/tacit knowledge, namely through more frequent exchanges between the parent and subsidiary companies, targeting specifically higher level local cadres. This will be easier to realise if the local labour knowledge gap is narrowed, and localisation policies are in place and effectively enforced.

2 | INTRODUCTION: SPECIAL ECONOMIC ZONES AND KNOWLEDGE TRANSFER

Over the past two decades, the substantial expansion of economic cooperation and foreign direct investment

(FDI) flows in the Global South provides novel ground for investigation, namely, to try understanding the extent to which processes and outcomes of KT between developing countries deviate from vertical North–South patterns. This is, however, an area that remains very under-researched despite a growing stream of studies unbundling the booming exchanges between countries within the Global South. Although other emerging economies such as India, Brazil, and Turkey have also surfaced as leading agents in SouthSouth cooperation, none stand to make an impact on the same scale as China owing to the much wider geographical scope and volume of its cooperation in the Global South. Beijing's cooperative engagements with the developing peers naturally showcase the most successful elements of its development experience, namely the emphasis on hard connectivity infrastructure and export-led industrialisation through special economic zones (SEZs). The latter is particularly coveted by developing countries across the south hoping to tap into China's unparalleled knowledge in operationalising SEZs as a successful industrialisation policy.

Economic zones comprise various modes such as free trade zones, industrial parks, and export processing zones. They are intended to facilitate rapid economic and industrial growth by leveraging tax incentives and streamlined procedures to attract FDI. Benefits to their host nations, however, go much beyond the attraction of FDI. Economic zones serve as a privileged vehicle for knowledge and technology transfer necessary to upgrading native manufacturing capabilities and fostering domestic value chains, which are critical to avoiding the enclave syndrome that afflicts many SEZs across the south. Other beneficial spillovers include employment opportunities for locals, stimulating soft and hard infrastructure development (Giannecchini & Taylor, 2018). Adjacent to their focal profit-making and industry-nurturing qualities, SEZs also enhance, socially and culturally, the local communities in which they operate. One manner through which this is achieved is by functioning as centres for the transfer of knowledge, technological proficiencies, vocational-skill upgrading, and best practices to the local workforce.

As of 2018, an estimated 147 countries were hosting special zones of one kind or another, with China alone hosting 2543 zones (Dodwell, 2019). China has been the most successful in using SEZs to attract foreign capital and effect structural transformation through the transfer of knowledge and technology. In Shanghai alone, there are at least 36 special zones, ranging from industrial estates, export processing zones, and high-tech parks to an automobile city. In the 1980s, Special zones became the driving force behind China's industrialisation and opening-up strategy by hosting small-scale experiments in economic reform in strategic coastal locations which spread across the country gradually instead of risking a nationwide reform.

The Chinese government actively endorses such sharing of 'wisdom' with other developing countries (Jiang, 2019). This is apparent in the official rhetoric in the context of the Forum of ChinaAfrica Cooperation (FOCAC) and the Belt and Road Initiative (BRI). In his opening speech at the 2015 FOCAC summit in Johannesburg, president Xi Jinping highlighted China's commitment to help increase African productivity by nurturing the continent's industrialisation, an endeavour that was also emphasised in the final declaration.[1.] Furthermore, in the 2015–2018 FOCAC Action Plan, US$10 billion in funds were committed to further develop economic and trade cooperation zones (ETCZ) and industrial parks on the continent.[2.] Moreover the creation of industrial parks and ETCZ along cross-border economic corridors appears to be 'an increasingly important dimension of international cooperation

Policy Implications

- For an impactful and sustainable industrialisation process, creative learning and innovation need to take root among the workforce, particularly at management levels.
- In host contexts characterised by low labour absorptive capacity, governments need to close the skills gap and take greater ownership of the knowledge transfer process rather than relying on automatic spillovers arising from foreign-investor training initiatives. This requires:
- In-depth knowledge of the labour force's capabilities, limitations, and potential to effectively devise a long-term strategy of labour upgrading in light of broad industrialisation goals, coupled with strong investment in vocational-training institutions aligned with the SEZs' needs;
- Complemented by the creation of institutional links or coordinating mechanisms bridging tertiary education and vocational schools with economic zones; and
- Drafting of conducive policies and regulations enforcing knowledge and transfer, namely through the localisation of cadres at management levels followed by monitoring mechanisms for effective and systematic implementation.

within the framework of the Belt and Road Initiative' (Xinhua, 2019), with the government playing an important role in promoting and facilitating outward investment into these SEZs. Chinese SOEs and private companies are also involving themselves directly in establishing, constructing, and operating SEZs in many developing host countries (Ding & Chuan, 2020), investing in manufacturing and other productive activities in SEZs across Africa and Asia.

As Chinese firms shift manufacturing to labour-intensive, low-wage production locations, countries in Asia and Africa are provided with a promising opportunity to climb the industrialisation ladder in a manner similar to China's previous path. Their governments aim at meeting the demand for inexpensive labour and low production costs through the replication of Chinese SEZ-led development approaches. However, the overall effectiveness of SEZs in achieving these benefits remains mixed (Farole, 2011; UNCTAD, 2019) because the performance of the zones vary and many remain below expectations, failing either to attract substantial investment or to generate promised economic impact (UNCTAD, 2019). Not all Chinese overseas SEZs are fully operational, although some have experienced teething problems and backlash. Occasional local issues have also emerged with political pushback from local businesses resenting the Chinese as well as frustration from members of the local community who had once lost their lands owing to unfair compensation in the initial construction of the SEZs (Alves, 2011; Venkateswaran, 2020). Environmental regulations and their enforcement can be laxer within the zones to attract investment, leading to heightened pollution and environmental degradation (UNCTAD, 2019). These and other issues, often caused or exacerbated by poor planning and governance in the process of establishing and implementing SEZs (Gauthier, 2018), have led to disputes and protests in many SEZs. Notwithstanding, it is possible that SEZ projects inspired or built by China in developing countries might succeed where others have failed, not only because of China's own successful experience with SEZs, but also because of Chinese government backing, the generous incentive packages provided, and the possibility that such zones may be more suitable for conditions in developing countries.

Despite the rapid expansion of China-inspired/China-supported SEZs in Africa and Southeast Asia, and a nascent stream of literature on the topic (Ding and Liao, 2020; Tang, 2019; Tang, 2015; 2019; 2019b, & 2020; Zhang et al., 2018), little is understood about the transfer process of the skills, knowledge, and technology from China to the host countries as well as the extent to which effective and sustainable outcomes ensue from such transfer (Knoerich et al., 2021). Although some studies discuss the merits of transnational knowledge and skill spillovers for FDIs and host nations, there is a paucity in the literature that comprehensively reviews this fluid dynamic within the context of specific nations. Particularly, how transnational knowledge and skills transfers occur within the context of the BRI. This paper proposes to help fill this gap by offering an analysis of workforce KT flows in two high profile economic zones in Africa and Southeast Asia: the East Industrial Zone (EIZ) in Ethiopia and the Sihanoukville Special Economic Zone (SSEZ) in Cambodia. Motivated by the broader aim of contributing to the understanding of knowledge transfer (KT) flows within the Global South, this article attempts to shed light on the following three interrelated questions: What modalities of KT are taking root in these Zones? What KT outcomes have they produced so far? And, finally, is it possible to discern a distinctive horizontal pattern of KT processes and outcomes compared with the North–South track? The article draws on secondary sources, primarily published research on Chinese SEZs in Africa and Southeast Asia, on EIZ and SSEZ, and qualitative primary data collected in Ethiopia and Cambodia.

The rest of the paper is structured as follows: First, we address the dynamics of KT to situate the research framework for this paper. Next, we discuss how SEZs contribute to development in host countries through KT. After explaining the data collection, we present the case studies of EIZ and SSEZ, focusing on the process and outcome of the knowledge and skills transfer, followed by concluding remarks.

Our cases demonstrate that, although the provision of training by Chinese investors has added value to the labour force, its transformative impact is limited because of the concentration on explicit KT modalities at lower skills levels and the top–down approach to KT adopted by Chinese companies. Such a situation is more conducive to knowledge reuse than knowledge creation, which is more likely to result in dependence on the knowledge sender, thus undermining the self-sustainability of the industrialisation process. This outcome is largely explained by the large absorptive capacity gap of the labour force in the host countries studied vis-à-vis China and the absence of more conducive industrial policies in host countries.

3 | THEORETICAL FRAME: WHAT DO WE KNOW ABOUT KNOWLEDGE TRANSFER DYNAMICS?

Knowledge transfer is a by-product of FDI and is ultimately the function of knowledge asymmetry between investor and host, in the sense that it results from the need to fill the knowledge gap between the two. Although scattered research on the topic emerged in the 1970s and 1980s, KT seems to have taken off as a steady stream of academic inquiry in the 1990s, when some of the seminal and most cited works were published (Nonanka, 1994; Simonin, 1999; Szulanski, 1996; Zander & Kogut, 1995). The number of annual publications on KT grew exponentially in the following decade, from nearly 30 in 1999 to more than 150 by 2006 (Graham, 2008:4). Albeit relevant research on KT has been conducted from the point of view of health care (Kramer & Wells, 2005; Thompson et al., 2006) and social sciences (Crewe & Young, 2002; Landry et al., 2001), the bulk of studies dissecting the dynamics and determinants of KT across borders originates from business and management subjects. Most findings derive from studying behavioural patterns of multinational corporations in foreign contexts, typically through subsidiaries, acquisitions, or joint ventures. Predictably, existing research has thus far focused primarily on KT flows from developed to developing countries, with China offering a particularly fertile ground for investigation. Over the past three decades, this stream of literature has enriched our understanding immensely, not only of how knowledge is vertically transferred within and between companies across boundaries but also how horizontal knowledge spillovers can take root and benefit the host economy more broadly.

Drawing on the literature given above, by vertical KT one understands the hardware and software knowledge that is passed on by one entity to another across boundaries through a direct/formal link, such as parent to local subsidiary company, in strategic partnerships, or assembler–supplier contracts. Conversely, horizontal KT refers to indirect/informal links (such as exposure to competitor products, trade shows, supplier contract discussions) that may lead to knowledge spillovers in related industries through mechanisms of competition and specialisation (Sinani & Meyer, 2004; Smarzynska, 2004). For this article, we shall focus on vertical KT only.

Much of the debate on vertical KT has been around the modalities and effectiveness of KT to which the concepts of explicit and tacit (or implicit) knowledge are central. The concept of tacit knowledge, originally developed by Polanyi (1958, 1966), refers to knowledge that is embedded in individuals/organisations which is difficult to articulate and therefore disseminate. It derives from cumulative experiential learning at the individual level and at the organisational level from communities of practice of norms and routines, which are difficult to codify and separate from the source. Knowledge in its explicit form, on the other hand, can be easily codified and disseminated across boundaries allowing by itself some degree of technological transfer (copy-paste/transplant). Although implicit knowledge 'adds more value to the organisation' (Liyanage et al., 2009), a dynamic interaction between explicit and tacit knowledge is necessary to produce creative learning, the kind of knowledge that leads to innovation (Nelson & Winter, 1982; Nonanka, 1994; Spender, 1996). Therefore, to be more effective, KT strategies should aim at effectively disseminating both explicit and implicit knowledge, particularly at management levels. The literature seems to converge on the benefits of nurturing frequent two-way interactive personal exchanges at higher skill levels, between the source and the receiver of knowledge as the most effective way of transferring tacit knowledge across firms (Buckley et al., 2005; Cavusgil et al., 2003; Lam, 2000). Effective transfer of implicit knowledge is more likely to generate creative learning patterns, stimulate local innovation, and lead to self-sustainability (Cavusgil et al., 2003; Madhavan & Grover, 1998), which are required for a more transformative impact on the local economy. Conversely, the transfer of explicit knowledge alone is more conducive to a knowledge-reuse (copy-transplant) output and a dependence path/enclave outcome.

The literature on KT tends to converge on several other factors affecting KT outcomes in the receiving country. Communication is one of them. For effective communication to take place, a common working language is needed; however, this is by no means sufficient, particularly when the transfer is happening between two different cultures. Cultural distance or asymmetries may impair the ability to decode and interpret information (Simonin, 1999), but also originate misunderstandings that further undermine communication. Basic issues, such as awareness of codes of conduct (i.e. to avoid offending the other) to greater understanding of local culture (i.e. how best to motivate the trainees), are examples of such communication barriers that go beyond language difficulties. The wider the cultural/language gap, the more complex and difficult it is to transfer knowledge effectively.

One other key proposition in mainstream literature is that KT is greatly affected by local absorptive capacity. The concept was first vented by Cohen and Levinthal (1990) referring to '(…) the ability of a firm to recognise the value of new, external information, assimilate it, and apply it to commercial ends (…)' (p. 128). This ability, he argues, is a function of preexisting related knowledge and the diversity of background between sender and recipient. Absorptive capacity determines the innovative capabilities of the recipient, and is path dependent (i.e. on prior investments in R&D, labour education, and broader circumstantial context such as institutions and regulations, market conditions, etc.). The mainstream take is that the lower the absorptive capacity of the recipient (wider knowledge gap with the sender) the less likely significant knowledge spillovers will ensue.

Drawing from the scientific wisdom above, this study will focus on vertical KT between China (sender) and Cambodia and Ethiopia (receivers) through the establishment of economic zones, considered privileged platforms for policy sharing and dissemination. The analysis will hinge on juxtaposing empirical findings from the two zones with the concepts and propositions expounded in this section.

4 | CHINA-LED SEZS AS A POTENTIAL TOOL TO PROMOTE SUSTAINABLE DEVELOPMENT GOALS

China's BRI has many potential synergies with the United Nations 2030 Sustainable Development Agenda, along with its Sustainable Development Goals (SDGs). SEZs have become an increasingly important dimension of international cooperation within the BRI along with infrastructure building, to provide Chinese state-owned enterprises (SOEs) and private companies with a controlled channel for building familiarity with and exposure to international markets and the global economy. Under the BRI and in line with China's 'Going Global' blueprint to expand its domestic economy and access untapped markets, Chinese firms were competitively handpicked by the Chinese Ministry of Commerce to venture into and further develop these SEZs (Giannecchini & Taylor, 2018; Rohne, 2013). These zones can involve multiple activities including, among others, energy, manufacturing, export processing, and logistics. They are not financed out of China's foreign aid budget, but they are subsidised by the Chinese state. The BRI framework aims to promote a parallel sustainable development strategy in other developing nations through the active sharing of working experiences, the transfer of technological capabilities, and training programmes to promote capacity building in host countries (Cao & Alon, 2020). Specifically, SEZs are a significant driver for promoting BRI's five connectivities (policy coordination, facilities connectivity, unimpeded trade, financial integration, and people-to-people bonds), a key platform for international capacity cooperation, an essential way for Chinese enterprises to go global in groups and to integrate into the world, as well as realise the model of mutually beneficial cooperation among countries (Warr & Menon, 2015; Huang, 2016; Akbari et al., 2018; Pang and Huo, 2019).

In the late 1990s, the development of overseas SEZs was pioneered by Chinese investors, and subsequently, the Chinese government announced the establishment of approximately 50 SEZs globally. Support was also provided to the Chinese companies which won the bids to build the zones by the government in the form of incentives, long-term loans, and subsidies (Brautigam and Tang, 2011). SEZs can be a useful tool for developing countries unable to upgrade infrastructure, human capital, and institutional frameworks across the entire economy and help overcome economic bottlenecks and conflicting priorities. If successfully implemented, SEZs can foster inclusive and sustainable industrialisation (SDG 9), promote sustained economic growth, and create decent jobs and income (SDG 8), which will result in improved health and well-being (SDG 3), and thus potentially help reduce poverty (SDG 1), hunger (SDG 2), and inequality (SDGs 5 and 10). If environmentally well managed, they can also increase resource and energy efficiency (SDGs 6, 7, 11, 12) and reduce greenhouse gases and other polluting emissions (SDGs 13, 14, and 15; UNDP, 2019).

From the recipient country's perspective, main drivers in setting up SEZs are employment creation and the upgrading of skills to fulfil the requirements of firms operating in the SEZs. Provision of skills training, capacity development, and human resource management help create a pool of well-trained workers that helps fulfil SDG 4 (quality education) and substantially increases the number of youths and adults with relevant skills, including technical and vocational skills, leading to higher employment rates, decent jobs, and entrepreneurship. In this paper, we will focus particularly on the knowledge and skills transfer to the local workforces in EIZ and SSEZ.

In most developing countries where Chinese SEZs have been implemented, the local workforce tends to be young, non-educated, and habituated to an agrarian way of life where daily tasks include herding sheep and tending crops. Therefore, knowledge and skills transfer is vital to acclimatising these labourers to handle

heavy industrial machinery and automised technology (Ding & Chuan, 2020). They will also need to build up their business management and communication skills (Tang, 2019) so that they could eventually take up managerial positions that are usually occupied by foreign or Chinese expatriates. Therefore, the successful transfer of skills, technology, and knowledge is key to upgrading the indigenous labour force and, as such, help realise the developmental goals of the host countries.

4.1 | Methodological note

This paper draws on published studies focusing on the case studies under analysis and field research carried out in Ethiopia and Cambodia. The primary collection method is through surveys and interviews with Chinese companies invested in the two SEZs.

In Ethiopia, fieldwork was conducted in Addis Ababa and the EIZ between April and May 2018. The fieldwork consisted of field observations and 10 semistructured interviews with key informants. These included three Ethiopian government officials, three local businessmen, two Chinese managers, and two local factory workers. The Chinese managers and local factory workers were all from the same company, Huajian, a shoemaker, and the largest exporter inside the zone. Owing to the much larger volume of published studies on EIZ, the collection of primary data was less extensive than the one conducted in Cambodia.

The data collection in Cambodia was conducted from August to September 2019 by surveying and interviewing top managers, middle managers, and staff selected from five factories of the SEZ in Sihanouk Ville (Sihanouk province). This was complemented by interviews with top managers/HR managers, middle manager/training managers, and staff/workers of a company known as Dara Sakor Resort located in the SEZ of Koh Kong province. To fully comprehend and examine the dynamics of knowledge and skills transfer from investors to the local workers employed within the zone, primary data were collected from five factories located in the SSEZ. Surveys and interviews were conducted to understand the process of KT (including training process, type of training, as well as the outcome of transnational KTs) with six top managers, nine middle managers, and nine workers. Individuals at the management level were Chinese professionals, and the workers were mostly locals (see Table 1 for the profile of respondents).

5 | CASE STUDY 1: KT IN THE EASTERN INDUSTRIAL ZONE, ETHIOPIA

The Ethiopian EIZ was officially announced in 2007 and formally launched in 2009 in the town of Dukem,

35 km to the southeast of Addis Ababa. The land plot covers an area of 233 ha leased for 99 years. The zone is fully owned and run by Jiangsu Qiyuan Group, a private Chinese steel pipe and aluminium producer. In the early years, the zone struggled to develop because of infrastructure financing issues, high transport costs, and lengthy customs handling at the Djibouti Port (which handles most of Ethiopia's overseas trade). It slowly became operational from 2010, with activities ranging from construction materials to garment, shoe, and leather processing, packaging, steel products, and automobile assembly (Gakunu et al., 2015). The zone's pace of development has accelerated significantly in recent years, owing to the construction of the Addis–Djibouti railway[3.] (by a Chinese company), which was completed in late 2016 and has a stop at Dukem. As of 2018, there were 83 companies in the industry zone, of which 56 had already started production (Xinhua, 2019). According to information collected in our fieldwork, by May 2018 the original land plot was fully occupied, and Jiangsu Qiyuan Group had started developing an additional plot of 137 ha to host new investors.[4.]

Huajian Group, which produces shoes for brands like Guess, Calvin Klein, Nina, and other brands, is often cited as the foremost example of success in EIZ. Huajian set up its factory in the zone in 2011 and began operation the following year. By 2015, it had created 3800 jobs and had become widely regarded as a model investor, because it provided free meals and training for its labour force and contributed greatly to Ethiopia's leather exports (Gakunu et al., 2015), reaching a total value of US$31 million in export revenue in 2017.[5.]

5.1 | KT and labour training in EIZ

Along with the attraction of FDI, the increasing share of manufactured exports, and improvements in the local investment climate, employment generation is a main contribution of the EIZ for Ethiopia. As of 2019, approximately 8000 employment opportunities had been created by the zone (Ding & Chuan, 2020). The estimated 87% workforce localisation rate (Zhang, et al., 2018)

leaves no doubt of the potential benefits to surrounding communities. Moreover, the training that is part of the employment process in the EIZ is vital for Ethiopia to transit into a fast-paced industrial environment, given that most of the labour force comprises young, non-educated workers from an agrarian way of life. As such, training is critical to upgrade their skills to handle industrial machinery. According to one survey, 60% of the labour force in the zone received training (Ding, 2018). On average, workers are trained for 40 hours (Ding & Chuan, 2020), with the length of training varying according to the target markets. Therefore, enterprises that export goods to Europe or North America tend to provide longer training to ensure that quality standards match the prime benchmarks of targeted markets, as compared with businesses that focus on the domestic market (Ding, 2018). Skills upgrading of factory workers happens mostly through on-the-job training and e-learning, varying from one week to one month in length. At upper levels, smaller scale, long-term (one to two years) training is undertaken in China, with an equivalent bond period in the factory in Ethiopia.

Hua Jian, for instance, imported approximately 300 technicians to begin production in the Ethiopian factory and train local workers (Chen, 2020). After this intensive training programme, many of the Ethiopian labourers were qualified to replace the expatriate workers. Over a period of seven years, the company additionally sent approximately 500 locals to its plant in Guangdong for a 3- to 12-month training course where they were inculcated with vital skills such as proficiency in Chinese and efficiency in meeting the targets set by managers (Tang, 2019b). The aim of this overseas training was to empower local employees to eventually take up managerial positions (Gakunu et al., 2015). Notwithstanding, our interviews and the existing literature suggest that management (managers, accountants, quality inspectors) remain mostly in the hands of Chinese cadres, and the few locals in managerial positions (mostly foremen) are in subordinate positions and seldom participate in decision-making (Ding, 2018).

According to our fieldwork[4] in Huajian (EIZ), the training of factory-floor workers has been the main vehicle

TABLE 1 Top managers, middle managers, and workers interviewed from five selected corporations in the SSEZ

Company name	Country of origin	Production	No. of top managers	No. of middle managers	No. of workers
Cambodian Gateway Underwear Co., Ltd	Hong Kong	Garment	1	2	2
Hongdou International Garment Co., Ltd	China	Garment	1	0	2
Colia Leather (Cambodia) Co., Ltd	China	Furniture	2	2	2
Romantic Leather (Cambodia) Co., Ltd	China	Leather Bags	1	3	0
Sinoproud (Cambodia) Co., Ltd	China	Garment	1	2	3
Total			6	9	9

Note: All the above selected companies in Sihanouk Ville are garment factories and have received investment by Chinese companies with most of their products, such as bags, luggage, underwear, and clothes, exported to EU markets.

of skills transfer, focusing on operational skills but also soft skills such as punctuality, productivity, and industriousness. This is done through short-term courses, lasting from one week to one month, through on-the-job training or e-learning. Training of local workers at upper levels appears to be limited. A few selected individuals (mostly plant-floor supervisors) have undergone long-term training, some in China (one to two years, with an equivalent bond period). Above that level, not much training occurs, and cadre exchanges between the parent and subsidiary companies seem to be rare and involve mostly Chinese cadres. One study indicates that, although workers perceive skills development as a key incentive to work in Chinese companies, they often think the training provided is insufficient and that prospects of promotion are rather slim, particularly at higher levels (Ding, 2018).

6 | CASE STUDY 2: KT IN SIHANOUKVILLE SPECIAL ECONOMIC ZONE, CAMBODIA

Established in 2008 and located in southwest Cambodia, the Sihanoukville Special Economic Zone (SSEZ) is considered the biological child of the Royal Government of Cambodia and the Chinese government, and one of largest SEZs in Southeast Asia (Chheang, 2017). The zone occupies an area of 11 km and is conveniently located 3 km from Sihanoukville airport and 12 km from its harbour, the only international port in Cambodia. SSEZ is a flagship BRI project and China has invested more than US$610 million in its construction. It is the only state-level overseas economic and trade cooperation zone backed by a bilateral governmental agreement and coordination mechanism at vice-ministerial level that aims at creating an ideal investment platform for enterprises (Chheang and Heng, 2019; Cheng, 2020). The SSEZ is a joint venture between two private companies, China's Hongdou Group and Cambodia International Investment Development Group (Wang et al., 2021).

The SSEZ was developed based on the Shenzhen SEZ model and is funded by the Shenzhen Foundation for International Exchange and Cooperation, a privatised foundation under the Chinese government (Bühler, 2019). This setting—compounded with investment-friendly provisions, such as income tax breaks for 6 to 9 years, complete import duty exemption on production apparatuses, and no curbs implemented on capital control—has incentivised Chinese businesses to station their manufacturing facilities in the SSEZ (Bühler, 2019). In 2015, East China's Jiangsu province opened a trade and economic representative office in the SSEZ, aiming to further boost trade and investment ties between the two countries. The SSEZ aspires to become a well-facilitated, fully functional, ecological model industrial zone with capacity for 300 enterprises and projected to create 80,000–100,0000 industrial jobs (Xinhua, 2019).

The zone has attracted businesses from nations such as Japan, Korea, the USA, and China, with most of the ventures focusing on industrial areas such as textiles and garments, electronic products, hardware, and machinery (Cheng, 2020; Heng & Cheng, 2019). According to a report by the Council for the Development of Cambodia (CDC, 2018), in 2018, the SSEZ exported products worth US$372 million and housed more than 160 factories with a registered investment capital of approximately US$918 million, creating 22,495 jobs. Most factories are Chinese and engage in garment manufacturing (Fifield, 2018). Goods such as steel piping, bicycles, wire hangers, sofa covers, plywood, and household products are also produced here. Most workers in the SSEZ are young rural-urban migrants from Cambodia's southern districts (Blau, 2017).

6.1 | Knowledge transfer and labour force training in SSEZ

Attracting FDI plays an important role in the long-term economic development of the country. To facilitate an investment-friendly environment, the Cambodian government has worked hard to maintain peace and political, social, and macroeconomic stability, develop fundamental infrastructure (hardware and software), reduce tax measures, and develop an industrial policy. As a result, FDI in Cambodia grew significantly: from US$ 3.138 billion in 2016 to US$ 6.388 billion in 2018 (CDC, 2018)[6]. Notably, over the past few years, Chinese companies have become the largest foreign investors in Cambodia (Buckley and Eckerlein, 2020). FDI is not only an important source of capital but also critical to enhancing competitiveness of the domestic economy through infrastructure development and transfer of knowledge, skills, and technology. It also creates employment opportunities for the locals and fosters domestic productivity.

Although there has been notable progress in education over the past 10 years, Cambodian labour has yet to reach the skill level required by the industrial sector (ADB, 2019). The low skill level of the workforce remains the main problem identified by the firms. Therefore, most of the factories surveyed have their own in-house training department or unit to meet the educational needs of their local employees or engage in staff orientation. Notably none of them send their workers to local training institutions, which suggests some misalignment between Cambodian training institutions and the labour needs of the zone. Based on the data we collected, on the investors' side, the principal impetus and expected outcome for the knowledge and skills transfer were twofold. On the business end, this was aimed at enhancing efficiency and market competitiveness, with the larger objective of augmenting profit margins. This process was vital for upgrading the hard and soft capabilities of the domestic workforce by encouraging workers to work harder, improve their work outputs, produce better quality goods, and boost their productivity to reach the set performance indicators such as attaining a larger market share.

Most of the firms train their technical staff and line managers through on-the-job and off-the-job training. Factory managers were recruited mainly from China where they received technical training before being sent to the factories in the SSEZ. Technical skills training focused mainly on designing bags and clothes, sewing techniques, ironing, and packaging. These skills were then transferred to the local workforce through supervisor-direct-train-the-subordinator or peer-to-peer training. Training in management skills of the local workforce was the second most common kind of KT, provided by four out of the five factories. Training here focused on local line and middle managers, with an emphasis on soft skills such as supervisory and management skills. One firm, Romantic Leather (Cambodia) Co., Ltd also sent workers to China for further training for a short duration of less than a month. Only three factories transferred leadership skills that involved teaching decision-making and analytical skills to middle managers. Mostly the purpose was to promote them to higher management levels and improve their capacity to lead their subordinates, improve their daily working processes, and refine their documentation skills. The two most common modes of transfer that are identified across all the factories are mentoring to transfer management skills and on-the-job training for the workers. Mentoring and on-the-job training are achieved through either peer-to-peer learning among the workers or where the supervisor directly instructs his subordinates. Table 2 presents a comparison of the transfer of skills across the five firms.

Thus far, the most evident benefits accrued from the SSEZ are undoubtedly economic profit and the strengthening of cooperation between the two countries to compete more effectively in regional and international markets, especially the opportunity to export manufactured goods to the EU and USA. The fact that the Cambodian government has left the establishment and management of the zone entirely to private-sector developers meant that there is no formal institutionalisation of KT processes, and each company is free to pursue their own training strategies, which naturally are driven by their narrow profit interests, rather than the interest of the labour force or the national development plan.

7 | DISCUSSION: KNOWLEDGE REUSE OR KNOWLEDGE CREATION?

In comparative terms, the two zones analysed in this study seem to share a few characteristics. Sectors invested are similar (garments, leather, and light manufacturing), most investors in the zone are Chinese companies, and the workforce appear to be largely unskilled as composed overwhelmingly of former rural dwellers. The zone in Cambodia, however, is significantly larger in area, number of companies invested, and the volume of investment and jobs created, and it benefits from being located much closer to exporting exit points (Sihanoukville port and airport). From the perspective of the host countries, the largest impact of these two zones is felt in FDI influx, job creation, increased export earnings, and improvement of the overall investment environment (hard and soft infrastructure). However, from a KT point of view, the potential for a more transformative impact is modest owing to evidence that in both zones the emphasis falls largely on explicit knowledge transfer.

TABLE 2 Comparison of the transfers of skills across the five SSEZ firms included in this study

Firm	In-house training unit	Mode of KT	Location of training	Skills	Number of trainees
Cambodian Gateway Underwear Co., Ltd	No	Mentoring; on-the-job training; orientation	Local	• Technical	Not provided
Hongdou International Garment Co., Ltd	Yes	Mentoring; on-the-job training	Local	• Technical • Management	600 50
Colia Leather (Cambodia) Co., Ltd.	Yes	Training; Mentoring; on-the-job training	Local	• Technical • Management • Leadership	1000 50 10
Romantic Leather (Cambodia) Co., Ltd	Yes	Mentoring; on-the-job training	China and Local	• Technical • Management • Leadership	16 4 16
Sinoproud (Cambodia) Co., Ltd	Yes	Training; mentoring; on-the-job training	Local	• Technical • Management • Leadership	64 160 80

Observations in both zones thus run contrary to the best practices unveiled in mainstream KT literature. Knowledge transfer mechanisms in the EIZ have thus far privileged the dissemination of explicit knowledge (hard and soft skills), mostly at lower skills levels and through on-the-job training. Implicit KT remains limited owing to the low level of mobility between parent company and subsidiary company involving indigenous cadres, particularly at higher levels. Even when these exchanges take place, evidence suggests that the beneficiaries remain in subaltern positions, indicating a rigid vertical hierarchy that leaves little margin for local ownership and the emergence of an innovative, localised managerial class. These observations clearly deviate from the findings of mainstream literature that intensive exchanges between the parent company and subsidiary are the most effective way to transfer implicit knowledge, especially at higher levels (Buckley et al., 2005; Lam, 2000).

The output appears slightly more promising in the SSEZ. Although the pattern of training seems similar (preference for short-term, on-the-job technical training), in Cambodia, Chinese companies seem to make a more consistent effort at training local cadres at management and, importantly, leadership levels. Although the mobility of local cadres with the parent company seems to be the exception, the use of mentorship to prepare locals for management and leadership roles may be a vehicle for transfer of implicit knowledge. According to mainstream literature on the topic (Buckley et al., 2005; Cavusgil et al., 2003; Lam, 2000), if sufficiently intense, this exchange between Chinese and local cadres may lead to a more effective diffusion of implicit knowledge at management levels and thus greater indigenous ownership. This will depend, however, on the intensity of exchanges and the frequency of mobility of high cadres between parent and subsidiary companies, which so far seems to be happening mostly one way (Chinese cadres sent from parent companies to SSEZ). Furthermore, this leadership mentoring accounts for a significantly smaller portion of training, which has yet to bear fruit, because most top positions remain in the hands of Chinese cadres. The limited implicit KT apparent in both case studies hinders a more efficient dynamic interaction between explicit and implicit knowledge at the recipient level which, according to the literature (Nelson & Winter, 1982; Nonaka, 1994; Spender, 1996), makes it less likely for knowledge creativity and innovation to take root at local levels and thus undermines the self-sustainability of the industrialisation process.

Notwithstanding, the impact of explicit KT in an eminently agrarian labour force is noteworthy. In addition to operational skills, key soft skills that were lacking, such as work ethics, have been instilled in the Ethiopian zone through the enforcement of rigid timetables with disciplinary measures, inscription of rules and regulations within the physical space of the working environment, and red banners proclaiming grand mottos such as "building harmonious enterprise" in Chinese, English, or Amharic (Ding, 2018). Through this method of industrial acclimatisation, these corporations guarantee the efficiency of their production operations and, at the same time, cultivate a consciousness of competence and self-discipline (Ding & Chuan, 2020) that was largely absent in the Ethiopian agrarian labour force. Our empirical research in Huajian corroborated that the transfer of soft and hard skills to factory workers has significantly improved work ethics, productivity, and product quality, and that this is something highly valued by local workers and governments officials because these are critical skills for the labour force as it changes to an urban–industrial context. Meaningfully, investors in the EIZ seem to have put a lot more effort into transferring soft skills related to work ethics (punctuality, industriousness, etc.) than in the SSEZ, which may indicate a lower level of skills (or a greater cultural gap) in Ethiopia than in Cambodia. The wide knowledge gap vis-à-vis China limits the absorptive capacity of the labour force (Cohen & Levinthal, 1990) and so undermines the multiplier effects of KT.

Notably, significant horizontal spillovers are taking root in Ethiopia via the high labour turnover because, once skills are acquired, workers tend to look for higher salaries elsewhere contributing to the dissemination of skills to indigenous factories outside the zone. At the management level, however, no significant horizontal spillovers appear to be taking place because Chinese-trained Ethiopian managers are found lacking in skills when hired by local companies (Tang, 2019), which attests to the inefficient transfer of explicit knowledge at higher levels. Further to this, according to our interviewees in Ethiopia, the knowledge being transferred is reportedly informed mainly by Chinese experiences with little effort of adjustment to local contexts, suggesting a top–down approach to KT that defies the horizontal mutual-benefit paradigm of South–South cooperation.

Based on the literature on KT, several factors explain the limits of KT in both zones. First, drawing on our research in the Huajian factory (EIZ), communication barriers, as highlighted by Simonin (1999), seem particularly challenging for two reasons: (a) the fact that the vehicle of KT is a third language (English), which both parties lack full command of, and (b) the significant cultural gap (both corporate and societal) that impairs effective adjustment of KT to the local context. Together they introduce a lot of noise in communication, limiting the scope and depth of the knowledge that can be effectively transferred. In addition, the high labour turnover in Ethiopia discourages companies from further investments in KT activities and especially regarding the training of local management cadres (Tang, 2019a) because this requires larger investments owing to longer training and mobility that is required. Second, there is a significant gap in the absorptive capacity of local labour in both countries vis-à-vis Chinese companies, particularly at managerial levels. As underlined by Cohen and Levinthal (1990), this knowledge gap results from the historically low investment in labour education in the recipient country (Ethiopia and Cambodia in this case) and the wide diversity in background (economic, social, cultural) between sender and recipient, which is particularly evident in the Ethiopian case. This wide gap in knowledge and background makes it very challenging for local labour to effectively absorb knowledge from China, which is light years ahead in its development stage. Third, this knowledge gap is compounded by poor strategic planning around knowledge spillover processes on the Ethiopian (Ding & Chuan, 2020) and Cambodian sides. For example, in Ethiopia there is no institutional mechanism ensuring that the curricula of universities and vocational-training institutes cater to the industries in the zones (Ding, 2018; Gukunu et al., 2015) or that the investors are connected with local professional institutions (Ding & Chuan, 2020). Moreover, industrial policies to ensure technology and KT from foreign investors necessary to develop domestic productive capabilities (i.e. through enforcement of joint ventures with local companies), which have proven critical in the sustainability of industrialisation processes in China and the Asian tigers, are lacking in Ethiopia (Hauge, 2019). Similar institutional and regulatory inefficiencies are also apparent in the Cambodian case study, namely the absence of coordinating mechanisms linking educational institutions and the SEZ and an overarching educational policy serving the national industrialisation strategy. The absence of this overarching coordinating effort in upgrading local skills undermines, for instance, existing high cadres' localisation policies.[7.] The large knowledge gap, combined with high turnover once skills are acquired, and lax policies thus explain investor concentration on short-term technical skills training at basic levels. A greater impact of KT is thus constrained by structural communication barriers, weak absorptive capacity of local labour, and poor strategic planning on the Ethiopian and Cambodian sides.

Although both zones have made strong contributions to Ethiopian and Cambodian exports of manufactured goods from the point of view of labour training, and drawing on findings in mainstream literature (Cavusgil et al., 2003; Madhavan & Grover, 1998), its potential for a transformative impact is, thus far, modest owing to the clear emphasis on explicit KT modalities at lower skills levels. As such, KT modalities and impact thus far appear more commensurable with a 'knowledge-reuse' output (copy-transplant), which is likely to lead to a dependence outcome. Although Chinese companies bear some responsibility for this state of affairs, in both countries this is also largely a function of local weak 'knowledge absorptive capacity' and wide manufacturing knowledge asymmetry, typical of largely agrarian societies changing to an early industrial stage but lacking in education, experience, and institutions. Notwithstanding, the KT patterns described above also suggest that explicit knowledge transfer has played a critical role in upgrading the skills of the local labour force (soft skills such as improved work ethics and hard skills such as operating industrial equipment). Although this may not seem meaningful in the broad picture, it is surely critical at this stage of development in both countries.

8 | CONCLUSION

Knowledge transfer is critical to developing countries' quest to upgrade their economy to higher value-added production and to successfully integrate global value chains, while acting as a developmental catalyst by contributing to the achievement of many SDGs as pointed out earlier. SEZs, if rightly leveraged, are a privileged medium to facilitate KT. Overall, despite the modest results, it is still too early to write off knowledge-creation outputs (i.e. local absorption of tacit knowledge, adapted to local context, and leading to innovation) taking root at later stages in both SEZs, which would be more conducive to a self-sustained and transformative outcome. This however will depend largely on upgrading local absorptive capacity, which entails more conducive local institutional and policy frameworks.

Our cases demonstrate that, although the provision of training by Chinese investors has added value to the labour force, in the end, its impact may fall short because the objective of the companies is to provide sufficient skills to increase productivity rather than ensure local empowerment, ownership, and self-sustainability. To change that scenario, both countries need to take ownership of the KT process rather than leave it to the Chinese companies and expect that automatic spillovers will ensue. This can be done through the institutionalisation of facilitating mechanisms and regulations and by ensuring its effective and systematic implementation. Such overarching guidance, as demonstrated by China's own SEZs experience, is more likely to produce creative learning and innovation, which is necessary for an impactful and sustainable industrialisation process.

Our analysis also demonstrates that, although the economic partnership with China may be rhetorically placed in the horizontal paradigm of South–South cooperation, the reality of labour KT patterns in these zones reflect a top–down approach. To some extent, this can also be attributed to the knowledge gap between China and Ethiopia and Cambodia, because many Chinese investors have pointed out the lack of skilled labour locally, particularly at managerial levels, to justify the continued reliance on Chinese cadres at top levels. A truly horizontal exchange pattern (i.e. two-way flow/mutual learning, adjustment of policies and strategies to the local context, empowerment of local cadres, and greater local ownership) requires a smaller absorptive capacity gap between partners, as demonstrated by the successful KT experience of the Singapore–China Suzhou industrial park. More than the nature of the partnership (North–South or South–South), the question for countries lower in the value chain is how to promote KT efficiently in fragile institutional frameworks compounded by weak knowledge absorptive capacity.

Going forward, as we get to know more about the exchange dynamics between China and its peers in the Global South, more comparative research is needed to gauge the impact and assess the effectiveness of KT in host economies and also further uncover the variables that determine its success or failure. To have a clearer grasp of the specifics of KT between China and other developing countries, a better understanding is also needed of the ways in which KT between China and the Global South differs from that with western counterparts, but also China's own KT experience at home.

ACKNOWLEDGEMENTS

The research of this paper was supported by Singapore Ministry of Education AcRF Tier-2 Grant entitled "Transnational Knowledge Transfer and Dynamic Governance in Comparative Perspective" [MOE2016-T2-02-87]. Special thanks to Gideon G. Jalata and the Economics and Finance Institute of The Ministry of Economy and Finance, Cambodia, for conducting the fieldwork in Ethiopia and Cambodia.

ORCID

Ana Cristina Alves ⓘ https://orcid.org/0000-0001-6744-1626
Celia Lee ⓘ https://orcid.org/0000-0002-0807-4018

ENDNOTES

1. Ministry of Foreign Affairs, 'Declaration and Action Plan of the Johannesburg Summit of the Forum on China-Africa Cooperation', 7 December 2015, www.tralac.org/news/article/8656-declaration-and-action-plan-of-the-johannesubrg-summit-of-the-forum-on-China-Africca'cooperation.html.

2. Ministry of Foreign Affairs, 'The Forum on China-Africa Cooperation – Johannesburg Action Plan (2016–2018)', www.fmprc.gov.cn/mfa_eng/zxxx_662805/51323159.shtml.

3. Personal Interview, Ethiopia Investment Commission officer, Addis Abeba, 11 May 2018.

4. Various personal interviews, EIZ Dukem and Addis Ababa, April–May 2018.

5. Owing to its stellar performance, in 2016 Huajian opened its own 133 ha industrial park in Lebu ('Ethio-China Light Industrial City', located West of Addis), raising the number of its local employees to 7000. In 2019, Huajian signed an agreement with the Ethiopia Industry Park Development Corporation to manage and operate Ethiopia's Jimma Industrial Park, centred in the agro-processing sector (coffee), which is expected to create another 15,000 jobs. Xinhua, 'Chinese firm signs agreement to manage Ethiopian industrial park', 31 May 2019, Xinhuanet, accessed (3 August 2021): http://www.xinhuanet.com/english/2019-05/31/c_138103636.htm.

6. Figures for first 11 months of both years.

7. In the interviews we conducted in Ethiopia (April–May 2018), it transpired that, although the law requires managers to be localised after three years, this was not enforced because of the lack of local skilled managers.

REFERENCES

Akbari, M., Azbari, M.E. & Chaijani, M.H. (2018) Performance of the firms in a free-trade zone: The role of institutional factors and resources. *European Management Review*, 16(2), 363–378.

Alves, A. (2011) *Chinese economic and trade co-operation zones in Africa: the case of Mauritius, SAIIA Occasional Paper No 47*. Available from http://www.saiia.org.za/occasional-papers/chinese-economic-and-trade-co-operation-zones-in-africa-the-case-of-mauritius [Accessed 11th October 2021].

Asian Development Bank (ADB) (2019) *ADB to improve skills, competitiveness of Cambodia's Labor force*. Available from: https://www.adb.org/news/adb-improve-skills-competitiveness-cambodias-labor-force [Accessed 5th September 2021].

Blau, G. (2017) *Cambodian SEZ index*. Unpublished internal report. Phnom Penh, Cambodia: Solidarity Center.

Brautigam, D. & Tang, X. (2011) China's investment in Africa's special economic zones. In: Farole, T. & Akinci, G. (Eds.) *Special economic zones: Progress, emerging challenges, and future directions*. Washington, DC: The World Bank.

Buckley, J. & Eckerlein, C. (2020) Cambodian Labour in Chinese-Owned Enterprises in Sihanoukville: An Insight into the Living and Working Conditions of Cambodian Labourers in the Construction, Casino and Manufacturing Sectors.

Buckley, P.J., Carter, M.J., Clegg, J. & Tan, H. (2005) Language and social knowledge in foreign-knowledge transfer to China. *International Studies of Management & Organization*, 35(1), 47–65.

Bühler, T.A. (2019) *Development in Sihanoukville under Chinese influence (Master's thesis) Chulalongkorn University*. Bangkok, Thailand: Chulalongkorn University.

Cao, M. & Alon, I. (2020) Intellectual structure of the Belt and Road Initiative research: A scientometric analysis and suggestions for a future research agenda. *Sustainability*, 12(17), 1–40.

Cavusgil, S.T., Calantone, R.J. & Zhao, Y. (2003) Tacit knowledge transfer and firm innovation capability. *Journal of Business & Industrial Marketing*, 18(1), 6–21.

Chen, X. (2020) 4. The BRI and Development. In: Chen, X., Miao, J.T. & Li, X. (Eds.) *Regional studies policy impact books: The Belt and Road Initiative as epochal regionalisation*, 2nd edition, Vol. 2, London, UK: Regional Studies Association, pp. 61-78. Available from: https://doi.org/10.1080/2578711X.2020.1823715

Chheang, V. (2017) *The political economy of Chinese investment in Cambodia, Trends. Southeast Asia No. 16*. Singapore: ISEAS.

Chheang, V. & Heng, P. (2021) Cambodian perspective on the Belt and Road Initiative. In: Liow, J.C., Liu, H. & Xue, G. (Eds.) *Research Handbook on the Belt and Road Initiative*. London: Edward Elgar, pp. 176–190.

Cohen, W.M. & Levinthal, D.A. (1990) Absorptive capacity: A new perspective on learning and innovation. *Administrative Science Quarterly*, 128–152.

Council for Development of Cambodia (CDC) (2018) *The report of investment activities in Cambodia, December 2018*, Phnom Penh.

Crewe, E. & Young, M.J. (2002) *Bridging research and policy: context, evidence and links*. ODI Working paper 173, UK. https://www.files.ethz.ch/isn/100449/wp173.pdf

Ding, F. (2018) *Work, employment, and training through Africa–China cooperation zones: Evidence from the Eastern Industrial Zone in Ethiopia* (pp. 1–28, Working paper No. 2018/19).

Washington, DC: China Africa Research Initiative, School of Advanced International Studies, Johns Hopkins University.

Ding, F. & Chuan, L. (2020) Chinese Eastern Industrial Zone in Ethiopia: Unpacking the Enclave. *Third World Quarterly*, 41(4), 623–627.

Dodwell, D. (2019) *China is the world leader in special economic zones but the results are erratic at best, with many being underused or failing to benefit the wider economy*. South China Morning Post: Available from: https://www.scmp.com/comment/opinion/article/3023067/china-world-leader-special-economic-zones-results-are-erratic-best [Accessed 11th October 2021].

Farole, T. (2011) *Special Economic Zones: Performance and Practice – with a focus on Sub-Saharan Africa*. Washington D.C.: International Trade Department, The World Bank.

Fifield, A. (2018) This Cambodian city is turning into a Chinese enclave, and not everyone is happy. Washington Post, 29 March 2018.

Gakunu, P., Demissie, A., Weigel, M., Zhuo, K. & Li, L. (2015) *If Africa Builds Nests will the Birds come? Comparative Study of SEZ in Africa and China*. Working Paper No 6/06, UNDP and International Poverty Reduction Center in China.

Gauthier, J.P. (2018) Potential and pitfalls of special economic zones. Presented at the Workshop on Chinese investment in developing-country special economic zones: impacts on labour and migration. The Transnational Law Institute and the Lau China Institute, King's College London, 9–10 July 2018

Giannecchini, P. & Taylor, I. (2018) The eastern industrial zone in Ethiopia: Catalyst for development? *Geoforum*, 88, 28-35. Helsinki, http://dx.doi.org/ https://doi.org/10.35188/UNU-WIDER/2020/917-4

Graham, P.J. (2008) *Knowledge transfer in theory and practice: A guide to the literature*. Saskatoon, Canada: Social Research Unit, Department of Sociology, University of Saskatchewan.

Hauge, J. (2019) Should the African lion learn from the Asian tigers? A comparative-historical study of FDI-oriented industrial policy in Ethiopia, South Korea and Taiwan. *Third World Quarterly*, 40(11), 2071–2091.

Heng, P. & Chheang, V. (2019) The political economy of China's maritime silk road initiative in Cambodia. In: Blanchard, J.M. (Ed.) *China's maritime silk road initiative and Southeast Asia. Palgrave studies in Asia-Pacific political economy*. Singapore: Palgrave Macmillan, pp. 163–190. https://doi.org/10.1007/978-981-32-9275-8_6

Huang, Y.P. (2016) Understanding China's Belt & Road Initiative: Motivation, framework and assessment. *China Economic Review*, 40, 314–321.

Jiang, Y. (2019) Chinese wisdom: new norms for development and global governance. In: Brown, K. (Ed.) *China's 19th party congress: Start of a New Era*. London: World Scientific Publishing Europe, pp. 177–203.

Knoerich, J., Mouan, L.C. & Goodburn, C. (2021) Is China's model of SEZ-led development viable? A call for smart replication. *Journal of Current Chinese Affairs*, 50(2), 248–262.

Kramer, D.M. & Wells, R.P. (2005) Achieving buy-in: building networks to facilitate knowledge transfer. *Science Communication*, 26(4), 428–444.

Lam, A. (2000) Tacit knowledge, organizational learning and societal institutions: An integrated framework. *Organization Studies*, 21(3), 487–513.

Landry, R., Amara, N. & Lamari, M. (2001) Utilization of social science research knowledge in Canada. *Research Policy*, 30(2), 333–349.

Liyanage, C., Elhag, T., Ballal, T. & Li, Q. (2009) Knowledge communication and translation–a knowledge transfer model. *Journal of Knowledge Management*, 13(3), 118–131.

Madhavan, R. & Grover, R. (1998) From embedded knowledge to embodied knowledge: New product development as knowledge management. *Journal of Marketing*, 62(4), 1–12.

Nelson, R.R. & Winter, S.G. (1982) The Schumpeterian trade off revisited. *The American Economic Review*, 72(1), 114–132.

Nonaka, I. (1994) A dynamic theory of organizational knowledge creation. *Organization Science*, 5(1), 14–37.

Pang, C. & Huo, J. (2019) Exploration of the theoretical framework into the development of overseas economic and trade cooperation zones and summary of China's practice. *Globalization*, 134(4), 19–28.

Polanyi, M. (1958) *Personal knowledge: Towards a post-critical philosophy*. Chicago: University of Chicago Press.

Polanyi, M. (1966) The logic of tacit inference. *Philosophy*, 41(155), 1–18.

Rohne, E. (2013) *Chinese-initiated special economic zones in Africa: a case study of Ethiopia's Eastern industrial zone*. Master Thesis. School of Economics and Management, Lund University.

Simonin, B.L. (1999) Ambiguity and the process of knowledge transfer in strategic alliances. *Strategic Management Journal*, 20(7), 595–623.

Sinani, E. & Meyer, K.E. (2004) Spill-overs of technology transfer from FDI: the case of Estonia. *Journal of Comparative Economics*, 32(3), 445–466.

Smarzynska Javorcik, B. (2004) Does foreign direct investment increase the productivity of domestic firms? In search of spill-overs through backward linkages. *American Economic Review*, 94(3), 605–627.

Spender, J.-C. (1996) Making knowledge the basis of a dynamic theory of the firm. *Strategic Management Journal*, 17(S2), 45–62.

Szulanski, G. (1996) Exploring internal stickiness: Impediments to the transfer of best practice within the firm. *Strategic Management Journal*, 17(S2), 27–43.

Tang, K. (2019a) *Lessons from East Asia: comparing Ethiopia and Vietnam's early-stage special zone development*, Working Paper No. 2019/5. China Africa Research Initiative, School of Advanced International Studies, Johns Hopkins University, Washington, DC.

Tang, X. (2015) *How do Chinese Special Economic Zones support economic transformation in Africa? Supporting economic transformation brief, ODI / UK aid*. Available from: http://set.odi.org/wp-content/uploads/2015/07/How-Chinese-SEZs-support-economic-transformation-in-Africa.pdf

Tang, X. (2019b) *Chinese manufacturing investments and knowledge transfer: a report from Ethiopia*. Working Paper No. 2019/3. China Africa Research Initiative, School of Advanced International Studies, Johns Hopkins University, Washington, DC.

Tang, X. (2019c) *Export, employment, or productivity? Chinese investments in Ethiopia's leather and leather product sectors*. Working Paper No. 2019/32. China Africa Research Initiative, School of Advanced International Studies, Johns Hopkins University, Washington, DC. Available from: http://www.sais-cari.org/publications

Tang, X. (2020) Co-evolutionary pragmatism: Re-examine 'China Model' and its impact on developing countries. *Journal of Contemporary China*, 29(126), 853–870.

Thompson, G.N., Estabrooks, C.A. & Degner, L.F. (2006) Clarifying the concepts in knowledge transfer: A literature review. *Journal of Advanced Nursing*, 53(6), 691–701.

UNCTAD (2019) *World investment report 2019: Special economic zones*. New York: United Nations.

Venkateswaran, L. (2020) China's Belt and Road Initiative: Implications in Africa, ORF Issue Brief No. 395, August, Observer Research Foundation.

Wang, S., Meng, G., Zhou, J., Xiong, L., Yan, Y. & Yu, N. (2021) Analysis on geo-effects of China's overseas: A case study of Cambodia Sihanoukville Special Economic Zone. *Journal of Geographical Sciences*, 31(5), 712–732.

Warr, P.G. & Menon, J. (2015) *Cambodia's special economic zones (October 2015)*. Asian Development Bank Economics Working Paper Series No. 459, Available at SSRN: https://ssrn.com/abstract=2708828 or https://doi.org/10.2139/ssrn.2708828

Xinhua (2019) *Economic zones expected to play bigger role in global BRI cooperation*. XinhuaNet. http://www.xinhuanet.com/english/2019-04/26/c_138009876.htm

Zander, U. & Kogut, B. (1995) Knowledge and the speed of the transfer and imitation of organizational capabilities: An empirical test. *Organization Science*, 6(1), 76–92.

Zhang, X., Tezera, D., Zou, C., Wang, Z., Zhao, J., Gebremenfas, E.A. et al. (2018) *Industrial park development in Ethiopia: Case study report*. Inclusive and Sustainable Industrial Development Working Paper Series, pp. 1–78, Working paper No. 21/2018). Vienna, Austria: United Nations Industrial Development Organization.

AUTHOR BIOGRAPHIES

Dr Ana Cristina Alves is Assistant Professor at the School of Social Sciences - Nanyang Technological University, Singapore, where she lectures on China–Africa relations, Chinese foreign policy, politics in the developing world, and foreign policy analysis. She holds a PhD in International Relations from the London School of Economics.

Dr Celia Lee is Research Fellow at the Nanyang Centre for Public Administration – Nanyang Technological University, Singapore. In addition to being a core member of the research team, she also teaches Globalisation and Talent Strategies, Innovation in the Public Sector, and An Applied Learning Approach to BRI for the Master Programmes.

How to cite this article: Alves, A.C. & Lee, C. (2022) Knowledge Transfer in the Global South: Reusing or Creating Knowledge in China's Special Economic Zones in Ethiopia and Cambodia? *Global Policy*, 13(Suppl. 1), 45–57. Available from: https://doi.org/10.1111/1758-5899.13060

Received: 11 August 2021 | Revised: 31 October 2021 | Accepted: 1 November 2021

DOI: 10.1111/1758-5899.13033

RESEARCH ARTICLE

Convergence or Divergence? China Invested Firms' E&E Evaluation of CSR in Southeast Asia

Jianxun Kong | Yidi Zhou

School of International Studies, Yunnan University, Kunming, Yunnan, China

Correspondence
Jianxun Kong, School of International Studies, Yunnan University, 2 North Cuihu Road, Wuhua District, Kunming, Yunnan 650091, China.
Email: kjx@ynu.edu.cn

Abstract

Using the 2019 China Invested Firms and Employees Survey (CIFES), this study explores the convergence of Chinese enterprise and employee (E&E) evaluation in Southeast Asian countries. The results show that convergence varies greatly across the nine Southeast Asian countries. Union organisations and economic factors play a key role in convergence. Firms with labour unions report a more effective corporate social responsibility (CSR) performance than others, while employees in the construction sector report their firms' CSR and those in the manufacturing and service sectors. Interestingly, the number of years worked by an employee correlates positively with their perception of firms' CSR performance.

1 | INTRODUCTION

Southeast Asia has played a key role in the 21st Century Maritime Silk Road and, as a consequence, the number of China-invested firms in the region has surged over the past few years. Chinese official statistics show that, in 2013, China's outward foreign direct investment (OFDI) in the ten ASEAN countries amounted to US$7.3 billion, with a total of more than 159,000 local employees (MOFCOM, 2014). After 6 years, the number soared to an estimated US$13 billion, with a total of 500,000 local employees in 2019 (MOFCOM, 2019). This is arguably evidence of the host countries' positive responses to the Belt and Road Initiative in the region. It is therefore not surprising that corporate social responsibility (CSR) activities of China-invested firms draw wide attention from both academia and the mass media (Mark & Zhang, 2017). For example, in the international business literature, most studies discuss the liability of foreignness (LOF) encountered by transitional enterprises in countries (Campbell et al., 2012; Mezias, 2002; Nachum, 2003), whereas cultural distance is widely recognised as a key factor affecting the CSR performance of transnational firms in host countries (Campbell et al., 2012; Gallén & Peraita, 2018;

Xiao, 2014). Likewise, some scholars argue that labour unions provide a platform to spur enterprises' CSR incentives (Chen et al., 2011; Chyz et al., 2013; Hirch, 1991; Matten & Moon, 2008) while others suggest that employees' orientation is highly related to CSR activities at the firm level (Bridoux et al., 2016; Rupp et al., 2013).

However, little has been discussed regarding the relationship between enterprises' self-reported CSR activities and local employees' perception of transitional firms in the host countries. Therefore, this study investigates the divergence and convergence of enterprises' CSR activities and employees' perceptions of CSR performance. The study also aims to understand how the variables of how the host country, labour union effect, types of industry, and employees' years of working in the firm may all play a role in the enterprise and employee (E&E) evaluation.

In terms of structure, this paper begins with an overview of previous studies on CSR performance. It then provides a brief account of the quantitative data of the 2019 China Invested Firms and Employees Survey (CIFES) and the methodological approach to analysis, which is followed by a subsection devoted to descriptive statistics of the key variables. The last section considers the substantive results of statistical modelling on the matching of organisation-reported CSR and individual perceived CSR, and how the matching varies across different countries in Southeast Asia. It also reports on findings of how union participation, types of industries, and length of work experience mediated the degree of matching between organisational and individual CSR performance. The conclusion summarises the key findings and our main arguments. The major limitations of the study are acknowledged, and further inquiries for future research are proposed.

2 | RESEARCH OVERVIEW

2.1 | Defining CSR

The discussion about the definition of corporate social responsibility has always been a focus point for most economic and management studies. Since it was first defined by Howard R. Bowen in his 1953 publication of *Social Responsibilities of the Businessman*, many discussions and definitions have been raised by other scholars in the following decades. In 1979, Archie B. Carroll (summarised most of the previous results and refined the definition of CSR, concluding that corporate social responsibility 'must embody the economic, legal, ethical, and discretionary categories of business performance' (Carroll, 1979, p. 499). Further, from a stakeholder's theory perspective, CSR creates sustained value depending on its relationship with various stakeholders (Seungwoo et al., 2017). For the consumers the companies serve, CSR is regarded as a strategy to improve the consumers' view and valuation of the products and services provided by the firms; thus, companies could generate more profit than the products' original value. Some scholars argue that CSR lowers capital costs (Milgrom & Roberts, 1986).

Other CSR-related studies argue that CSR could be a firm's sustainable determinant of survival in its long-and short-term development (Feng et al., 2018). Waddock and Graves (1997) suggested that an enterprise's good economic performance could effectively use alternative sources, which would create investment opportunities in social performance areas, including donations, volunteering programmes, and environmental protection, among others. However, few studies have examined the relationship and interaction between labour unions and CSR. Moreover, the existing studies on unions and CSR are mostly theoretical, arguing that the role of labour unions in CSR is either important or, as stated above, is less effective. Matten and Moon (2008) proposed a conceptual framework for CSR performance, which argues that labour unions contribute to 'implicit' CSR that is functionally equivalent to 'explicit' voluntary CSR performance. Campbell (2007) states that firms are regarded as more socially

responsible because they have an institutionalised dialogue with labour unions and other participants inside and outside the enterprises.

2.2 | Labour unions

Previous studies on labour unions have mainly focused on their influence on employee management, protection of workers' rights, and the rise of wages. Because of these multiple functions, labour unions are believed to be effective bridges between employees and firms. It can serve as an efficient way for a company's marketing and production, as well as a powerful leverage for employees to bargain for higher wages and better working conditions. On the contrary, some researchers argue that labour unions do not appear to work as efficiently as they ought to do, playing a weak, even negative role in company production and management.

In a study analysing the effects of the existence of labour unions on corporate performance and insolvency, Karier (1985) argued that when the union organisation rate in industries with relatively high economic concentration increases, the union wages increase, but the profit decreases. It is possible that labour unions promote corporate insolvency. In a similar vein, Lewis (1986) found that unions raise workers' wages by around 10–20 per cent. In addition, Hirsch (1991) argued that the demand for short-term wages by labour unions reduces the investment of companies in the future, making it difficult for companies to survive. Similarly, Connolly et al. (1986) noted that unions reduce profitability by restricting R&D investments and negatively affect growth.

The brighter side is that the enterprise owner may use labour unions as a governance to monitor the manager to reduce agency costs. This is supported by Chen et al.'s (2011) finding that the union premium is stronger when the union faces a more favourable bargaining environment. Further, the union was found to have a positive relationship with various operational leverage measures. Schwab and Thomas (1998), for example, argued that workers use unions to supervise managers as insiders of the enterprise, and to play a role in recognising and monitoring corporate policies and future plans as soon as shareholders do. Similar findings have been reported by Chyz et al. (2013). These findings suggest that unions provide a platform for employees to negotiate their profits while increasing the costs of equity by reducing the firm's operational flexibility.

2.3 | Labour unions, CSR, and employee identification

A survey of the literature shows that previous CSR studies have mainly focused on how and why companies do well in their CSR performance. As a result, little attention has been given to the levels of individuals involved in CSR. CSR influence on employees has been found to be highly related to how an individual is oriented (Bridoux et al., 2016; Rupp et al., 2013). Thus, more studies pay attention to the individual and internal levels within a company, which affects the company's CSR behaviour or is affected by the company's CSR. A study on micro-CSR was conducted recently, focusing mainly on individual levels (Rupp & Mallory, 2015). Nonetheless, it seems to provide little insight into the effectiveness of labour unions on CSR performance.

Each company is formed and run by individuals in the organisation; hence, an individual employee's support and effort are crucial for a company to survive and prosper. Unfortunately, however, our review of the studies on employees and companies' CSR performance shows that most of the results are concerned with the relationship and interaction between companies and their employees. Since other factors might affect employees' views and thoughts about the company's CSR performance, there is an urgent need to determine how other variables may contribute to the company's CSR performance. To bridge this research gap, we investigate the effect of labour unions on employees' attitudes towards Chinese CSR performance. As noted above, labour unions play an important role in managing employees and protecting their rights (Schwab & Thomas, 1998). We have also argued that, as an internal organisation, a labour union provides an internal platform balancing the relationship between the company and employees, connecting them as well as an organisation for employees to communicate and affect employee identification. Since a labour union is an internal collective within a company formed by a majority of its employees, labour unions affect employees' thoughts towards their own working attitude and comments on the company's overall behaviour from a collective perspective. If we take the labour union as a group, employee identification with in-groups can elicit cooperative behaviour even in the absence of interpersonal communication among group members. Within the in-group category, individuals develop a cooperative orientation towards shared problems (Brewer & Gardner, 1996).

As our project studies Chinese enterprises in 18 Belt and Road countries, we were in a perfect position to carry out a cross-country analysis of the matching quality of the E&E evaluation of their CSR performance, based on all the data collected from different industries in 16 countries. Meanwhile, our analysis shows that there has been a dramatic change in data among different companies from different categories of industry. To date, few studies in the field have discussed the influence of industry on the evaluation of a company's CSR performance. For example, Vashchenko (2014) examined industry factors in CSR performance. However, the study is based on research on leading companies in the industry Vashchenko (2014). Unlike that study, the present project can generate all employees' as well as the enterprises' evaluation data about their companies' CSR performance. It is therefore necessary to focus on employee identification involving the effects of labour unions in such a special business environment – the employees are not Chinese nationals – and to take account of industry factors that have a huge impact on the matching quality of evaluation difference with E&E evaluations. Therefore, our survey shows many differences among countries and political systems, as well as among industries, which result in different cultural backgrounds, education levels, and even worldviews among the employees in those Chinese companies. We argue that Chinese companies' CSR performance must not only satisfy the local community's requirements, but also meet the standards of their employees, who are also citizens of the host countries. In doing so, the companies could do well in marketing, as well as company and human resource management.

3 | DATA AND METHOD

3.1 | CIFES description

Due to the lack of time-series data, it is impossible to empirically investigate the changing patterns of CSR performance over time. However, we can compare the status quo at a given time by using cross-sectional data collected over a certain period. Based on data from the first wave of the CIFES collected in 2019, this study aims to extend the existing CSR studies to match the quality between firms' self-reports and employees' recognition, which will be discussed as the E&E evaluation of CSR performance for the remainder of this article. It will also examine how the matching quality is affected by country differences, union participation, type of industry, and working length of employees. CIFES took the China Invested Firms List released by MOFCOM as the sample frame, and used proportionate sampling techniques across 18 countries in South and Southeast Asia, the Middle East, and Africa. The data used in this analysis consists of 539 firms and 7,744 local employees in the nine ASEAN member countries, excluding Brunei. Data were collected during fieldwork using a computer-assisted personal interview (CAPI) system.

3.2 | Response variables

CSR is measured using nine parallel items in both E&E questionnaires. The questions asked about: (1) local educational programmes; (2) vocational training programmes; (3) healthcare; (4) infrastructure; (5) religious facilities; (6) water purification programmes; (7) recreational facilities; (8) cultural exchange programmes; and (9) social services. The response types are dichotomous, where '1' refers to a positive answer and

'0' refers to a negative one, both at organisational and individual levels.

3.3 | Explanatory variables

The labour union in the CIFES data is measured at the enterprise level to identify whether firms with labour unions have distinctly different CSR performance compared to those without union.

The industrial sector in the CIFES data can be divided into four categories: agriculture (including mining),' construction, manufacturing, and services.

The working experience in the CIFES data at the individual level is measured by years of working at the current enterprise. This study collapses the variable into five sub-groups: (1) 1 year or less;, (2) 2 years; (3) 3 years; (4) 4 years; and (5) 5 years or more.

3.4 | Methods

As detailed above, the observed indicators of CSR items are dichotomous. Therefore, the construction of the two CSR latent variables with categorical observed indicators was carried out using the item response theory (IRT) models (Baker & Kim, 2004; Muthén & Muthén, 2010) in the Mplus statistical package. Then, the mean scores of firms' self-reports and employees' perceptions are used to analyse the matching quality, and to compare how the matching degree may vary across different subgroups of the explanatory variables.

4 | RESULTS

4.1 | Summary of CSR items

As noted above, while most CSR researchers view activity as a substantive aspect of firm strategy in response to community demand and pressures from a variety of stakeholders (Waddock et al., 2002), others focus on employees' reactions to their firms' CSR programmes (Jones, 2011). The CIFES survey enables us to extend the research to compare the firms' self-reported CSR activities and related perceptions from their employees, referred to as E&E evaluation (see above). Parallel CSR activities involve a variety of community-level assistance. Figure 1 displays the percentage of firm-reported, employee-accepted, expected CSR donations according to the various CSR domains. Aid in education and social service facilities are two of the most outstanding areas where Chinese firms in Southeast Asia launch non-profitable CSR activities. For instance, around half of Chinese firms (48.95 per cent) reported aid in local education programmes. Nearly four out of ten firms (39.78 per cent) assisted in the improvement of community facilities for social services, followed by aid in cultural exchange programmes (33.17 per cent), religious facilities (21.33 per cent), and infrastructure (20.49 per cent). Comparatively, a much lower percentage of firms reported to have provided aid to local communities in the fields of healthcare (15.27), vocational training (18.05), recreational facilities (17.05), and water cleaning programmes (9.57).

Regarding the degree of employees' perceptions of their firms' CSR activities, more than four of ten (43.28 per cent) employees responded positively to their firms' aid in the healthcare sector, while the lowest was aid to religious facilities (28.79 per cent). Other areas are somewhere between the two extremes: 42.30 per cent to cultural exchange programmes, 39.43 per cent to local education, 38.87 per cent to social service facilities, 34.63 per cent to recreational facilities, 32.29 per cent to water cleaning, and nearly the same percentage to infrastructure (32.07 per cent). Overall, these results clarify the varied degree of matching quality between firm-reported and worker-accepted CSR activities across the nine items. For instance, CSR in healthcare, vocational training, and water cleaning demonstrate larger gaps (at least 20 per cent) between firm reports

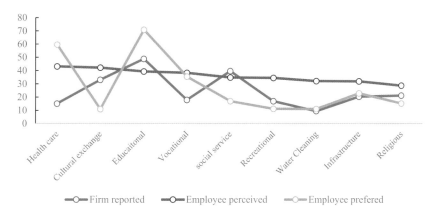

FIGURE 1 Chinese firms' CSR performance, by sector (per cent). *Source*: China Invested Firms and Employees Survey (CIFES), 2019. All data in this study were derived from the same source unless otherwise specified

and employee acceptance. On the contrary, CSR in cultural exchange programmes, social services, and religious facilities delineates high matching quality between the two levels of firms and employees.

Unlike the somewhat steady rate of perception, employees' preferences for their firms' CSR initiatives differ substantively across the nine items. As for multiple-choice items, around 71 per cent and 59.74 per cent of interviewed workers expected their firms to provide aid in education and healthcare, respectively, followed by 35.55 per cent in vocational training. Therefore, the largest gap between what Chinese firms have done and what local employees expect occurs on the item of healthcare, because only 15.27 per cent of Chinese firms reported provision with aid, but nearly six out of ten (59.74 per cent) of the employees expressed their preference in this field. Great gaps exist in terms of assistance in education and social service facilities.

These results have major implications for China-invested firms in general, and for those in Southeast Asian countries in particular. First, CSR performance as corporate diplomacy may not always be visible to stakeholders (e.g. employees and residents). This is particularly true with aid to educational programmes and social service facilities. Second, CSR activities in healthcare, vocational training, recreational programmes, and water cleaning are more likely to be perceived more favourably than activities in other items. Third, most local employees expressed high expectations that their firms undertake more CSR activities in education-related programmes healthcare assistance.

4.2 | Cross-country comparison

As stated above, the internationalisation of Chinese firms has soared since the launch of the Belt and Road Initiative in 2013, and Southeast Asia has become one of the regions where Chinese firms surged most dramatically. Scholars have been interested in studying Chinese firms in Southeast Asia. For example, Tong

(2014) argues that the Chinese business retains a highly centralised authority structure despite the size, while Cooke (2014) analyses the relationships between institutional actors and patterns of human resources management practices of Chinese multinational firms in Southeast Asia and in other regions as well. This sub-section focuses on the CSR performance of Chinese firms from a cross-country comparative perspective of the nine ASEAN members.

The sub-sample of Chinese firms and local employees in Southeast Asia accounts for 61.98 per cent and 58.50 per cent, respectively, of the total CIFES data in the first survey. Figure 2 shows the mean CSR factor scores for both E&E levels across the nine Southeast Asian countries. On the one hand, the mean scores of enterprise CSR differ genuinely among the nine countries. For instance, Chinese firms in Indonesia have the highest score (0.829) of CSR performance, while their counterparts in Singapore display the lowest (−0.649). The scores from other countries fall somewhere between these two extremes. Chinese firms in Myanmar also reported a considerably high percentage of CSR activities (0.533), while those in Lao PDR and Vietnam are at a moderate level, with mean scores of 0.043 and 0.005, respectively. The mean scores of Thailand, the Philippines, Cambodia, and Malaysia are also rather negative, indicating that the CSR activities in these countries are less reported than in other countries, especially Indonesia and Myanmar. On the other hand, the distinction of employees' perceived CSR performance across the nine countries does not differ significantly, with the highest being Lao PDR (0.278) and the lowest being Malaysia (−0.340). Local employees in Myanmar and the Philippines also present positive evaluations of Chinese firms' CSR in their respective countries.

Regarding the matching quality of CSR performance between enterprises' self-reports and employees' perceptions, Chinese firms and their host country employees present good matches in Vietnam (0.005; 0.038), Cambodia (−0304; −0.259), and Malaysia (−0.396; −0.340), whereas the largest gap was found

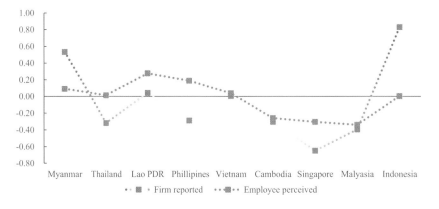

FIGURE 2 Firm and employee CSR factor mean scores, by country

in Indonesia (0.829; 0.004), as in Myanmar (0.533; 0.091) and the Philippines (−0.288; 0.190). Unlike the substantive gaps in Indonesia and Myanmar, where firm-reported CSR performance is higher than the employees' perceptions, the gaps in Thailand, Lao PDP, the Philippines, and Singapore are reversed, namely, the employees' perceived CSR is remarkably higher than the firms' self-reports in these countries.

As can be seen in Figure 2, the E&E evaluation in Vietnam, Cambodia, and Malaysia displays the best match, whereas that in Indonesia shows the widest disparity. Interestingly, the Vietnamese employee comment curves were slightly higher than the enterprises' self-reports. This seems to indicate employees' high satisfaction with Chinese companies' CSR performance in Vietnam. The variability of the diplomatic relationship between China and Vietnam in the past may explain why Chinese companies were apparently more cautious and prudent in marketing, careful to perform CSR.

Similarly, the perfect match in Cambodia and Malaysia is presumably attributable to these two countries' historical and cultural closeness to China. Cambodia and China have agreed to establish a comprehensive strategic partnership of cooperation, in addition to the historical ties between the royal family of Cambodia and the Chinese government. The overall impression of Cambodian citizens towards China and Chinese enterprises has become increasingly amicable, leading to a high matching quality of E&E evaluation.

With regard to Malaysia, the large Malaysian Chinese population size could be the decisive factor. To be precise, citizens with Chinese ethnic backgrounds account for about 20 per cent of Malaysians, and it is plausible to assume that this cohort of Malaysians share similar beliefs and values with those Chinese companies operating in Malaysia. In addition, Malaysia is one of the first countries to respond positively to China's Belt and Road' initiative. Thus, the finding about the best E&E evaluation match in Malaysia does not come as a surprise.

In contrast, it is worth noting that the data in its neighbour, Indonesia, show a low degree of matching. This can be partly explained by the bilateral relationship between China and Indonesia, which has always been a tough challenge, especially in terms of their South China Sea dispute. We assume that the poor national image of China among Indonesian citizens contributes to the low matching quality of the E&E evaluation.

2011). More recently, the influence of labour unions on firm CSR activities has been widely discussed, given that some scholars consider union participation as stakeholder activity that affects firms' CSR performance (Chun & Shin, 2018). As to the empirical results, there are diverse perceptions on whether labour unions act an incentive or a disincentive role in firms' CSR activities. Rather than discussing union participation in positive and negative terms, this section contributes to the debate by showing how union participation affects the matching quality between firms' self-reported and workers' perceived CSR activities.

Overall, the summary statistics of the CIFES data show that for Chinese firms in Southeast Asian countries, 34.6 per cent of the interviewed firms have a labour union as opposed to none in the remaining 65.4 per cent. Further analysis indicates that the majority of those without unions are small-scale business entities. Presumably, the relatively low rate of union existence is also because it takes time for new registered companies to establish their own labour unions, although an increasing number of Chinese firms were registered in Southeast Asian countries soon after the Belt and Road Initiative was launched. In this connection, it can be expected that in the coming years, a large number of newly registered Chinese firms will set up their union organisations.

As an important internal stakeholder inside the company, employees oversee the actual work of their companies. Since employees are always positively involved in discussions about the origins, results, and influences of CSR that their companies bring to society, there is a direct link between CSR and employees' organisational identification (De Roeck & Delobbe, 2012; Jones, 2010; Kim et al., 2010). Thus, the concept of employee identification with companies' CSR performance has been introduced (Glavas & Godwin, 2013). As shown in Figure 3, for Chinese firms with unions, the firm-reported CSR mean score is 0.319, which is considerably higher than the mean score of firms without unions (−0.194). The mean score difference between these two types of Chinese firms was 0.513. This result appears to prove the role of union existence in firms' decisions and actions in CSR performance. At the individual level, employees working in firms with unions also perceived a higher mean score (0.103) than those who worked for firms without unions (mean score 0.053). This finding coincides with the pattern of firms' CSR performance.

4.3 | Union influence

Some prior studies advocated CSR activities as a firm strategy to improve consumer evaluation of product quality (Milgrom & Roberts, 1986), or to reduce the price of business (Beatty & Ritter, 1986; Ghoul et al.,

4.4 | Cross-sector comparison

In the CSR literature, many previous studies analyse CSR performance by the economic sector. Researchers into the energy economy categorise the long list of CSR indicators into three pillars – social

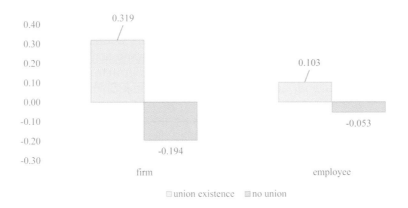

FIGURE 3 Firms and workers CSR mean scores, by union existence

TABLE 1 Firms and workers' CSR mean scores, by economic sector

	Manufacturing	Construction	Service
Enterprise-reported CSR	−0.004	−0.281	−0.066
Employee-perceived CSR	−0.006	0.014	−0.091

issues, environmental issues, and economic issues – and therefore advocate that the CSR in this sector is driven by the mixed motivation of firms' incentives and stakeholders' demand. Weber and Lin (2014) identified the advantages and disadvantages of CSR in the financial sector, given the nature of the financial sector as an environment-friendly economy. In contrast, the mining sector is intensely related to the environment and state ownership in many countries, especially in developing economies. From an empirical study of the Zambian copper mining sector, Phiri et al. (2018) concluded that CSR performance in the mining sector is influenced by the 'stark power asymmetries in the relationship between the state, civil society, and mining companies, which are exacerbated by a number of factors' (p. 26).

Instead of adding empirical evidence to the existing literature from any specific economic sector, this section intends to compare the matching quality of E&E evaluation towards CSR performance over different economic sectors – the construction, manufacturing, and service industries. Among the total Chinese firms in Southeast Asia in the CIFES survey, more than half (56.75 per cent) came under the economic sector of services. Manufacturing and construction accounted for 27.40 per cent and 15.85 per cent, respectively. Table 1 shows a significant difference between construction and the other two sectors at the firm level. While the firm-reported CSR means score is as low as −0.281, the mean scores of manufacturers and services are moderate (−0.004 and −0.066). Meanwhile, employee-perceived CSR displays a reversed pattern across the three economic sectors: construction business with highest scores of 0.014, followed by the manufacturing (−0.006) and service sectors (−0.091). These results

present substantial differences regarding the degree of matching quality across the three economies. The E&E evaluation of CSR performance in manufacturing and service matches to a great extent, whereas it is immensely mismatched in the construction sector.

4.5 | Influence of the working experience

In the growing body of CSR literature, firm owners' working experience has been discussed as a key explanatory factor. For example, Pei (2017) study uses the effect of a firm owner's years of working in the model to estimate its net effect on CSR performance. However, little research has investigated how years of working may affect employees' perceptions of CSR performance. Therefore, this subsection is intended to pin down this effect and to examine the mediating effect of employees' experience on the matching quality of firm and employee CSR perception. For the interviewees of Chinese firms in Southeast Asia in the CIFES data, 23.52 per cent worked in the current enterprise for 5 or more years, 12.58 per cent for 4 years, 19.45 per cent for 3 years, and 28.95 per cent for 2 years. The remaining 15.51 per cent worked in the current firm for 1 year or less.

Figure 4 displays CSR performance of firms and employees across different groups, grouped by length of employment at the firm. Two clear patterns can be observed in the Figure. First, the mean scores of both the firms' and the employees' evaluation of CSR performance demonstrate a positive correlation with the length of employees' employment. For those who have worked in the current firm for 1 year or less, the CSR mean scores of both firms and employees are at the

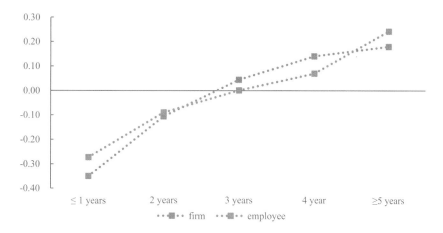

FIGURE 4 Firms and workers CSR mean scores, by years of employment

lowest (−0.351; −0.273). As years of working increase, the CSR mean score of both the firms and the employees grow steadily until the scores reach 0.179 and 0.242, respectively, for those who have worked for 5 year or more. Second, the CSR mean scores of firms and employees match to a great extent over the five groups by years of employment, suggesting that employees' working experience is most probably the best explanatory factor for the matching quality of CSR between the firm and employee levels.

5 | CONCLUSION

As mentioned at the beginning, CSR is a corporate integrated responsibility to achieve and enhance their social influence to satisfy society's expectations for local enterprises (Carroll, 1979). CSR also creates sustained value depending on its relationship with various stakeholders (Seungwoo et al., 2017). For companies that are new to the host country, CSR plays an important role in their marketing and manufacturing processes. Good CSR performance would improve the company's impression among the host country citizens, in addition to creating convenience for them to live in different countries and cultures. More specifically, with the trend of the host countries' requirement of the localisation of foreign enterprises, many host countries' citizens are involved in foreign companies' manufacturing and marketing. Thus, for those who are not only the employees of a foreign company but also native residents of their homeland, it is necessary to determine their attitudes towards the company's overall behaviour, especially CSR performance. In this study, we find that there are differences between the company's report and the employee's comments on the company's CSR performance. Factors such as country, labour union existence, economic sector, and length of the employee's working experience played an important role in influencing the E&E

evaluation matching quality. In conclusion, Chinese companies in countries such as Vietnam, Cambodia, and Malaysia accomplished CSR with both sides (enterprise and employee) satisfied to a substantive degree, while those in other Southeast Asian countries display a large disparity between firm and employee levels. Second, the existence of labour unions led to a wider gap between E&E evaluations. Moreover, the E&E evaluation of CSR performance in manufacturing and service matches to a great extent, whereas it is immensely mismatched in the construction sector. Finally, employees' working experience is most probably the best explanatory factor affecting matching quality, as the length of employment increases, the gap between both sides narrows.

In his 'pyramid of corporate social r=', Archie Carroll (1991, p. 42) depicted the top level of CSR as philanthropic responsibilities, and advocated that firms are expected to be good corporate citizens by contributing 'financial and human resources to the community and to improve the quality of life'. Following Carroll's philanthropic CSR activities, this study contributes to the research on the UN's sustainable development goals (SDGs) by exploring Chinese firms' donations in goods or cash to local communities. The aid spreads across the fields of health, education, infrastructure and culture, and coincides with a number of sustainable development goals, such as no poverty, good health and well-being, clean water and sanitation, decent work, and economic growth.

This study also contributes to the CSR literature in general and Chinese firms' CSR performance in Southeast Asian countries in particular, especially in the context of the Belt and Road Initiative. Despite the long tradition of empirical investigation of transnational firm CSR volunteerism activities and the organisational implications and policy recommendations to the home country, very few studies have addressed the matching quality of firm-reported and employee-perceived CSR performance, and factors that affect the degree of the match. The present study fills this research gap by investigating how Chinese firms in different Southeast Asian countries vary in the matching quality of their E&E evaluations, and how the degree of matching differs across different economic sectors of Chinese firms. The results of this study shed light on the effect of employees' years of work, as they indicate that a steady team of employees can help improve a firm's reputation in the host country.

6 | POLICY IMPLICATIONS

Local employees expect Chinese firms to put more aid in the fields of healthcare, education, and training as CSR performance.

As far as the enterprise itself is concerned, the enterprise should establish an employee medical insurance system in medical assistance, enterprise medical fund, medical insurance and other aspects. In terms of employee education and training, employee vocational skills training should be combined with compensation and benefits. Staff with excellent professional skills should be given corresponding material rewards and job promotion, in order to encourage employees' enthusiasm to participate in training programme, so as to improve employees' loyalty to the enterprise. In addition, firms should pay attention to contracts related to the training programme to ensure employee loyalty. Governments on both sides should establish corresponding policies to protect companies' business operations, including tax incentives, and should open a positive foreign policy planning dialogue between each other.

The average performance of Chinese firms' CSR activities in Myanmar and Indonesia is higher than that in other Southeast Asian countries, but they are less visible to local employees. In this regard, it is suggested that enterprises should establish external publicity mechanism, formulate corresponding implementation measures, and ensure the performance of corporate social responsibility activities in various ways to enhance the social responsibility awareness of local social and economic development, so as to improve the local employees' loyalty and enterprise recognition.

The longer local employees work in the firm, the more they recognise its CSR activities, indicating that long-term workers play an important role in the evaluation of firms' CSR performance. It is suggested that employers should provide extra benefits to long-term workers, such as more promotion and vocational training opportunities, developing viable policies in labour protection, employee healthcare, skills training, compensation and benefits for relevant employees, as well as more opportunities and full respect for those employees to participate in the process of company policy making, to arouse enthusiasm and increase engagement between both sides. Further, governments can institute certain policies to make it more convenient to obtain the relevant visas and length-of-stay permissions for both employees and employers to travel and receive training, if needed, in the companies' headquarters in China.

ACKNOWLEDGMENTS
The authors would like to thank the anonymous reviewers and the editors for their insightful comments and constructive feedback on the earlier drafts of this manuscript. Special thanks to Professor Hong Liu for his ideas and times on topic selection.

REFERENCES
Baker, F.B. & Kim, S.H. (2004) *Item response theory: parameter estimation techniques.* Marcel Dekker, Inc. Available from: https://doi.org/10.1201/9781482276725

Beatty, R.P. & Ritter, J.R. (1986) Investment banking, reputation, and the underpricing of initial public offerings. *Journal of Financial Economics*, 15, 213–232. Available from: https://doi.org/10.1016/0304-405X(86)90055-3

Bowen, H.R. (1953) *Social responsibilities of the businessman.* New York: Harper and Borthers.

Brewer, M.B. & Gardner, W. (1996) Who is this "We"? Levels of collective identity and self representations. *Journal of Personality and Social Psychology*, 71(1), 83–93. Available from: https://doi.org/10.1037/0022-3514.71.1.83

Bridoux, F., Stofberg, N. & Hartog, D.D. (2016) Stakeholders' responses to CSR tradeoffs: When other-orientation and trust trump material self-interest. *Frontiers in Psychology*, 6, 1992. Available from: https://doi.org/10.3389/fpsyg.2015.01992

Campbell, J.L. (2007) Why would corporations behave in socially responsible ways? An institutional theory of corporate social responsibility. *Academy of Management Review*, 32(3), 946–967. Available from: https://doi.org/10.5465/AMR.2007.25275684

Campbell, J.T., Eden, L. & Miller, S.R. (2012) Multinationals and corporate social responsibility in host countries: does distance matter? *Journal of International Business Studies*, 43(1), 84–106. Available from: https://doi.org/10.1057/jibs.2011.45

Carroll, A.B. (1979) A three-dimensional conceptual model of corporate performance. *Academy of Management Review*, 4, 497–505. Available from: https://doi.org/10.2307/257850

Carroll, A.B. (1991) The pyramid of corporate social responsibility: Toward the moral management of organizational stakeholders. *Business Horizons*, 34(4), 39–48. Available from: https://doi.org/10.1016/0007-6813(91)90005-G

Chen, H.J., Kacperczyk, M. & Ortiz-Molina, H. (2011) Labor unions, operating flexibility, and the cost of equity. *Journal of Financial & Quantitative Analysis*, 46(1), 25–58. Available from: https://doi.org/10.1017/S0022109010000645

Chun, H.M. & Shin, S.Y. (2018) The impact of labor union influence on corporate social responsibility. *Sustainability*, 10(6), 1922. Available from: https://doi.org/10.3390/su10061922

Chyz, J., Leung, W.S.C., Li, O.Z. & Rui, O.M. (2013) Labor unions and tax aggressiveness. *Journal of Financial Economics*, 108(3), 675–698. Available from: https://doi.org/10.2139/ssrn.1498663

Connolly, R.A., Hirsch, B.T. & Hirschey, M. (1986) Union rent seeking, intangible capital and market value of the firm. *Review of Economics and Statistics*, 68, 567–577. Available from: https://doi.org/10.2307/1924515

Cooke, F.L. (2014) Chinese multinational firms in Asia and Africa: Relationships with institutional actors and patterns of HRM practices. *Human Resource Management*, 53(6), 877–896. Available from: https://doi.org/10.1002/hrm.21612

Feng, Y., Chen, H.H. & Tang, J. (2018) The impacts of social responsibility and ownership structure on sustainable financial development of China's energy industry. *Sustainability*, 10, 301. Available from: https://doi.org/10.3390/su10020301

Gallén, M.L. & Peraita, C. (2018) The effects of national culture on corporate social responsibility disclosure: A cross-country comparison. *Applied Economics*, 50(27), 2967–2979. Available from: https://doi.org/10.1080/00036846.2017.1412082

Ghoul, S.E., Guedhami, O., Kwok, C. & Mishra, D.R. (2011) Does corporate social responsibility affect the cost of capital? *Journal of Banking & Finance*, 35(9), 2388–2406. Available from: https://doi.org/10.1016/j.jbankfin.2011.02.007

Glavas, A. & Godwin, L. (2013) Is the perception of "goodness" good enough? Exploring the relationship between perceived corporate social responsibility and employee organizational identification. *Journal of Business Ethics*, 114(1), 15–27. Available from: https://doi.org/10.1007/s10551-012-1323-5

Grimes, P.W. & Lewis, H.G. (1986) *Union relative wage effects: a survey*. University of Chicago Press. Available from: https://doi.org/10.2307/1059441

Hirch, T. (1991) Firm investment behavior and collective bargaining strategy. *Industrial Relations: A Journal of Economy and Society*, 31, 95–121. Available from: https://doi.org/10.1111/j.1468-232X.1992.tb00300.x

Jones, B. & Nisbet, P. (2011) Shareholder value versus stakeholder values: CSR and financialization in global food firms. *Socio-Economic Review*, 9(2), 287–314. Available from: https://doi.org/10.1093/ser/mwq033

Jones, D.A. (2010) Does serving the community also serve the company? Using organizational identification and social exchange theories to understand employee responses to a volunteerism programme. *Journal of Occupational and Organizational Psychology*, 83, 857–878. Available from: https://doi.org/10.1348/096317909X477495

Karier, T. (1985) Unions and monopoly profits. *Review of Economics and Statistics*, 67, 1335–1364. Available from: https://doi.org/10.2307/1928432

Kim, H.R., Lee, M., Lee, H.T. & Kim, N.M. (2010) Corporate social responsibility and employee–company identification. *Journal of Business Ethics*, 95(4), 557–569. Available from: https://doi.org/10.1007/s10551-010-0440-2

Mark, S.S. & Zhang, Y. (2017) From impediment to adaptation: Chinese investments in Myanmar's new regulatory environment. *Journal of Current Southeast Asian Affairs*, 36(2), 71–100. Available from: https://doi.org/10.1177/186810341703600203

Matten, D. & Moon, J. (2008) Implicit and Explicit CSR: a conceptual framework for a comparative understanding of corporate social responsibility and marketing: an integrative framework. *Academy of Management Review*, 33(2), 404–424. Available from: https://doi.org/10.2307/20159405

Mezias, J. (2002) Identifying liability of foreignness and strategies to minimize their effects: the case of labor lawsuit judgments in the United States. *Strategic Management Journal*, 23(3), 229–344. Available from: https://doi.org/10.1002/smj.220

Milgrom, P. & Roberts, J. (1986) Price and advertising signals of product quality. *Journal of Political Economy*, 55, 796–821.

MOFCOM (2014). *Statistical yearbook of Chinese outward foreign direct investment (2013)*. China Statistics Press.

MOFCOM (2019). *Statistical yearbook of Chinese outward foreign direct investment (2019)*. China Statistics Press.

Muthén, L. & Muthén, B. (2010) *Mplus user's guide*. Muthén and Muthén.

Nachum, L. (2003) Liability of foreignness in global competition? Financial service MNEs in the city of London. *Strategic Management Journal*, 24(12), 1187–1208. Available from: https://doi.org/10.1002/smj.347

Pei, C.W. (2017) How does CEO work experience and myopic behavior influence CSR engagement? *Management and System*, 24(3), 361–392.

Phiri, O., Mantzari, E. & Gleadle, P. (2018) Stakeholder interactions and corporate social responsibility (CSR) practices: evidence from the Zambian copper mining sector. *Accounting, Auditing & Accountability Journal*, Available from: https://doi.org/10.1108/AAAJ-04-2016-2540:26.

Roeck, K. & Delobbe, N. (2012) Do environmental CSR initiatives serve organizations' legitimacy in the oil industry? Exploring employees' reactions through organizational identification theory. *Journal of Business Ethics*, 110(4), 397–412. Available from: https://doi.org/10.1007/s10551-012-1489-x

Rupp, D.E. & Mallory, D.B. (2015) Corporate social responsibility: psychological, person-centric, and progressing. *The Annual Review of Organizational Psychology and Organizational Behavior*, 2, 211–236. Available from: https://doi.org/10.1146/annurev-orgpsych-032414-111505

Rupp, D.E., Shao, R., Thornton, M.A. & Skarlicki, D.P. (2013) Applicants' and employees' reactions to corporate social responsibility: the moderating effects of first-party justice perceptions and moral identity. *Personnel Psychology*, 66(4), 895–933. Available from: https://doi.org/10.1111/peps.12030

Schwab, S.J. & Thomas, R. (1998) Realigning corporate governance: shareholder activism by labor unions. *Michigan Law Review*, 96, 1018–1094. Available from: https://doi.org/10.2307/1290082

Seungwoo, O., Ahreum, H. & Junseok, H. (2017) An analysis of CSR on firm financial performance in stakeholder perspectives. *Sustainability*, 9, 1023. Available from: https://doi.org/10.3390/su9061023

Tong, C.K. (2014) Centripetal authority, differentiated networks: the social organization of Chinese firms in Singapore. In: Tong, C.K. (Ed.) *Chinese business: rethinking Guanxi and trust in Chinese business networks*. Singapore: Springer, pp. 21–40.

Vashchenko, M. (2014) Organizational CSR portfolio: exploration and evaluation. *Business & Professional Ethics Journal*, 33(4), 351–369. Available from: https://doi.org/10.5840/bpej201512319

Waddock, S., Bodwell, C. & Graves, S. (2002) Responsibility: the new business imperative. *Academy of Management Executive*, 16(2), 132–148. Available from: https://doi.org/10.5465/ame.2002.7173581

Waddock, S.A. & Graves, S.B. (1997) The corporate social performance-financial performance link. *Strategic Management Journal*, 18, 303–319. Available from: https://doi.org/10.1002/(SICI)1097-0266(199704)18:4<303:AID-SMJ869>3.0.CO;2-G

Weber, O. & Lin, H. (2014) CSR reporting and its implication for socially responsible investment in China. In: Wendt, K. (Ed.) *Responsible investment banking: risk management frameworks, sustainable financial innovation and softlaw standards*. Springer, pp. 417–426. Available from: https://doi.org/10.1007/978-3-319-10311-2_27

Xiao, H.-J. (2014) Does institutional distance matter in transnational firms CSR performance in host countries? *Journal of Quantitative and Technical Economics*, 4, 50–67.

AUTHOR BIOGRAPHIES

Jianxun Kong is research professor of quantitative sociology at Yunnan University. He started his academic career at the Institute of Southeast Asian Studies, Yunnan Academy of Social Sciences in 1996. His current research interests are Southeast Asian Studies in general and political sociology in Southeast Asia in particular.

Yidi Zhou is a graduate student and concurrent research assistant at School of International Studies, Yunnan University. She finished her undergraduate education at the University of California, Los Angeles with a major in Asian Studies. Her current research orientation is Southeast Asian Studies.

How to cite this article: Kong, J. & Zhou, Y. (2022) Convergence or Divergence? China Invested Firms' E&E Evaluation of CSR in Southeast Asia. *Global Policy*, 13(Suppl. 1), 58–68. Available from: https://doi.org/10.1111/1758-5899.13033

Received: 11 August 2021 | Revised: 9 February 2022 | Accepted: 16 February 2022

DOI: 10.1111/1758-5899.13083

RESEARCH ARTICLE

Polycentric Urbanization and Sustainable Development in China

Eric J. Heikkila[1] | Ying Xu[2]

[1]Sol Price School of Public Policy, University of Southern California, Los Angeles, California, USA

[2]School of Public Administration, Hunan University, Changsha, China

Correspondence
Ying Xu, School of Public Administration, Hunan University, No. 2 North Lushan Road, Yuelu District Changsha, China Changsha Hunan Province 410082, China.
Email: xuyingefface@gmail.com

Abstract

This paper addresses urbanization in the context of China's efforts to meet its commitments regarding the United Nations' Sustainable Development Goals (SDGs). This paper focuses specifically on governmental policies to promote polycentricity, with multiple urban centers of a similar scale within metropolitan areas, rather than a traditional single, dominant central business district. Polycentric urban forms have the potential to reduce average commuting times, thereby impacting greenhouse gas emissions. Polycentricity may also enhance access to employment and other opportunities for marginalized households. To this end, we examine the nexus between emerging polycentric urbanization patterns in Chinese cities and modes of governance at the national and local levels. Changsha, in Hunan province, is selected as a case study to illuminate the issues. Our analysis shows that fiscal considerations and other national and local governance imperatives can play a crucial role in determining how urbanization evolves. While China is unique in many ways, there are also important commonalities with other countries in the global South that are experiencing rapid urbanization, so the insights generated here may be more broadly applicable.

1 | THE IMPORTANCE OF CHINESE POLYCENTRICITY TO SUSTAINABLE DEVELOPMENT

In 2015, the United Nations General Assembly set 17 Sustainable Development Goals (SDGs). Of those, SDG 11 addresses urbanization directly, which calls on UN member countries to 'Make cities and human settlements inclusive, safe, resilient and sustainable'. SDG 11 does not stand in isolation, however. Because human settlements are the locus of so much of contemporary life, urbanization outcomes are inextricably linked to many of the other SDGs. For example, the evolving urban economy influences SDG outcomes in terms of poverty (SDG 1), economic growth and employment (SDG 8), industrialization (SDG 9), and consumption and production patterns (SDG 12). Likewise, the ongoing spatial dispersal of urban activities will impact climate change (SDG 13), the availability of water and sanitation (SDG 6), energy supplies (SDG 7), and other infrastructure (SDG 9). Urban governance also influences efforts to reduce inequality (SDG 10), foster public health (SDG 3), provide quality education (SDG 4), promote gender equality (SDG 5), and build effective institutions (SDG 16, 17). In short, as urban populations grow, urbanization policies are critical factors in determining SDGs outcomes.

The polycentric urban development is considered as a key tool to promote social cohesion, economic competitiveness, and environmental sustainability (Veneri & Burgalassi, 2012). According to the guiding principles of 'European Spatial Development Perspective'

(ESDP), polycentric development is a pre-requisite for sustainable and balanced development (CSD, 1999). More recently, the report entitled 'An agenda for a re-formed cohesion policy' (better known as the 'Barca report'), which is a guiding document for EU new co-hesion policies, highlighted the role of networked poly-centric regions in order to promote balanced territorial development and to overcome the disadvantages aris-ing from large urban agglomerations (Barca, 2009). The SDGs-related implications of polycentric urban development are multifaceted and complex, but many scholars view polycentric urban development in gen-erally positive terms (Boarnet, 2010; Heikkila, 2020; Landis et al. 2019).

The critical importance of urban development for meeting the SDGs is magnified by the rapid pace of urbanization, especially in the global South. It is in the global South, where a flood of urbanization is now fully underway, with its urban population doubling from 1990 to 2020, with comparable increases continuing over coming decades (United Nations, 2018). Even within this frame, China's urbanization has been astonishing, with the urban share of its population leaping from 26.5 per cent in 1990 to 63.9 per cent by 2020, and an antici-pated 80 per cent by 2050 (National Bureau of Statistics of China, 2021; United Nations, 2018). Following the as-tonishing urbanization process, the built-up area has greatly enlarged from 12,200 to 60,721 km^2, and more than 0.6 billion population flowed into cities (National Bureau of Statistics of China, 2021). Thus, because of its huge size and its rapid transformation, the Chinese urbanization pattern would play a critical role in achiev-ing SDGs.

The polycentric urban development having arisen in many Chinese cities in the last decade, such as Beijing (Huang et al. 2017; Qin & Han, 2013; Zou et al. 2015), Shanghai (Murakami & Chang, 2018), Hangzhou (Wen & Tao, 2015; Yue et al. 2010), and Guangzhou (Wu, 1998). According to the calculation by Liu and Wang (2016), approximately 60 per cent of all 318 cities are intra-city polycentric in structure. Most of these poly-centric cities are medium- or small-sized, and are less developed than the leading cities liking Beijing and Shanghai, which have encountered severe agglomera-tion diseconomies in their historical city centers, there-fore necessitating polycentric development. The driving forces of polycentric urban spatial configuration forma-tion in medium- and small-sized Chinese cities remain to be determined. This is at least in part attributable to state-dominated practices. Nevertheless, the existing state power-based theories of causation for polycentric urban development, such as urban planning, infrastruc-ture investment, and new town development, cannot fully explain the phenomenon of prevailing polycentric-ity in Chinese cities (Murakami & Chang, 2018). That is, there is a lack of empirical research on the man-ner in which polycentric urban development has been

Policy implications

- Fiscal considerations and other national and local governance imperatives play a crucial role in determining how urbanization evolves.
- The fundamental economic drivers of urbani-zation manifest themselves in China much the same as anywhere else, which can result in the dissipation of economic rents accruing from the scarcity value of urban land.
- China's unique governance system does provide significant capacity for staunching the economic rent dissipation with equali-tarianism principle, which is embodied as: (i) tight regulation of intra-urban competition by higher-level governments; (ii) regular auditing of preferential treatments to prevent monopo-lization; and (iii) diversified resource endow-ment for location decisions.

configured by state-led endeavors. The role of gover-nance has not been adequately researched.

In view of the great significance of polycentricity to sustainable development and achievement of SDGs, this paper aims to examine the role of governance in the formation of polycentric urbanization patterns in China, therefore, contributing to the understanding of the causation of polycentric urban development. The extant literature has provided a horizontal overview of polycentric urban development, but this must be en-riched by in-depth case studies to examine how the for-mation processes unfold in specific localities (Liu et al. 2018; Liu & Wang, 2016). Changsha is selected as the studying case in this research.

2 | OVERVIEW OF THE POLYCENTRIC URBANIZATION AND SUSTAINABLE DEVELOPMENT

Polycentric cities are generally characterized as hav-ing one or more urban centers/sub-centers beyond the traditional central business district (CBD) (Liu & Wang, 2016; Veneri & Burgalassi, 2012). The polycentricity, although remaining a rather ambiguous concept, has been extensively highlighted in academic research and policy agendas (Liu & Wang, 2016; Veneri & Burgalassi, 2012). It can be conceptualized at multiple geographical scales, ranging from intra-city to inter-city, or even trans-regional scales (Davoudi, 2003; Hall & Pain, 2006; Liu et al. 2018; Parr, 2004; Taylor et al. 2009). This concept can also be interpreted from ei-ther morphological or functional perspectives (Green, 2007; Hoyler et al. 2008; Yue et al. 2019; Zhao et al.

2017). The research literature has demonstrated that polycentric urban development occurs in major cities and urban regions, liking greater Cleveland, Beijing, Mexico City, Lima, Greater South East of UK, etc. (e.g. Arribas-Bel & Sanz-Gracia, 2014; Bogart & Ferry, 1999; Burger, 2010; Feng et al. 2009; Fernandez-Maldonado et al. 2014; Liu et al. 2018).

Urban forms and spatial structures are thought to reduce the environmental pressure of regions. In transportation, Bertolini (2010) believes that polycentricity can reduce private vehicle flows and hence emissions between centers. Lee and Lee (2014) hold the similar view, because polycentric urban form can decrease commuting distance by enhancing land use mixtures. Also, Veneri and Burgalassi (2012) found polycentric urban form is characterized by the highest use of public transport which is carbon emission friendly. Specific to industry development, the polycentric urban form will decentralize firms in CBDs, and scholars have confirmed that industrial gatherings exacerbate environmental pollution and emissions (Verhoef & Nijkamp, 2002; Zeng & Zhao, 2009). Polycentric urban form is considered that can protect open spaces and reduce the emission efficiency of the urban heat island effect (Debbage & Shepherd, 2015; Ewing & Rong, 2008).

Scholars believe that there is a positive relationship between polycentric urban form and economic performance. A polycentric structure has been regarded as an effective approach to mitigate the impacts of agglomeration diseconomies (Fujita & Thisse, 2002; Meijers & Burger, 2010). Cities with larger subcenters and a more balanced distribution among these subcenters are often conceived to be more productive (Li & Liu, 2018; Liang & Lu, 2019).

Research has also shed light on the causes of polycentric urban development. The driving force for the formation of new sub-centers has principally been interpreted as agglomeration diseconomies, arising from traffic congestion, increased land rent, and rising commuting costs (Ahlfeldt & Wendland, 2013; Anas & Kim, 1996; Lucas & Rossi-Hansberg, 2002; McMillen & Smith, 2003). Meanwhile, improvements in private transportation and telecommunications reduce the importance of agglomeration, further encouraging firms to disperse geographically (Arribas-Bel & Sanz-Gracia, 2014; Pfister et al. 2000).

The effects of state-led practices have also been extensively researched. Multiple-center urban planning or development strategies are regarded as playing a critical role in forming polycentric urban structures (Liu & Wang, 2016; Xie et al. 2018). City governments' participation in land and housing development of new towns has greatly promoted the formation of polycentric cities, as demonstrated in Korean and Chinese cases (Lee & Shin, 2012; Liu & Wang, 2016). Murakami and Chang (2018) argued that the transfer of land-use rights from local governments to property developers greatly

predetermines the long-term trajectory of polycentric development. Additionally, municipal infrastructure investment in suburban areas facilitates the development of polycentric urban structure. For example, Garcia-López et al. (2017) verified the positive effect of railroads on the formation of urban sub-centers.

3 | RESEARCH STRATEGY

3.1 | The case study of Changsha

Changsha is the capital of Hunan province in south-central China. The total area of the city is 11,816 km^2, with 2150.9 km^2 constituting the urban region (Changsha Statistics Bureau, 2019). This urban region comprises inner five districts: Yuelu, Kaifu, Furong, Tianxin, Yuhua. In 2020, Changsha had a household-registered population of 10.06 million, ranking 17th among China's most populated cities, and its GDP had reached 12.14 trillion RMB, ranking it 13th nationally (National Bureau of Statistics of China, 2021).

Changsha is selected as the studying case for two reasons. First, its polycentric urban configuration is evident, and its polycentric urban development process is complete and intensive enough to provide a persuasive case. Second, Changsha is neither a leading city in China nor one that is lagging behind in terms of economic growth or urban population. Third, Changsha did not receive any unique privilege or policy support from the central government for urban development. The polycentric urban development process in Changsha is aligned with other Chinese cities. Thus, the research findings with the case of Changsha therefore may be applicable to many other cities in China.

3.2 | Interview and data collection

The primary research method in this study is a field survey, comprising semi-structured interviews and direct observations. Snowball sampling was employed to ask respondents in the preliminary interview to recommend suitable government departments and participants for a further semi-structured interview. Seventeen in-depth interviews and a focus group meeting were conducted from November 2015 to October 2019 in Changsha. There are four categories of respondents in the interviews, which include: (i) government officials who are responsible for investment attraction affairs (Commerce Bureaus of Kaifu, Yuhua, and Yuelu districts); (ii) office leasing and sales managers of office building developers (BOFO International Plaza, North Star Time Square, and Jinmao ICC); (iii) department heads of newly incoming firms that are in charge of site selection (Hengfeng Bank, PwC Accounting, and DHC Software); and (iv) office-broking manager from a real estate consultancy company (Cushman & Wakefield). The participants of the focus group meeting are all staff members from commerce bureaus of Kaifu.

They were asked to respond to the questions relevant to 'intra-urban competition situations for mobile investment', 'competitive endeavors taken by governments', 'the impact of incentive schemes on decision-making', 'the factors affecting site selection', 'the interaction between incoming firms and governments', etc. Archive studies, retrieval of census, and secondary data collection from government sectors and professional websites were conducted to supplement the research.

4 | THE RISE OF INTRA-URBAN COMPETITION AMONG URBAN DISTRICTS

In 1994, China reformed the tax-sharing system with respect to taxes levied by the central and local governments, reserving the largest and most stable parts of tax revenue for the central government (Wong & Zhao, 1999). As a result, local governments throughout China encountered severe fiscal deficits. The prosperity of real estate development provided an alternative channel of revenue for local governments through leasing of state-owned land (Li et al. 2011). The resulting land leasing income has become an indispensable supplement to local fiscal revenue. For instance, the nationwide land leasing income in 2018 was 6.51 trillion RMB, which accounted for 35.5 per cent of the revenue in China's general public budgets (Ministry of Finance of the People's Republic of China, 2019).

Nevertheless, there is limited and decreasing available land for leasing in inner cities. As presented in Table 1, the land leased for real estate development in Changsha has been low and decreasing following the peaks in 2005 and 2007. Thus, local governments, especially at the district level in inner cities, have been obliged to seek other sources of income to offset budgetary deficits.

In view of this, attracting advanced producer service firms has become the optimum choice for district-level governments, owing to these companies' minimal land occupation, non-polluting nature, and high tax revenue. For example, the five urban districts in Changsha have all prioritized the development of finance, commerce and trade, cultural creativity industries, etc., as shown in Table 2.

Consistent with the emphasis on the development of advanced producer service industries, each urban district has proposed to build an urban center or sub-center (i.e., known as 'financial centers', 'quasi-CBDs', and 'international new towns' in regional strategic planning) to accommodate prospective advanced producer service firms (Table 3). These planned urban centers are portrayed by local states as promising harbingers of the future and advertised extensively with iconic slogans such as 'The Bund', 'Wall Street' and the like. The five urban districts of Changsha have invested heavily in the infrastructure and public facilities of these designated places, as well as attracting private investment in high-rise office buildings, large shopping malls, and five-star hotels by means of land write-downs, cash rewards, and other methods. Thus, these proposed urban centers/sub-centers in the five urban districts of Changsha are taking shape physically in the short term under public-private joint efforts.

The homogeneity in prioritized industries and urban center/sub-center development among the five urban districts has inevitably led to intensive intra-urban competition for economic growth in Changsha. Thus, these districts compete with each other to attract not only incoming firms but also extant firms in other districts. This is somewhat surprising, as this dissipation of economic rents might not be expected in a more centralized governance system. Consequently, the global top 500 companies and financial enterprises have become the focus of competition among the urban districts.

5 | THE STATE-LED INVESTMENT ATTRACTION SYSTEM IN INTRA-URBAN COMPETITION

5.1 | The involved government sectors and incentive schemes

The five urban districts have all made extensive endeavors to attract mobile investment to succeed in the intra-urban economic competition. As argued by Baybeck et al. (2011), learning and economic competition lead to the diffusion of policy across local authorities. Thus, the district-level governments imitate the effective competitive policies of neighboring governments.

TABLE 1 The area of land leasing for real estate development in Changsha

Year	2003	2005	2007	2009	2011	2013	2015	2017
leasing land (10,000 m²)	789.72	1007.59	973.23	392.92	331.17	458.99	106.68	205.85

Source: Changsha Statistics Bureau (2019).

TABLE 2   The competitive policies of the five urban districts in Changsha

Urban district	Competitive incentive policies
Furong District	The incentive measures to promote economic development in Furong District (2013)
Tianxin District	The measures to promote financial industry development in Tianxin District (2014) The incentive measures to promote regional economic development (2014)
Kaifu District	The provisional incentive measures of economic development in Kaifu District (2014) The incentive measures to promote financial industry development in Kaifu District (2016)
Yuhua District	The incentive measures to promote regional industry development in Yuhua District (2014) The incentive measures to promote financial industry development in Yuhua District (for trial implementation) (2015) The incentive measures to promote cultural industry development in Yuhua District (for trial implementation) (2015) The incentive measures to promote professional service industry development in Yuhua District (for trial implementation) (2015)
Yuelu District	The schemes of promoting headquarter economy development in Yuelu District (2012) The schemes of promoting cultural industry development in Yuelu District (2013) The incentive measures to promote regional economic development in Yuelu District (2014) The policy suggestions of developing service industry development in core area of Xiangjiang New District (2014) The policies of promoting service industry development in Yuelu District (2015)

Source: collected from the official websites of five urban districts respectively.

TABLE 3   Prioritized industries and proposed urban centers in the urban districts of Changsha

Urban district	Priority industries	Proposed urban center
Furong District	Finance, Commerce & Trade, Tourism	Furong CBD (traditional central business district of Changsha)
Tianxin District	Finance, Trade & Logistics, Cultural Creativity, Hotel & Catering, Tourism, IT, Agency	Nanhu New Town (financial bund of Xiang river)
Kaifu District	Finance, Cultural Creativity, Trade & Logistics,	Changsha Financial & Commercial Zone (regional financial center and 'Wall Street of Central China')
Yuhua District	Commerce & Trade, Finance, Cultural Creativity, Tourism	High-Speed Rail New Town (Regional CBD of Changsha)
Yuelu District	Finance, Cultural Creativity, Tourism, Trade & Logistics, IT, Health, Agency	Riverside New Town (financial center of Hunan province)

Source: collected from official documents and government websites of the five urban districts

Consequently, all five urban districts deploy essentially the same competitive strategies.

For the involved government departments, the main functions of investment attraction have been partially devolved from the Commerce Bureau to produce a model known as 'one bureau and two centers' (i.e. the Commerce Bureau, the Modern Service Industry Development Center, and the Financial Affairs Center). The Commerce Bureau was originally the only authority responsible for investment attraction affairs, the Modern Service Industry Development Center is a newly established agency to specifically facilitate the settlement and subsequent service of incoming firms, and the major duty of the Financial Affairs Center has shifted from supervision to attraction of financial business. Additionally, other government departments are required to undertake part of the function of investment attraction. For example, the Bureau of Industry and Information Technology

has been endowed with the new responsibility of attracting high-technology enterprises. The financial and taxation sectors are also required to estimate the future fiscal income of new investment, while the judicial department takes charge of investment contract reviews.

In terms of the inputted manpower resources, the deputy principal or above in each urban district is appointed to specifically take charge of promoting investment attraction, and, aside from the staff originally allocated to investment attraction, a portion of staff from other government sectors has been requested to temporarily shift their obligations to this aspect of government. For instance, a respondent from the Yuhua district-level government stated that 'my colleagues, originally working in the Statistical Bureau, were dispatched to other cities to contact and lobby potential investors for several months, aiming to enhance the staff resource of investment attraction''. Comments such as this would not be out of place in the context of traditional economic development functions in the United States.

Additionally, local authorities have announced competitive policies with various incentive schemes to attract incoming firms, with several having formulated additional competitive policies specifically to financial and cultural industries. Table 2 lists the competitive incentive policies of the five urban districts in Changsha.

The incentive schemes of such competitive policies are generally categorized into: (i) *monetary subsidies* in the form of cash rewards for new investment and relevant intermediaries, monetary subsidies for buying or renting office space, and development fund support; (ii) *tax relief* via tax credits or individual income tax abatement for senior executives; (iii) *administrative assistance* in terms of regulatory flexibility, one-on-one service from major government officials; (iv) *business-operation assistance* via low-interest loans, labor recruitment, and training support; and (v) other incentives such as priority provision of public housing and quotas of top schools. Furthermore, renowned companies, especially those from Fortune Global 500 and China's top 100 companies, are eligible to negotiate directly with district- or city-level governments on a case-by-case basis for particular preferential treatments that go beyond the normal privileges.

In summary, to succeed in intra-urban economic competition, every district-level government has designated several sections with large numbers of civil servants to engage in works related to investment attraction. Meanwhile, they also provide a variety of incentive schemes to attract mobile business. Correspondingly, the extant and incoming firms actively communicate and negotiate with different urban districts to seek the most beneficial incentive packages. As one interviewee said, 'once [our company] decided to enter into Changsha, we began to negotiate with different urban districts for possible investment, and make them bid against each other to offer the best incentive package''.

5.2 | The supplemental role of private partnership

During the intra-urban competition process, private enterprises are also intimately involved in the state-led investment attraction system. To secure more sales/rents to incoming firms, office building developers have to cooperate with relevant government sectors in various investment attraction affairs, such as data collection, investment promotion activities, brand advertisement of districts, and others. For example, developers are requested to provide space and other assistance in their office buildings for district-level governments to set up service hubs, which perform on-site administrative service provision, information collection from office buildings and settled firms, and related tasks. Property management companies of office buildings that may influence the location choice of firms are also brought into the state-led investment attraction system through staff training, model selection, industry association, and monetary reward.

Even when incoming firms directly access office building developers or real estate brokerage companies for site selection, these private agencies still encourage incoming firms to contact district-level governments, as the preferential treatment offered by urban districts facilitates deals between them. Meanwhile, these private agencies can acquire intermediary rewards from district-level governments, according to the urban districts' competitive incentive policies.

6 | THE SPATIAL CONSEQUENCE OF STATE-LED INVESTMENT ATTRACTION

In the intra-urban competition for mobile investment, all urban districts fight for advanced producer service firms with the unique state-led investment attraction system. Following the Chinese institutional settings, this operates with a prominent characteristic of *equalitarianism*, which is a means of preventing the kind of economic rent dissipation alluded to earlier.

First, higher tiers of government (city-level) have formulated legislation to prevent fierce intra-urban competition among urban districts. According to the regulation set by the Changsha Leading Group Office of Investment Attraction,[1] the urban district that first contacts an incoming firm has the privilege of prior negotiation. The number of urban districts that can join in the negotiation with a given firm is no more than two. If district-level governments are found to contravene the regulation, they would be penalized by disqualification from yearly assessment, decreased funding support, circulation of criticism notices, or even by their principal governors being held personally accountable.

Second, the preferential treatments offered by each urban district are strictly inspected in year-end audits by high-level government. The relevant administrative governors are held accountable if the treatments are beyond a reasonable level of generosity, such as exorbitant monetary subsidies or excessive deregulation. This constraint on preferential treatment, especially the various kinds of monetary subsidies, can prevent the affluent urban districts from winner-take-all situation with a cycle of higher monetary inputs leading to more investment influx to themselves only.

Third, the resource endowments of urban districts for location decisions of incoming firms tend to be diversified, not limited by the traditional rule of geographical advantage. That is, every urban district has its own comparative advantages that are attractive to incoming firms with various preferences. This is what one finds in the United States, as documented for example by Giuliano et al. (2019) for their case study of Los Angeles. In the case of Changsha's Furong district, where the traditional CBD is located, it has the advantage of a central location and comprehensive business facilities. Yuelu district is further away from the traditional city center, but endowed with the privileges of a state-level new area (Hunan Xiangjiang New Area) in the aspects of land supply, taxation, etc. Yuhua district offers a wider range of producer service businesses for incoming firms, as it has more advanced industrial development with numerous industrial enterprises. Therefore, despite the convergence of monetary subsidies, each urban district is able to provide its unique preferential treatments.

Consequently, the state-led investment attraction system with equalitarian features allows every urban district to gain an equitable portion of firms during the intra-urban competition process. That is to say, the extant and incoming firms are (re)located into different urban districts, rather than concentrating in traditional CBDs. The distribution of the advanced producer service firms in Changsha has unmistakably supported this argument.

Taking financial enterprises (including banks, insurance companies, and securities enterprises) in Changsha as an example, Table 4 presents the time-series changes of their provincial or national headquarter office locations from 2004 to 2019. In 2004, Changsha was a typical monocentric city, with half of its financial enterprises located in the traditional Furong CBD. This spatial configuration remained unaltered until 2009. Subsequently, as more financial enterprises set up regional headquarters in Changsha, these enterprises gradually dispersed into different localities, instead of congregating in the traditional city center. This trend was especially prominent during the period of 2014 to 2019. For instance, at the end of 2014, not a single financial enterprise had placed its headquarters in Yuelu district, but ten enterprises did so in the following five years, coinciding with the establishment of state-level Xiangjiang New Area. Changsha has thus evolved from a single-center city to a polycentric urban development with multiple centers.

Moreover, of all 96 financial enterprises in Changsha at the end of 2014, more than half (49 enterprises) moved their headquarters in the subsequent five years (2015–2019), while only three enterprises had done so before this period. Furthermore, 36 out of those 49 enterprises were relocated into other urban districts. This sharp increase in office relocation of financial enterprises is evidently in accordance with the rise of intra-urban competition for advanced producer service firms. This kind of transformation indicates the intensive restructuring of urban spatial distribution of advanced producer service firms towards polycentricity.

Generally, the state-led investment attraction strategy in Chinese institutional settings has the prominent characteristic of equalitarianism, which ensures that every urban district accommodates an almost equal share of advanced producer service firms, especially financial enterprises and Global 500 firms. In other words, the extant and incoming firms are distributed among the proposed urban centers of different districts via the state-led investment attraction in intra-urban competition. It follows that the state-led investment attraction system engenders the emergence of polycentric urban development among Chinese cities.

7 | CONCLUSION

Meeting the UN Sustainable Development Goals poses a daunting but essential challenge for all countries. As the world continues on its relentless path of urbanization, the resulting urban development patterns will be a crucial factor in determining whether each country's SDG commitments are met. Increasingly, metropolitan regions are polycentric in form, and this trend may be a positive one, balancing opposing forces of agglomeration economies and congestion effects. Ultimately, local governance will determine whether this process is well managed and fruitful.

TABLE 4 The number of financial enterprises' headquarters in urban districts of Changsha

Urban district and proposed urban center	2004	2009	2014	2019
Furong District (Furong CBD)	17 (50%)	29 (44.6%)	38 (39.6%)	33 (28.7%)
Tianxin District (Nanhu New Town)	7 (20.6%)	16 (24.6%)	23 (24.0%)	21 (18.2%)
Kaifu District (Changsha Financial & Commercial Zone)	6 (17.6%)	9 (13.8%)	14 (14.6%)	22 (19.1%)
Yuhua District (High-Speed Rail New Town)	4 (11.7%)	11 (16.9%)	21 (21.8%)	29 (25.2%)
Yuelu District (Riverside New Town)	0 (0%)	0 (0%)	0 (0%)	10 (8.7%)
Total	34	65	96	115

Source: collected from the website www.tianyancha.com

Using Changsha as a case study, this research uncovers two key findings. First, inner urban authorities all put emphasis on the advanced producer service industry development as the alternative fiscal revenue channel to replace land leasing. This homogeneity in priority industries gives rise to intensive intra-urban economic competition, in which urban districts within a city compete with each other for mobile investment. They adopt a distinctive state-led investment attraction strategy, by devoting several government sectors with large numbers of civil servants to investment attraction and offering a variety of incentive schemes to attract incoming firms. The fundamental economic drivers of urbanization manifest themselves in China much the same as anywhere else. We find this not only in the push and pull of agglomeration economies and congestion effects, but also in the tendency for potential firms to play off one local jurisdiction against another, as a means of extracting the most favorable terms. This can result in the dissipation of economic rents accruing from the scarcity value of urban land.

The second key finding is that China's governance system does provide significant capacity for staunching this economic rent dissipation. This is most evident in the so-called *equalitarianism* principle, which is embodied as: (i) tight regulation of intra-urban competition by higher-level governments; (ii) regular auditing of preferential treatments to prevent monopolization; and (iii) diversified resource endowment for location decisions. It should also be noted that those rent-dissipating behaviors are themselves a fairly direct result of fiscal imperatives imposed by the national level government, especially the 1994 tax-sharing reforms that left local governments to scurry for fiscal revenues through land-leasing arrangements of state-owned urban land.

The findings of this research have greatly enhanced our understanding of the causes of polycentric urban development. The findings are derived from a case study in transitional China, however, and thus are only partial evidence to be applied to cities in other countries. That is, the particularity of Chinese cities and their institutional setting may impose restrictions on the generalizability of the research findings. Nevertheless, this is an exploratory study that will lead to subsequent research examining the polycentric urban spatial configuration from the perspectives of intra-urban competition and investment attraction systems. This kind of research calls for more extensive empirical studies with examples from different developed and developing countries to seek more general conclusions. Attainment of the UN Sustainable Development Goals hangs in the balance.

ENDNOTE

1. Changsha Leading Group Office of Investment Attraction is a city-level governmental agency that is responsible for citywide investment attraction affairs, including complaint handling from incoming firms, coordination among urban districts, etc. The mayor normally takes the post of group leader.

REFERENCES

Ahlfeldt, G.T. & Wendland, N. (2013) How polycentric is a monocentric city?: centers, spillovers and hysteresis. *Journal of Economic Geography*, 13(1), 53–83. https://doi.org/10.1093/jeg/lbs013

Anas, A. & Kim, I. (1996) General equilibrium models of polycentric urban land use with endogenous congestion and job agglomeration. *Journal of Urban Economics*, 40(2), 232–256. https://doi.org/10.1006/juec.1996.0031

Arribas-Bel, D. & Sanz-Gracia, F. (2014) The validity of the monocentric city model in a polycentric age: US metropolitan areas in 1990, 2000 and 2010. *Urban Geography*, 35(7), 980–997. https://doi.org/10.1080/02723638.2014.940693

Barca, F. (2009) An Agenda for a Reformed Cohesion Policy, Independent Report prepared at the request of Danuta Hubner, Commissioner for Regional Policy. Available from http://www.ecostat.unical.it/Dorio/Corsi/Corsi%202017/Politiche%20Sviluppo%20Locale/Materiale%20poleco/report_barca_v0306.pdf [Accessed 29 January 2022]

Baybeck, B., Berry, W.D. & Siegel, D. (2011) A strategic theory of policy diffusion via intergovernmental competition. *The Journal of Politics*, 73(1), 232–247. https://doi.org/10.1017/S00223816100000988

Bertolini, L. (2010) Integrating mobility and urban development agendas: a manifesto. *disP - the Planning Review*, 46(1), 16–26. https://doi.org/10.1080/02513625.2012.702956

Boarnet, M. (2010) Planning, climate change, and transportation: thoughts on policy analysis. *Transportation Research Part A : Policy and Practice*, 44, 587–595.

Bogart, W. & Ferry, W. (1999) Employment centres in greater Cleveland: evidence of evolution in a formerly monocentric city. *Urban Studies*, 36, 2099–2110. https://doi.org/10.1080/0042098992566

Burger, M.J. (2010) Functional polycentrism and urban network development in the greater south east, united kingdom: evidence from commuting patterns, 1981–2001. *Regional Studies*, 44, 1149–1170. https://doi.org/10.1080/00343400903365102

Changsha Statistics Bureau (2019) *2018 Changsha Statistical Yearbook*. Beijing: China Statistics Press.

Committee on Spatial Development (CSD). (1999) European spatial development perspective: towards balanced and sustainable development of the territory of the EU, postdam. Presented at the Informal Meeting of Ministers Responsible for Spatial Planning of the Member States of the European Union.

Davoudi, S. (2003) European briefing: polycentricity in European spatial planning: from an analytical tool to a normative agenda. *European Planning Studies*, 11(8), 979–999. https://doi.org/10.1080/0965431032000146169

Debbage, N. & Shepherd, J.M. (2015) The urban heat island effect and city contiguity. *Computers Environment and Urban Systems*, 54, 181–194. https://doi.org/10.1016/j.compenvurbsys.2015.08.002

Ewing, R. & Rong, F. (2008) The impact of urban form on US residential energy use. *Housing Policy Debate*, 19(1), 1–30. https://doi.org/10.1080/10511482.2008.9521624

Feng, J., Wang, F. & Zhou, Y. (2009) The spatial restructuring of population in metropolitan Beijing: toward polycentricity in the post-reform era. *Urban Geography*, 30, 779–802. https://doi.org/10.2747/0272-3638.30.7.779

Fernandez-Maldonado, A.M., Romein, A., Verkoren, O. & Pessoa, R.P.P. (2014) Polycentric structures in Latin American metropolitan areas: Identifying employment sub-centres. *Regional Studies*, 48, 1954–1971. https://doi.org/10.1080/00343404.2013.786827

Fujita, M. & Thisse, J.F. (2002) Agglomeration and market interaction. CORE Discussion Papers. http://hdl.handle.net/2078.1/4255

Garcia-López, M.-À., Hémet, C. & Viladecans-Marsal, E. (2017) Next train to the polycentric city: the effect of railroads on sub-center formation. *Regional Science and Urban Economics*, 67, 50–63. https://doi.org/10.1016/j.regsciurbeco.2017.07.004

Giuliano, G., Kang, S. & Yuan, Q. (2019) Agglomeration economies and evolving urban form. *The Annals of Regional Science*, 63(3), 377–398. https://doi.org/10.1007/s00168-019-00957-4

Green, N. (2007) Functional polycentricity: a formal definition in terms of social networks analysis. *Urban Studies*, 44(11), 2077–2103. https://doi.org/10.1080/00420980701518941

Hall, P. & Pain, K. (2006) *The polycentric metropolis: Learning from mega-city regions in Europe*. London: Earthscan.

Heikkila, E. (2020) *China from a U.S. policy perspective*. New York: Routledge.

Hoyler, M., Kloosterman, R.C. & Sokol, M. (2008) Polycentric puzzles – emerging mega-city regions seen through the lens of advanced producer services. *Regional Studies*, 42(8), 1055–1064. https://doi.org/10.1080/00343400802389377

Huang, D., Liu, Z., Zhao, X. & Zhao, P. (2017) Emerging polycentric megacity in China: an examination of employment subcenters and their influence on population distribution in Beijing. *Cities*, 69, 36–45. https://doi.org/10.1016/j.cities.2017.05.013

Landis, J., Hsu, D. & Guerra, E. (2019) Intersecting residential and transportation CO_2 emissions: metropolitan climate change programs in the age of Trump. *Journal of the American Planning Association*, 39(2), 206–226. https://doi.org/10.1177/0739456X17729438

Lee, S. & Lee, B. (2014) The influence of urban form on GHG emissions in the US household sector. *Energy Policy*, 68, 534–549. https://doi.org/10.1016/j.enpol.2014.01.024

Lee, Y.S. & Shin, H.R. (2012) Negotiating the polycentric city-region: developmental state politics of new town development in the Seoul capital region. *Urban Studies*, 49, 855–870. https://doi.org/10.1177/0042098011411947

Li, J., Chiang, Y. & Choy, L. (2011) Central-local conflict and property cycle: a Chinese style. *Habitat International*, 35(1), 126–132. https://doi.org/10.1016/j.habitatint.2010.06.002

Li, Y. & Liu, X. (2018) How did urban polycentricity and dispersion affect economic productivity? A case study of 306 Chinese cities. *Landscape and Urban Planning*, 173, 51–59. https://doi.org/10.1016/j.landurbplan.2018.01.007

Liang, W. & Lu, M. (2019) Growth led by human capital in big cities: Exploring complementarities and spatial agglomeration of the workforce with various skills. *China Economic Review*, 57, pp101113. https://doi.org/10.1016/j.chieco.2017.09.012

Liu, X., Derudder, B. & Wang, M. (2018) Polycentric urban development in China: a multi-scale analysis. *Environment and Planning B*, 45(5), 953–972. https://doi.org/10.1177/2399808317690155

Liu, X. & Wang, M. (2016) How polycentric is urban China and why? A case study of 318 cities. *Landscape and Urban Planning*, 151, 10–20. https://doi.org/10.1016/j.landurbplan.2016.03.007

Lucas, R.E. & Rossi-Hansberg, E. (2002) On the internal structure of cities. *Econometrica*, 70(4), 1445–1476. https://doi.org/10.1111/1468-0262.00338

McMillen, D.P. & Smith, S.C. (2003) The number of subcenters in large urban areas. *Journal of Urban Economics*, 53, 321–338. https://doi.org/10.1016/S0094-1190(03)00026-3

Meijers, E.J. & Burger, M.J. (2010) Spatial structure and productivity in US metropolitan areas. *Environment and Planning a-Economy and Space*, 42(6), 1383–1402. https://doi.org/10.1068/a42151

Ministry of Finance of the People's Republic of China. (2019) The report of China's financial revenue and expenditure in 2018 [online]. Avaialbe from http://www.gov.cn/xinwen/2019-01/23/content_5361095.htm [Accessed 5 Febuary 2020]

Murakami, J. & Chang, Z. (2018) Polycentric development under public leasehold: a spatial analysis of commercial land use rights. *Regional Science and Urban Economics*, 71, 25–36. https://doi.org/10.1016/j.regsciurbeco.2018.05.001

National Bureau of Statistics of China (2021) *2020 China Statistical Yearbook*. Beijing: China Statistics Press.

Parr, J. (2004) The polycentric urban region: a closer inspection. *Regional Studies*, 38(3), 231–240. https://doi.org/10.1080/003434042000211114

Pfister, N., Freestone, R. & Murphy, P. (2000) Polycentricity or dispersion? Changes in center employment in metropolitan Sydney, 1981 To 1996. *Urban Geography*, 21(5), 428–442. https://doi.org/10.2747/0272-3638.21.5.428

Qin, B. & Han, S.S. (2013) Emerging polycentricity in Beijing: Evidence from housing price variations, 2001–05. *Urban Studies*, 50(10), 2006–2023. https://doi.org/10.1177/0042098012471979

Taylor, P.J., Evans, D.M., Hoyler, M., Derudder, B. & Pain, K. (2009) The UK space economy as practised by advanced producer service firms: identifying two distinctive polycentric city-regional processes in contemporary Britain. *International Journal of Urban and Regional Research*, 33(3), 700–718. https://doi.org/10.1111/j.1468-2427.2009.00857.x

United Nations (2018) *World urbanization prospects: the 2018 revision [online]*. Available from: https://population.un.org/wup/Download/ [Accessed 13 May 2021]

Veneri, P. & Burgalassi, D. (2012) Questioning polycentric development and its effects. Issues of definition and measurement for the Italian NUTS-2 regions. *European Planning Studies*, 20(6), 1017–1037. https://doi.org/10.1080/09654313.2012.673566

Verhoef, E.T. & Nijkamp, P. (2002) Externalities in urban sustainability – environmental versus localization-type agglomeration externalities in a general spatial equilibrium model of a single-sector monocentric industrial city. *Ecological Economics*, 40(2), 157–179. https://doi.org/10.1016/S0921-8009(01)00253-1

Wen, H. & Tao, Y. (2015) Polycentric urban structure and housing price in the transitional China: evidence from Hangzhou. *Habitat International*, 46, 138–146. https://doi.org/10.1016/j.habitatint.2014.11.006

Wong, K.K. & Zhao, X.B. (1999) The influence of bureaucratic behavior on land apportionment in China: the informal process. *Environment and Planning C*, 17(1), 113–126. https://doi.org/10.1068/c170113

Wu, F. (1998) Polycentric urban development and land-use change in a transitional economy: the case of Guangzhou. *Environment and Planning A*, 30(6), 1077–1100. https://doi.org/10.1068/a301077

Xie, X., Hou, W. & Herold, H. (2018) Ex post impact assessment of master plans – the case of Shenzhen in shaping a polycentric urban structure. *International Journal of Geo-Information*, 7, 252–265. https://doi.org/10.3390/ijgi7070252

Yue, W., Liu, Y. & Fan, P. (2010) Polycentric urban development: the case of Hangzhou. *Environment and Planning A*, 42(3), 563–577. https://doi.org/10.1068/a42116

Yue, W., Wang, T., Liu, Y. & Zhang, Q. (2019) Mismatch of morphological and functional polycentricity in Chinese cities: an evidence from land development and functional linkage. *Land Use Policy*, 88, https://doi.org/10.1016/j.landusepol.2019.104176 104176.

Zeng, D.Z. & Zhao, L.X. (2009) Pollution havens and industrial agglomeration. *Journal of Environmental Economics and Management*, 58(2), 141–153. https://doi.org/10.1016/j.jeem.2008.09.003

Zhao, M., Derudder, B. & Huang, J. (2017) Examining the transition processes in the Pearl River Delta polycentric mega-city region through the lens of corporate networks. *Cities*, 60, 147–155. https://doi.org/10.1016/j.cities.2016.08.015

Zou, Y., Mason, R. & Zhong, R. (2015) Modeling the polycentric evolution of post-Olympic Beijing: an empirical analysis of land prices and development intensity. *Urban Geography*, 36(5), 1–22. https://doi.org/10.1080/02723638.2015.1027121

AUTHOR BIOGRAPHIES

Eric J. Heikkila is a professor at the USC Price School of Public Policy. His research is both quantitative and qualitative in nature, and his scholarly writings address a wide range of topics on urban development and public policy.

Ying Xu is a professor of School of Public Administration at the Hunan University. He has published extensively on Chinese urbanization, sustainable urban development, and public housing.

How to cite this article: Heikkila, E.J. & Xu, Y. (2022) Polycentric Urbanization and Sustainable Development in China. *Global Policy*, 13(Suppl. 1), 69–78. Available from: https://doi.org/10.1111/1758-5899.13083

Received: 13 August 2021 | Revised: 15 November 2021 | Accepted: 16 November 2021

DOI: 10.1111/1758-5899.13037

Sustainable Development Goals and their Fit with Good Governance

Andrew Massey ⓘ

International School for Government,
King's College London, London, UK

Correspondence
Andrew Massey, King's College London
– International School for Government,
Third Floor, Virginia Woolf Building, 22
Kingsway, London WC2R 2LS, UK.
Email: andrew.1.massey@kcl.ac.uk

Abstract

This Policy Insight paper places the UN's Sustainable Development Goals (SDGs) in the context of good governance. It explores what constitutes *Good Governance*, from a public administration perspective, and charts the manner in which SDGs and good governance are linked, before suggesting ways in which governments may achieve the aims of the SDGs. It argues none of the other 15 SDGs can be achieved without the coordination and delivery of SDGs 16 and 17. These are at the core of effective public administration and the provision of good governance. Without sufficient numbers of appropriately trained, competent and incorrupt public administrators, working at the local level, none of the other SDGs are widely achievable. We need to recognise, however, important political issues and definitions of good governance are socially constructed and culturally bound; to seek to impose one version on all others risks failure. The paper discusses some of the criteria used by different stakeholders to judge standards of public services. There is a short discussion about how actual and desired levels of performance are set and by whom and to what extent improvement can be measured by a rise or fall in service standards. In other words, whether perceptions of improvement can be objectively measured. The paper draws on cases from the UN's annual public service innovation awards as examples.

1 | INTRODUCTION AND CONTEXT: PUBLIC ADMINISTRATION AND THE SDGS

There have been sundry public policy lessons to be drawn from the global experience of the Covid pandemic, but conceivably the most valuable is the enduring realisation that we exist within the 'seamless web of circumstance'. By this it is meant that 'the shockwave Covid-19 delivered to the social, economic and political systems of the world; the outburst of social justice protests; the continuing angst regarding climate change; and deepening political and social polarization', remain inextricably linked together in many unforeseen and unforeseeable ways (Massey, 2021, pp. 1–4; Plowden Report, 1967). It is a situation that deepens the perception of the importance and interrelatedness of the SDGs. Within this challenging environment, policy makers are facing the implementation of the 2030 UN agenda. As noted elsewhere, 'the statist responses to these challenges, although supported by many, nonetheless were often in conflict with the individualist perspective of market-oriented old-style NPM supporting politicians' and herein lies an outlook for alternative public policy futures (Massey, 2021, p. 1). There is an extensive literature on good governance and its position within the institutions of the state and economy, but for the purpose of this Policy Insight, constrained by subject and word limitations, the narrow focus of contemporary public administration structures is adopted.

That noted, however, Rhodes (1997) has long-argued that interconnectedness and unequal but over-lapping networks in a series of differentiated polities and multi-level governments is the context in which public administration is centred:

- Any organisation is dependent upon other organisations for resources.
- In order to achieve their goals, the organisations have to exchange resources.
- Although decision-making within the organisation is constrained by other organisations, the dominant coalition retains some discretion. The appreciative system of the dominant coalition influences which relationships are seen as a problem and which resources will be sought.
- The dominant coalition employs strategies within known rules of the game to regulate the process of exchange.
- Variations in the degree of discretion are a product of the goals and the relative power potential of interacting organisations. This relative power potential is a product of the resources of each organisation, or the rules of the game and the process of exchange between organisations (Rhodes, 1997).

What we are exploring in these terms is the exercise of power through networks. Cairney (2012) (citing Lukes, 1986) argues that power 'can refer to an extraordinarily wide range of concepts and arguments' (p. 48). The delivery of the SDGs in a context of good governance touches many of these concepts. These can include:

- The ability to get what you want despite the resistance of others.
- The power to influence the choice of others.
- The power to influence an actor's decision-making environment.
- Power as a resource or capacity and the exercise of power.
- Power based on popular support, used legitimately or illegitimately.
- The power to change or obstruct.
- Power as knowledge or embedded in language.
- Reputational power.
- The ability of a social class to realise its interests.
- Decision or non-decision-making.
- The three 'dimensions' of power.
- Sources of power, economic, military, governmental, cultural.
- Power diffusion or concentration.
- Who gets what, when, how.
- Power or systemic luck.
- Inequalities of power related to gender, ethnicity, class sexuality (Cairney, 2012).

The foregoing list leads into discussions about the source and nature of power as well as its exercise in the realm of public administration and discussions of this in more detail may be found in Cairney's, 2012 book, but is beyond the scope of this paper.

It is clear that the delivery of the 2030 agenda can only succeed with the commitment of accomplished, trustworthy and dedicated public administrations across the globe, but the enduring questions to be answered are, how do societies recruit and train these cadres? And what policy insights are afforded by this quest? The template established in ancient China was for a merit-based principle of recruitment and this formed the modernist Weberian approach in many countries. In recent years, however, challenges to this have included calls for 'representative bureaucracy', that is, public administrations that represent societies in a number of ways that may include race, sex, ideology, language, culture and family wealth (Bradbury & Kellough, 2010; Fernandez, 2020; Johnston, 2020). Different states have approached this challenge in different organisational ways. For example, Singapore founded the Civil Service College (CSC) in 2001 as part of the Prime Minister's Office and all officials receive up to 100 h work-related and personal development training a year. The UK, which had abolished its own Civil Service College (more recently named the National School for Government) and privatised the premises at Sunningdale Park, has awoken to the need for continuous training and development for officials and is seeking to establish a Virtual Campus (Cabinet Office, 2021). The criteria for the recruitment and selection of public officials in many societies has undergone rigorous scrutiny and reform over the last generation (Hondeghem, 2015). Consequently, in the next section of this paper, the SDGs are placed within the context of governance and indeed, 'good governance'. It then explores the political and wider context of this, using the example of the UN's Public Service Innovation Awards, an illustration of the argument in favour of good governance.

2 | THE SUSTAINABLE DEVELOPMENT GOALS

The Sustainable Development Goals (SDGs) are lauded as seeking to 'transform our world' (UN, 2015). Even a cursory reading suggests that if fully implemented, they will lead to global good governance. The 2030 agenda was adopted by all UN Member States in 2015, and 'provides a shared blueprint for peace and prosperity for people and the planet, now and into the future' (UN, 2015) it is the culmination of years of work by the UN and its members. The starting point may be seen as the 1992 Earth Summit, with steady progression from there. For example, in June 1992, at the Earth

Summit in Rio de Janeiro, more than 178 countries adopted Agenda 21, a 'comprehensive plan of action to build a global partnership for sustainable development to improve human lives and protect the environment' (UN, 2015). The SDGs and Agenda 2030 can be directly traced from this point via:

- The Beijing World Conference on Women, 1995.
- The Millennium Declaration in September 2000 at UN Headquarters in New York. This led to the elaboration of eight Millennium Development Goals (MDGs) to reduce extreme poverty by 2015.
- The Johannesburg Declaration on Sustainable Development and the Plan of Implementation, adopted at the World Summit on Sustainable Development in South Africa in 2002, reaffirmed the global community's commitments to poverty eradication and the environment.
- At the UN Conference on Sustainable Development (Rio+20) in Rio de Janeiro, in June 2012, Member States adopted the outcome document 'The Future We Want' in which they decided, inter alia, to launch a process to develop a set of SDGs to build upon the MDGs and to establish the UN High-level Political Forum on Sustainable Development.
- In 2013, the General Assembly set up a 30-member Open Working Group to develop a proposal on the SDGs.
- In January 2015, the General Assembly began the negotiation process on the post-2015 development agenda, culminating in the adoption of the 2030 Agenda for Sustainable Development.
- Transforming our world: the 2030 Agenda for Sustainable Development with its 17 SDGs was adopted at the UN Sustainable Development Summit in New York in September 2015 (UN, 2015).

In summary, the seventeen SDGs finally agreed to are:

1. No poverty.
2. Zero hunger.
3. Good health and well-being.
4. Quality education.
5. Gender equality.
6. Clean water and sanitation.
7. Affordable and clean energy.
8. Decent work and economic growth.
9. Industry, innovation and infrastructure.
10. Reduced inequality.
11. Sustainable cities and communities.
12. Responsible consumption and production.
13. Climate action.
14. Life below water.
15. Life on land.
16. Peace and justice strong institutions.
17. Partnerships to achieve the goal.

As the product of many hours of discussion and compromise, the SDGs are a bland statement of the obvious. No politician is going to seek preferment campaigning in favour of hunger, poverty, poor health, inequality and illiteracy. But it is the statement of intent that is backed with a series of 17 core goals supported by 169 targets. Each target has between one and three indicators used to measure progress toward reaching them. In total 232 approved indicators that will gauge observance of each of the principal 17 goals (UN, 2019).

There are some obvious overlaps and contradictions. For instance, achieving zero hunger, clean water and sanitation, economic growth and industry can conflict with SDGs 13, 14 and 15. But those countries that have done the most in recent years to raise their citizens out of poverty, for example, China and India, are also attempting to intensely tackle the environmental problems resulting from increased industrialisation and urbanisation. The contradictions here were brought into stark focus at the COP26 in Glasgow, where the commitment to eliminating coal was nuanced from 'phase out' to 'phase down' at the insistence of India and China (BBC News, 2021). It is clear that none of the other 15 SDGs can be achieved without the coordination and delivery of SDGs 16 and 17. These are at the core of public administration and the delivery of good governance. Without sufficient numbers of appropriately trained, competent and incorrupt public administrators, none of the other SDGs are widely achievable. But we need to recognise important political issues and definitions of good governance are socially constructed and culturally bound; to seek to impose one version on all others is to risk failure.

3 | GOVERNANCE AND GOOD GOVERNANCE

'Governance' is not a new term. Henry IV used it in 1399 to justify his usurpation of the English throne, arguing there had been a 'default of good governance' (Richards & Smith, 2002). For the purpose of this paper, 'governance' is the term that refers to the activities and processes of government. It reflects the fragmentation of the state, as reflected by the multiplicity of policy networks that have evolved round core functions and departments (Klijn & Koppenjan, 2016). These are a form of private government of public services with welfare state services being delivered by packages of organisations (Osborne et al., 2021). As noted elsewhere, in its modern usage, *governance* has several interpretations (Frazer-Moleketi, 2005; Massey, 2005a), but it may be argued that governing is the 'totality of interactions, in which public as well as private actors participate, aimed at solving societal problems or creating societal opportunities' with specialist institutions being created for this purpose (Kooiman, 2003, p. 4). Its modern usage allows it to be defined as:

> A descriptive label that is used to highlight the changing nature of the policy process in recent decades. In particular it sensitises us to the ever-increasing variety of terrains and actors involved in the making of public policy. Thus governance demands that we consider all the actors and locations beyond the 'core executive' involved in the policy-making process. (Richards & Smith, 2002, p. 15)

It may be seen from this widely accepted definition, that there are several variabilities of governance; for example, governance in the form we use it here (governing through governance); but also corporate governance, health governance and numerous others. Just as with Cairney's inventory of types of power, so we can also see a list of different kinds of governance.

'Governance', therefore, signifies the multiple inclusions of civil society with economic, professional and social interest groups into a reflection of what it means to govern and to make and implement public policy (Massey, 2010). The work of some (Western and African) scholars makes clear, however, that inclusion is frequently neither comprehensive nor on an equal basis (Anyang'Nyong'O, 2002). Some groups and networks are dominant and civil society struggles to hold them to account. It follows, therefore, that there exists both *good* governance and *bad* governance, with the latter falling short of those elements such as accountability, transparency and opportunity to achieve the redress of grievance that lie at the heart of enlightenment notions of what it means to be well-governed. The SDGs may be viewed from this context, especially SDGs 16 and 17. We now need to explore what is meant by 'good governance'. There are several perspectives.

The Council of Europe defined good governance in terms of twelve traits. These combine and contribute to the different elements of 'best practice' in public administration:

1. Participation, representation, fair conduct of elections.
2. Responsiveness.
3. Efficiency and effectiveness.
4. Openness and transparency.
5. Rule of law.
6. Ethical conduct.
7. Competence and capacity.
8. Innovation and openness to change.
9. Sustainability and long-term orientation.
10. Sound Financial management.
11. Human rights, cultural diversity and social cohesion.
12. Accountability, (Council of Europe, 2008).

These are fairly well-defined, though somewhat overlapping and repetitive. It may be inferred that several of these informed the articulation of the SDGs. But to truly capture the essence of good governance, it is useful to draw on a range of White papers, guides and policy statements, to distil it down and propose seven fundamental features. Good governance, therefore, begins with transparency and democratic accountability in government institutions, NGOs and other civil society institutions involved in governance. They may aspire to possess:

1. A commitment to reduce corruption wherever it may be found. The difficulty is that one person's corruption is often another's 'fair fee'. Perceptions of this are rooted in cultural understandings and misunderstandings.
2. The rule of law; fair and enforceable legal frameworks: to operate regardless, or rather beyond the boundaries of, race, ethnicity, religion, culture and politics. To respect and support individual human rights (Omelicheva, 2004).
3. Connected to which is transparency; there are a range of definitions and different understandings here, there needs to be due cognisance of personal privacy, state secrets, and commercial confidentiality.
4. Equity; especially equality under the rule of law and accountability to an independent judiciary.
5. Accountability is at the heart of good governance. But there are many kinds. Answerability, amendatory, redress of grievance, sanctions. Accountable not just for their individual actions, but also in terms of their management, project implementation, financial management, and information disclosure;
6. Effectiveness and efficiency; this has been at the heart of new public management, reengineering and public value reforms, especially those that are citizen focused; they are ethically operationalised to ensure there is no conflict with democracy, and other aspects of good governance.
7. Consultation and participation; participation by all sectors of society and all levels. Embracing the diversity and range of interests (cited in Massey, 2010).

Taken at face-value these are fine-sounding aims, but to put them into practice it is necessary to constantly define and redefine terms to take account of the political, cultural and temporal context. For example, the tension between individual human rights as against group or collective rights, an issue much to the fore in societies where there is substantial inequality. It is impossible to divorce decision-making in the real world from the context of history, struggle, ethnicity, wealth and power. It is perhaps more fruitful to explore ways of confronting these realities and making them work in favour of good governance than to adopt some abstract notion that pretends they do not exist (Pyper et al., 2010).

Many of these traits and explanations are something of a tick-box exercise when we seek to understand if good governance has been achieved. We also need to caution against applying culturally specific versions of good governance as a form of ideal type against which to measure other societies. Boyne (2003, p. 233) defines good governance as 'a closer correspondence between perceptions of actual and desired standards of public service'. But it is often difficult to know when this is achieved. Boyne, but also Pyper et al. (2010) discuss various measurements, such as:

1. Through meeting specific narrow targets – as set and evaluated against key performance indicators.
2. Through meeting broader outcome focused goals.
3. Through delivering services using less resources – best value, of the kind developed over a generation in terms of new public management and its successor perspectives such as public value (Bozeman, 2007; Brandsen et al., 2018).
4. Through better and increased public participation – citizens as customers, democracy through consumption.

There is an obvious link here to the issues raised by the SDG targets, indeed it raises a related set of concerns, such as:

1. The different criteria used by different stakeholders to judge standards of public services, and how are the criteria selected.
2. The consensus, if any, there is on these criteria and their relative importance within the networks of the differentiated structures of multi-level governance. That is the major powers and interests that exercise hegemony and the local, often under resourced institutions of public administration.
3. The fact that preferences vary by gender, sex, age, ethnicity, income and location.
4. The methods by which actual and desired levels of performance set and the way this varies over time and place and is dependent upon a variety of resources.
5. The extent improvement is measured by a rise or fall in service standards, which is reflective of the local and national regulatory framework.
6. The extent to which politically important perceptions (rather than actual) improvement can be accurately measured.
7. It is probably not possible to globally achieve all these targets in a context of good governance by 2030, which means recourse to renegotiated goals that have to be delivered locally, but coordinated in some way to become effective.

The UN and its members can, and does, harness innovative techniques and technologies such as digital era governance to seek to attain the 2030 goals. There is a degree of learning and mimosis connected to this, such as the example set by Australia's development of digital era government (Evans et al., 2019).

Innovation may be both managerial and public service innovation (PSO) and often utilises the technical Innovation of data and e-governance (Evans et al., 2019). Borins (2001) explored the difficulty of defining public sector innovation and the difficulty public institutions have of developing it, especially that from middle managers. There is still no universally accepted definition of public service innovation, though Chen et al. (2020, p. 7) have developed a useful classification, arguing it is, 'the development and implementation of a novel idea by a PSO to create or improve public value within an ecosystem'. They argue that this, 'definition emphasises three attributes – novelty, development and implementation, and ecosystem – and one outcome – public value' (Chen et al., 2020, p. 7). But as Cinar et al. (2019) argue, there remain many barriers to innovation in the public sector and it is instructive to seek out examples, especially successful examples that have lessons to read across into other settings.

Examples of public sector (top-down and bottom-up) innovation and exploration of what works is evidenced by the UN Public Service Awards. The 11 winners of the immediate pre-covid awards, presented in June 2019 at Baku, Azerbaijan, were from Argentina, Australia, Austria, Brazil, Chile, Costa Rica, Indonesia, Kenya, Portugal, the Republic of Korea, and Thailand and represented a range and depth of public provision devoted to improving the delivery of services in an innovative and sustainable way, improving the lives of thousands and in some cases millions of citizens (UN, 2019). Mindful of the current global context of a pandemic and social conflict, the 2021 UNPSA award's four categories, which have been identified as:

1. Fostering innovation to deliver inclusive and equitable services for all including through digital transformation.
2. Enhancing the effectiveness of public institutions to reach the SDGs.
3. Promoting gender-responsive public services to achieve the SDGs.
4. Institutional preparedness and response in times of crisis.

The United Nations Public Service Awards is designed to reward the achievements and 'contributions of public service institutions that lead to a more effective and responsive public administration in countries worldwide' promoting 'the role, professionalism and visibility of public service' (UN, 2021). It also serves to educate with regard to contextually specific 'best practice'. In recent years it has been closely linked to the SDGs and notions of good governance. To this end, it is important to remember that the configuration of a state's public administration reflects the political and social values of a country (Massey, 2005b, 2010). SDGs 16 and 17 demonstrate that public administration and public servants are fundamental in promoting and maintaining a society's cohesion and prosperity. Public administration is 'central to the continuation of the social contract of all but the most totalitarian of societies. Along with the rule of law and a properly functioning civil society (itself guaranteed by and a guarantor of effective public administration) it is the mechanism by which the constitutional settlements of states are made to work (Massey, 2010).

The SDGs and the 2030 Agenda are an attempt by the UN and its members to avoid the errors of previous reform programmes that sought to remake much of the rest of the world in the image of the West, after the fall of the Soviet Union. It was a period of 'policy transfer' in the guise of mimetic and coercive isomorphism.

> By this is meant that the Bretton Woods institutions (and many Western governments) took the view that the policy of liberalisation including privatisation had been 'good' for those economies that had taken it the furthest, the US, UK, Australasia and the Tiger economies of the Far East. The reasoning followed; therefore, it would also be 'good' for the former Soviet Union and Africa. Advisors from the World Bank and other influential NGOs pushed African governments into copying Western patterns of liberalisation and state restructuring (mimetic isomorphism), while often loans, aid and favourable trading agreements were contingent upon such reforms (coercive isomorphism) (see Kwama, 2008, for an example). Some informed social science research has subsequently shown this approach to be overly simplistic. The successful policy transfer of liberalisation and New Public Management to Malaysia, South Korea and Singapore reflected very different socio-political constructions and relationships between the political elite and civil society, even then the transfer took place *mutatis mutandis* and was not a straight copy but a significant re-interpretation of the western approach. (Massey, 2010, p195, also citing Common, 2001)

In other words, the success of public sector reform in the global south was because strong, highly competent public administrations implemented reforms in a way that reflected local custom and culture and was sensitive to what worked. The implementation of the 2030 agenda and the SDGs will only be similarly successful if there is a comparable recognition of local context. Agenda 2030 is an example of global thinking that has to be enacted locally. Singapore restructured in a way that was distinctively Singaporean, likewise South Korea, Malaysia, Hong Kong, China and Japan (Common, 2001).

4 | CONCLUSIONS

The then UN Secretary General, Ban Ki-Moon launched the SDGs in 2015 with the observation that they are a 'shared vision of humanity and a social contract between the world's leaders and the people', as 'the 2030 Agenda for Sustainable Development (was) adopted unanimously by 193 Heads of State' (UN, 2015). He referred to it as a 'to-do list for people and the planet, and a blueprint for success', designed to 'wipe out poverty, fight inequality and tackle climate change over the next 15 years' (UN, 2015). The policy insight of this and previous waves of reform is the imperative to 'think global and act local'. By this is meant the need to approach reform using global benchmarks of good governance, but to ensure they are delivered with due sensitivity being accorded to local context. In this the implementation of the SDGs 16 and 17 are the key platform from which the others can be launched.

ORCID
Andrew Massey https://orcid.org/0000-0002-2311-7944

REFERENCES

Anyang'Nyong'O, P. (2002) *Democracy and political leadership in Africa in the context of NEPAD.* Paper to the Japan Institute for International Affairs Conference at the World Summit on Development, Johannesburg, 31 August, 2002.

BBC News. (2021) Available at: https://www.bbc.co.uk/news/uk-59284505 [Accessed 15 November 2021]

Borins, S. (2001) Encouraging innovation in the public sector. *Journal of Intellectual Capital*, 2(3), 310–319.

Bozeman, B. (2007) *Public values and public interest: Counterbalancing economic individualism.* Georgetown University Press.

Bradbury, M. & Kellough, J. (2010) Representative bureaucracy: assessing the evidence on active representation. *The American Review of Public Administration*, 41(2), 157–167.

Brandsen, T., Steen, T. & Verschuere, B. (Eds.) (2018) *Coproduction and co-creation: Engaging citizens in public service delivery.* Routledge.

Cabinet Office, Government Skills and Curriculum Unit, and Civil Service HR (2021) *The new curriculum and campus for government skills*, Published 15 January 2021. Cabinet Office.

Cairney, P. (2012) *Understanding public policy, theories and issues.* Palgrave Macmillan.

Chen, J., Walker, R.M. & Sawhney, M. (2020) Public service innovation: A typology. *Public Management Review*, 22(11), 1674–1695.

Cinar, E., Trott, P. & Simms, C. (2019) A systematic review of barriers to public sector innovation process. *Public Management Review*, 21(2), 264–290.

Common, R. (2001) *Public management and policy transfer in South East Asia.* Ashgate.

Council of Europe (2008) *12 Principles of good governance.* Available at: https://www.coe.int/en/web/good-governance/12-principles

Evans, M., Dunleavy, P., McGregor, C. & Halupka, M. (2019) Towards digital era governance: Lessons from the Australian experience. In Massey, A. (Ed.) *A research agenda for public administration*. Edward Elgar, pp. 146–161.

Fernandez, S. (Ed.) (2020) Representative bureaucracy and performance. In *Public service transformation in South Africa*. Palgrave, pp. 1–21.

Fraser-Moleketi, G. (2005) *The world we could win: Administering global government*. IOS Press.

Hondeghem, A. (2015) *Leadership and culture: comparative models of top civil servant training*. Palgrave Macmillan.

Johnston, K. (2020) Debate: failing to learn? The impact of new public management on public service innovation. *Public Money & Management*, 40(6), 473–474.

Klijn, E.H. & Koppenjan, J.F.M. (2016) *Governance networks in the public sector*. Routledge.

Kooiman, J. (2003) *Governing as governance*. Sage.

Kwama, K. (2008) article in, *The Standard*, Nairobi, 26 February 2008.

Lukes, S. (Ed.) (1986) *Power*. New York University Press.

Massey, A. (2005a) Multilevel governance. In Fraser Moleketi, G. (Ed.) *The world we could win: Administering global governance*. IOS Press, pp. 1–17.

Massey, A. (2005b) *The state of Britain: A guide to the UK public sector* (3rd edition). Chartered Institute of Public Finance and Accountancy, pp. 1–60.

Massey, A. (2010) Lessons from Africa: New public management and the privatization of Kenya Airways. *Public Policy and Administration*, 25(2), 194–215.

Massey, A. (2021) The seamless web of circumstance. *Public Money & Management*, 41(1), 1–4.

Omelicheva, M. (2004) *"Global civil society?" An empirical portrayal*. Paper to the Annual Meeting of the American Political Science Association, APSA.

Osborne, S., Nasi, G. & Powell, M. (2021) Beyond co-production: Value creation and public services. *Public Administration*, 99(1), 641–657. https://doi.org/10.1111/padm.12718

Plowden Report. (1967). *Children and their primary schools, a report of the Central Advisory*. Central Advisory Council for Education (England).

Pyper, R., Miller, K. & McTavish, D. (2010) Changing modes of official accountability in the UK. In Brandsen, T. & Holzer, M. (Eds.) *The future of governance: selected papers from the fifth transatlantic dialogue on public administration*. National Center for Public Performance, pp. 187–206.

Rhodes, R.A.W. (1997) *Understanding governance: policy networks, governance, reflexivity and accountability*. Open University Press.

Richards, D. & Smith, M. (2002) *Governance and public policy in the UK*. Oxford University Press.

United Nations. (2015) Sustainable development. Available at: https://www.un.org/sustainabledevelopment/blog/2015/12/sustainable-development-goals-kick-off-with-start-of-new-year/

United Nations. (2019) United Nations Public Service Forum and Awards Ceremony 2019. Available at: https://publicadministration.un.org/en/UNPSA2019

United Nations (2021), https://publicadministration.un.org/unpsa/database/Winners/2019-Winners

AUTHOR BIOGRAPHY

Andrew Massey is the Professor of Government and Academic Director of the International School for Government, King's College London. He has worked in a range of comparative public policy and public administration fields. His main areas of research include issues around the reform and modernization of government and governance.

How to cite this article: Massey, A. (2022) Sustainable Development Goals and their Fit with Good Governance. *Global Policy*, 13(Suppl. 1), 79–85. Available from: https://doi.org/10.1111/1758-5899.13037

Received: 10 August 2021 | Accepted: 16 August 2021

DOI: 10.1111/1758-5899.13015

BOOK REVIEW

Food Insecurity in Small Island Developing States

Food Security in Small Island States by John Connell and Kristen Lowitt (eds.), Singapore: Springer Natur Singapore. 2020. 318pp. ISBN 978-981-13-8255-0 (hc); 978-981-13-8258-1 (pb); 978-981-13-8256-7 (ebook). €124.79 (hc), €88.39 (pb), €71.68 (ebook).

Sustainable development and governance in the Global South were long issues associated with Africa. In the last decade, particularly after the existential threat to the Maldives was brought to international attention through a 2011 documentary about its then president, Mohamed Nasheed, small island developing states (SIDS) have been recognised as some of the most seriously challenged in the Global South. Not only do SIDS face submersion due to rising sea levels, but on a more immediate timescale salinization will reduce limited freshwater availability on islands and much of the limited land resources for domestic agriculture will disappear. In the meantime, sea temperature change threatens to destroy marine life and the availability of both the fishing industry as an economic resource and as an alternative local source of food. Regional climate systems are changing too and subjecting more SIDS to extreme weather events. SIDS face significant challenges in balancing these threats with growing populations. It should be no surprise that they have come to the forefront in international pressure to halt climate change. But climate change is only one of several major challenges to the SIDS.

As the contributors to John Connell and Kristen Lowitt's edited volume *Food Security in Small Island States* show, SIDS also face other serious problems regarding food security that preceded the awareness of the challenges of climate change. The contributors examine a wide array of these challenges, all grouped together loosely as representing globalisation. Globalisation, it is argued, is gradually reducing the diversity of the production of land and sea as everyone in the SIDS has been absorbed into the cash economy. The case studies have been drawn from the Pacific and the Caribbean, where many of the SIDS, identified by the United Nations as including 52 states and territories, are located. The volume leaves out SIDS with a population of a million or more, such as Cuba, to reduce independent variables, although Papua New Guinea with just over eight million people is a frequent reference point. All the case studies included here are characterised by their small size, over-dependence on commerce, particularly imports, their limited resources, and their environmental vulnerability.

Post-independence economic development turned many SIDS away from self-sufficiency and made them heavily dependent on imports of processed foods and drinks, making up a third of the value of all imports by the SIDS (p. 12). This has made these states more insecure regarding their food supply and dependent on outside sources which has raised the issue of food sovereignty, wherein everyone has a right to food and decisions about food markets should be made by the people dependent on them. The shift from subsistence to import dependence has led to health crises in many of the SIDS, due to nutritional and other health problems, including micronutrient deficiencies, child stunting, and obesity (p. 262). Moreover, things have gone from bad to worse in 2020–21. We still had not heard of COVID when the present volume went to press in January 2019 (p. vi). But in most SIDS, COVID will act as a risk multiplier, worsening the existing sustainability challenges.

The key contribution of the volume is the collective assessments of responses in different SIDS to the food security challenges they all face. The various case studies reveal a diverse panoply of options where SIDS have attempted to transform small island food systems to make them more resilient and sustainable. Much of the adaptation and resilience is enabled at the level of the household, food insecurity being, in many SIDS, a problem not of food production or distribution, but rather of livelihood insecurity (p. v). Food insecurity in the SIDS is thus particularly reliant on bonding social capital between producers and the function of knowledge networks within the local community (p. 255). If policy change is going to be effective, it needs to elicit buy-in from practitioners and local communities and to develop socially robust knowledge (p. 18).

Some of the larger geopolitical factors related to SIDS remains unexplored here, in part because many developments, such as ¨COVID, are very recent, the volume being the product of a 2015 special issue of *Regional Environmental Change* with additional chapters solicited afterwards. In the years since, China's ambitious One Belt One Road vision for its trade corridors across Eurasia and the counter-response by the Quad states (the US, Australia, Japan, and India) has afforded new resources and aid to SIDS that would have otherwise not been available. As different powers vie for regional footholds, atolls become valuable assets to barter for development aid, China's numerous projects in the Maldives provides a very good example. Elsewhere, such as in Papua New Guinea, interest shown by China has led to Japan and Australia upping the ante with better offers of aid. Such competition by the great powers may go far in providing additional sources of support for strategically placed SIDS. This is particularly true of nutritional challenges as public health often figures prominently in showcase aid projects.

Regarding food insecurity per se, the situation in many SIDS, at least in the Pacific examples, is not yet as bad as it is in parts of Africa and South Asia (p. 32). Nevertheless, how far the SIDS will meet their sustainable development goals is perhaps more immediately dependent on the overall rate of climate change, which is effectively out of the control of local governments. The governments of SIDS can adapt to rising ocean levels only so far and for only so long. Certainly, some of the problems faced by small island states are shared by coastal populations on larger land masses, such as the deltaic population of Bangladesh. Nevertheless, while coastal populations elsewhere might be displaced and fragile states in particular unable to cope, the populations of the SIDS have nowhere else to go. While the present volume successfully lays out the scope of the issue of food insecurity and policy responses to food vulnerability that SIDS can undertake themselves, the larger existential challenge SIDS face depend for their resolution on how far more powerful states with larger industrial and commercial bases can continue to co-operate on reducing carbon emissions. Without global solutions, whether local innovations and adaptation are effective in responding to the challenges of food insecurity locally or not will be a moot issue.

Michael W. Charney

SOAS, the University of London, London, UK

Correspondence
Michael W. Charney, SOAS, the University of London, 10 Thornhaugh St. Russell Sq.,WC1H 0XG, London, UK.
Emails: mwcharney@googlemail.com; mc62@soas. ac.uk

AUTHOR BIOGRAPHY

Michael W. Charney is Professor of Asian and Military History at SOAS, the University of London where he works on colonialism, security, violence, and refugees in Africa and Asia in the Centre for International Studies and Diplomacy of the School of Politics and International Studies and in the School of History, Religions, and Philosophy.